THE
MOSQUITO
IN THE
USAAF

THE
MOSQUITO
IN THE
USAAF

DE HAVILLAND'S WOODEN WONDER
IN AMERICAN SERVICE

TONY FAIRBAIRN

AIR WORLD

AIR WORLD

THE MOSQUITO IN THE USAAF
De Havilland's Wooden Wonder in American Service

First published in Great Britain in 2021 by
Air World
An imprint of
Pen & Sword Books Ltd
Yorkshire – Philadelphia

ISBN 978 1 39901 733 6

Typeset by SJmagic DESIGN SERVICES, India.
Printed and bound in the UK by CPI Group (UK) Ltd, Croydon, CR0 4YY

Pen & Sword Books Limited incorporates the imprints of Atlas, Archaeology,
Aviation, Discovery, Family History, Fiction, History, Maritime, Military, Military
Classics, Politics, Select, Transport, True Crime, Air World, Frontline Publishing, Leo
Cooper, Remember When, Seaforth Publishing, The Praetorian Press, Wharncliffe
Local History, Wharncliffe Transport, Wharncliffe True Crime and White Owl.

For a complete list of Pen & Sword titles please contact

PEN & SWORD BOOKS LIMITED
47 Church Street, Barnsley, South Yorkshire, S70 2AS, England
E-mail: enquiries@pen-and-sword.co.uk
Website: www.pen-and-sword.co.uk

Or
PEN AND SWORD BOOKS
1950 Lawrence Rd, Havertown, PA 19083, USA
E-mail: Uspen-and-sword@casematepublishers.com
Website: www.penandswordbooks.com

Contents

Foreword

By Brigadier General Elliott Roosevelt
USAAF (Ret)

Dear Fairbairn

In answer to your questions regarding the use by US reconnaissance outfits of the Mosquito aircraft, I am glad to supply the following information.

When preparing for the invasion of North Africa from July to November 1942, the 3rd Photo Group trained for combat at Steeple Morden, England. We were equipped with three squadrons of F-4s (Lightnings) and one squadron of B-17s. Early on we discovered the B-17 was useless for reconnaissance flying alone over enemy territory. I started to bombard higher headquarters to re-equip the B-17 squadron with Mosquitoes, having flown one over at Benson in August 1942. I appealed to our Ambassador, Mr Winant, to help me get some British aircraft. He tried hard, but the RAF had urgent need for all they could get, but we succeeded in speeding up the Canadian manufacture of Mosquitoes. Finally, after the invasion of North Africa in November 1942 the RAF allocated two production aircraft to my 3rd Photo Group. I took delivery of the first one at Benson and flew it to Algiers. Later this plane was lost in a landing accident which occurred when a lieutenant colonel on the staff of the 12th Air Force Headquarters was being checked out. The second British Mosquito was delivered to us in North Africa, and was used successfully in many photo missions over Italy and Sicily in the months leading up to the invasions. Gradually, in 1943 we started receiving Canadian-built Mosquitoes in the US recon units. In 1943, the 90th Photo Wing (Recon) was formed, in North Africa, of the RAF and American Recon outfits, and it included a Free French Squadron and a South African Air Force Squadron.

When I was transferred from Italy to England in January 1944 and asked to organise the 325th Recon Wing I equipped the Alconbury and Watton units with Mosquitoes. These units were under the command of Colonel Leon Gray. They flew many successful reconnaissance missions on daylight and night operations. They flew in many counter-espionage agents to be parachuted over various targets at night. They also were used effectively in advance of bomber formations to drop 'window' to confuse the enemy.

I consider the Mosquito to have been the most successful multi-purpose aircraft produced during the Second World War. The only criticism I ever made of the plane was the tendency of the Rolls Royce engines to overheat on hot, humid days when delayed while waiting for take-off. This is not a valid fault to find, as in the air I always found the plane to be more than reliable.

My rating of the planes used for reconnaissance purposes in the Second World War is as follows:

1. Mosquito
2. Spitfire
3. Lightning (F-4, F-5)
4. P-51 Mustang
5. B-25 Mitchell (used only in night photo missions)
6. B-26 Invader (used only in night photo missions)

Entirely unsatisfactory: the B-17 – used experimentally, with disastrous results in North Africa.

As you are well aware, all aircraft used for reconnaissance purposes were stripped of all armament and armour plating in order to achieve maximum effective speed and altitude. In the latter part of 1944 and in 1945, the advent of German jet aircraft and the high priority given by the Luftwaffe to shooting down reconnaissance planes necessitated the use of single or double fighter escorts on missions. These planes acted as spotters to advise the recon pilot of the approach of enemy planes.

From an operational standpoint, the reconnaissance units in the Mediterranean and European theatres, throughout the war, experienced a higher rate of loss than either the fighter or bomber units.

I hope the above random thoughts have proved useful to you in your research.

Yours sincerely

Elliott Roosevelt
Hill House, Little Somerford,
Wiltshire, England
26 August 1977

Author's Note

I first became interested in the USAAF Mosquito story in 1977 when co-authoring with Stewart Evans an article for *Aircraft Illustrated* on Joseph Kennedy's fatal mission of 12 August 1944 in an explosive-filled US Navy Liberator drone over Suffolk, England. Kennedy's aircraft was the focal point of a fairly exotic formation of aircraft that included at least one Mosquito in US 8th Air Force markings. The type in USAAF service was completely new to me and immediately struck me as worth some research.

Enquiries to *Air Force Magazine* and the 25th Bomb Group Association in the USA brought to light a steady stream of veterans who had flown or serviced the Mosquito and who were eager to share their memories. I also established contact with USAF historian and author Dana Bell and began a fruitful and enjoyable exchange of information that sparked all manner of leads, clues and pointers on the subject.

Here at home in the UK my research took me to the then Public Record Office (now the National Archives), where I located a file entitled *Mosquitoes for the USAAF.* This contains documents dating from 1943 tracing the progress of US bids to obtain quantities of Mosquitoes, in various marks, for their own use.

The correspondence continued apace with an RAF delegation in Washington playing a lively role in the negotiations for Mosquitoes for the Americans. In October 1943 they wrote to the Air Ministry in Whitehall setting out a request for revised quantities of bomber, PR and fighter-bomber airframes and adding: 'As you know, the Mosquito question has a slightly political flavour since Col Roosevelt commands the American PR unit in North Africa and I think [General] Arnold will be very pleased if you can meet this latest programme.'

This first reference to Elliott Roosevelt highlights the pivotal role played by the US President's son in the Americans' eager bid for Mosquitoes. I therefore set out to contact ER and, with the help of the American Embassy, tracked him down in retirement to, of all places, Little Somerford, Wiltshire, England. His answer to my request for information forms the foreword to this book. Before I was able to speak to him in person my Air Force career took me out of the country and by the time I returned to the UK three years later he had moved on himself. In retrospect it was a missed opportunity, but I console myself with the thought that he may have been neither willing nor able to add to the information he had provided. At the turn of the millennium I moved to Wiltshire myself and took the opportunity to visit Hill House, where he had lived, now a care home. There was no trace of ER himself but I was told that the lady who had typed some of his correspondence, Joan Wigmore, was living in the village. Joan proved to be the wife of an ex-RAF Hercules navigator from the nearby Lyneham air base. She remembered ER well, confirmed she had done some of his typing, which included his wartime experiences, and described him as a pleasant and approachable man. In his letter to me that forms the foreword, ER appears a little confused when he says '… in 1943 we started receiving Canadian-built Mosquitoes in the US recon units'. Early Canadian production airframes (termed F-8s by the USAAF) found their way to the USA for test and evaluation but it was not until 1944 that *British*-produced Mosquitoes began to equip the US recon units in the UK.

A word, first, about the Joan Eleanor missions; although these began in great secrecy under the aegis of the 25th BG at Watton in 1944, the operation was very soon taken over by the 492nd BG at Harrington. For the sake of continuity and clarity I have confined their description to the 492nd's activities.

Looking next at the 416th NFS, its eventual re-equipment with the Mosquito NF.XXX proved more protracted than the seemingly steady flow of PR.XVIs and it did not enter USAAF service until 1945. Its career as a night fighter with the Americans was thus a short one. Prior to that, the squadron flew the Bristol Beaufighter, under a sort of reverse Lend-Lease arrangement, from the date that it was declared operational. A particularly gratifying feature of the story is the close and good-natured co-operation between Brits and Americans, and I have therefore taken the liberty of describing the 416th's operations from activation in February 1943 to inactivation in November 1946.

Turning finally to the Mosquito itself, the Americans, like everyone else, found it a challenging aircraft to fly, primarily because of its inherent swing on take-off and landing. The comments of two people who flew it acknowledge this foible:

> If one of these big fans stops … the aeroplane starts to grow horns.
> Keith Skilling, after flying Mosquito KA114
> at the Canadian Warplane Heritage airshow in June 2013

THE MOSQUITO IN THE USAAF

The Mosquito has been called the most versatile aircraft ever made. Certainly its range, speed and high-altitude performance all combined to put it far ahead of anything else available at the time of its introduction into service in September, 1941 … However, the Mosquito, like most other things in this world, had its shortcomings and these for the most part were associated with getting it off and back on to the ground.

> Lettice Curtis, Air Transport Auxiliary pilot in the Second
> World War

Despite being a bit of a handful, the observations of three American pilots perhaps sum up the US view:

The performance characteristics of the airplane … were considered to be exceptionally good.

> W E 'Bill' Gray Jr, NACA test pilot, after flying KB186
> at Langley, USA, in October and November 1944

We who flew the Mossie were extremely proud that we had been privileged to fly this unique craft.

> Lt John Green, 653rd Bomb Sqn, February 1944

My pilots loved this beautiful bird – as undoubtedly a common feeling shared by their RAF counterparts.

> Col Joseph A Stenglein, Commander,
> 25th Bomb Gp, August 1944

Chapter 1

The Roosevelt Thread

Born in 1910, the son of the future President of the United States, Elliott Roosevelt's (ER) military career has rightly been described as meteoric. Enlisting in the USAAC in 1940 as a captain, he left five years later as a brigadier general. He is a key figure – arguably *the* key figure – in the USAAF's energetic quest for Mosquitoes in particular and for helping to shape that service's forthcoming aerial reconnaissance policy and operations as a whole. Ironically, though, he began life in uniform as a humble procurement officer at Wright Field, Dayton, Ohio, the hub for Air Corps research, development and materiel. While there he met Maj. George Goddard, the Air Corps' acknowledged expert in aerial photography. Goddard's work impressed ER and probably marks the very start of his interest in reconnaissance throughout the war.

Active involvement in survey and reconnaissance work soon followed for ER and some years later he recalled the details of his assignment:

> I was at Wright Field up until March of 1941, and then I was transferred over to Bolling Field [SE Washington, DC] for a special intelligence course under Captain Lauris Norstad, who is now one of the high-ranking generals in the Army, to serve as an intelligence officer of the 21st Reconnaissance Squadron, which had been assigned to Newfoundland to do anti-submarine patrols of the North Atlantic waters, and to guard our shipping lanes against German submarine activity. We arrived in Newfoundland and I received an additional assignment from Washington ordering me to take charge of all planning and execution of the survey of the North Atlantic possibilities for establishment of bases across the North Atlantic for the delivery of fighter and bomber aircraft to England.

Based at Gander with Douglas B-18 Bolos, the work took in Labrador, Iceland, Baffin Island (lying between Greenland and the Canadian mainland), and Greenland itself. ER's name crops up in the survey of what

1

would become a major transatlantic staging post – Goose Bay, Labrador – recommendations for the construction of which were passed to the Canadian Government in August 1941. Of his time in what he termed 'woebegone' Newfoundland he added:

> I was required to learn by the hardest way, which was through the taking of photographs of the terrain and the establishment of whether that terrain would be satisfactory for bases, and after the pictures were developed then we had to go back and go ashore from PBY aircraft and land on those areas and survey them on foot. That was my first contact with photographic survey work.

During his time in Newfoundland the crucial part played by the weather and its forecasting in the movement of transatlantic air and sea traffic stood him in good stead when some three years later he would command weather reconnaissance units. A survey flight to East Greenland in August 1941 was ER's last task and in September the 21st Recon Sqn returned to the USA.

Back on home soil, ER received orders to attend a navigation course at Kelly Field on 10 September, followed by an aerial navigation course at Brooks Field, both in Texas. Later in the year, on 15 December, he was posted to the 6th Recon Sqn at Muroc Dry Lake, California, flying B-18 Bolos. He describes subsequent events:

> Until late in January [1942], I served first with the 6th and then the 2nd [Recon Sqns] then, unexpectedly, secret orders came through directing that I report to the commander of the 1st Mapping Group at Bolling Field in Washington. There was so much secrecy surrounding my orders and the nature of my future assignment, that my hopes were really soaring. Must be something big and important. Surely some sort of overseas assignment …

He was certainly correct about the location of his next assignment.

Before setting off on his new appointment ER had a chance, or perhaps engineered, encounter with a certain Col Dwight Eisenhower, then chief of staff of the Sixth Army in Texas, but who in November 1942 would be appointed Supreme Commander Allied Expeditionary Force, North African Theatre. Eisenhower asked ER to visit him and took a keen interest in the latter's survey work in the frozen north. It would not be long before their paths crossed on the African continent.

2

Meanwhile, in February 1942, ER's work with the 1st Mapping Gp turned out to be the Special Reconnaissance Mission to Africa. 'I was due off to North Africa, one of two navigators assigned to the photographic mapping of the terrain as part of something identified as Project RUSTY,' he later recalled. The assignment was a sensible use of the experience he had gained in Newfoundland and would occupy him from March until May 1942.

The objectives of Project Rusty were summarised in an Air Staff memo for General Arnold dated 28 April 1942:

> The object of the RUSTY project is photographic reconnaissance of the Cape Verde Islands, Dakar, and the French West African coast. Its base is at ACCRA [on the British Gold Coast, now Ghana] and its present equipment consists of one B-17B which is not in operational condition. The Director of Photography has suggested to Col Cullen, Commanding Officer of RUSTY, that P-38s be sent to ACCRA for his use. This proposal is replied to unfavourably ... and request is made that three pilots from the 7th Photographic Squadron be flown to ACCRA with planes to follow as soon as possible.

No P-38s were authorised (the 7th Photo Sqn was an operational training unit at Colorado Springs) but two specially modified B-17s were allotted to the project and George Goddard describes their equipment and their work:

> They were stripped down and equipped with the latest navigational aids and three wide angle mapping cameras locked together to form a single tri-lens camera. Under suitable weather conditions, Elliott's expedition could make photographic strips from horizon to horizon for hundreds of miles in a day. And they did just that, although one of the B-17s disappeared on a flight between Puerto Rico and Trinidad and was never found. The other, with Elliott on board, went on down the coast of South America to Natal, Brazil, then across the ocean to Liberia. From there they spanned the African continent.

Conditions for aerial survey in Africa for the B-17 (nicknamed *Blue Goose* because of its colour scheme) proved challenging 'owing to inaccurate maps, poor weather data and low visibility' stated a classified project report back to Gen. Arnold in Washington. *Blue Goose* was worked hard and did fine work until damaged beyond repair in a crash landing. Despite losing two aircraft, Rusty was rated a success and in April ER could celebrate his promotion to major.

Returning to the USA in early summer 1942, ER spent some recovering from amoebic dysentery contracted in Africa, but on 11 July he took over command of the 3rd Photographic Group from Maj. Harry Eidson, equipped with F-4 and F-5 Lightnings, at Colorado Springs, and earmarked for overseas operations. The group comprised the 5th, 12th, 13th, 14th and 15th PR Sqns, the latter with B-17s. In August the group began moving to England, calling first at Membury, Berkshire, and then consolidating at Steeple Morden, Cambridgeshire. Here the group split up, the 13th and 14th Sqns remaining in England (Mount Farm, then Chalgrove) for the rest of the war while the 5th, 12th and 15th Sqns flew out to North Africa via Gibraltar over the period late November–early December. ER's 3rd Photo Gp was officially located at La Senia, Algeria, on 10 December 1942. On Christmas Day 1942 a move was made to Algiers, where the unit would remain for six months. Assigned to the 12th Air Force, the group followed closely in the footsteps of the Operation Torch landings of 8 November. It would also undergo some changes of designation, as follows:

B-17 41-24440 *I Got Spurs* of 15th Recon & Mapping Sqn, 3rd Photo Gp. (AAM)

4

May 43 – 3rd Photographic Reconnaissance & Mapping Group
Nov 43 – 3rd Photographic Group (Reconnaissance)
May 45 – 3rd Reconnaissance Group

While in North Africa the group provided photographic intelligence in support of the campaigns for Tunisia, Pantelleria, Sardinia and Sicily. Between November 1942 and the ending of the North African campaign in May 1943 ER's Group lost five F-4s to enemy action.

At this point it is timely to introduce ER's initial 'hands on' experience of the Mosquito. In his foreword to this book he claims to have taken delivery of one at Benson and flown it to Algiers after Operation Torch. He goes on to say that a second machine was delivered to him in North Africa that was subsequently used for PR missions in the months leading up to the invasion of Italy. Sharp and Bowyer in *Mosquito* state that in May 1943: 'A Mk IV was in American hands at Algiers, and on its nose was inscribed "Pilot – Colonel Roosevelt". The President's son thought very highly of the aeroplane, but it was dogged by engine trouble. Another Mk IV in American hands was lost on a flight to Britain for major overhaul.' Unfortunately, it is difficult to be precise about which airframes ER had access to but there are

B-17 41-24440 of 15th Recon & Mapping Sqn. Nickname has been altered from *I Got Spurs* to *I Had Spurs*. Behind is a P-38/F-4 Lightning. (usmilitariaforum)

one or two clues. The record card for DZ368 states: 'Mk IV, taken on charge by USAAF 6.11.42. Preparation for USAAF via Benson, Cat "E" 20.5.43'.

Chris Hansen, ER's biographer, says that the 5th PRS Lightnings and 15th Mapping Sqn's Flying Fortresses:

> were augmented by a single Mosquito Mk IV that Elliott Roosevelt and Harry Eidson (crewing as pilot) borrowed from the RAF in Gibraltar on the way. There were three on the peninsula, and it seems remarkable that Elliott was able to finagle one without worrying excessively about transition training or other finer points. Elliott and Eidson used that Mosquito to fly the first three missions over hostile territory – the Lightnings were having trouble getting established. Roosevelt said later that Eidson was the first pilot to survive five missions, and the sortie list suggests most of these were flown with Roosevelt in the borrowed Mosquito during November and December. The Mosquito 'proved itself wonderful for the work it was to do' and so began Roosevelt's long quest for more.'

Other references say that the 3rd Photo Gp 'carried out some intensive survey work over the Sardinian coastline in January 1943 with two PR Mosquitoes borrowed from the 544 Sqn detachment at Gibraltar. Despite appeals from 544 Sqn for the return of their aircraft, the US 3rd Photo Gp held on to them throughout the winter. ER let it be known that he would willingly exchange his Lockheed Lightnings for PR Mosquitoes.' This is all quite possible because 544 Sqn certainly had a Gibraltar detachment from October 1942 onwards, but pinpointing which individual aircraft were involved is elusive.

From the time of the Torch landings in November 1942 and the surrender of the Axis forces in May 1943 there were five USAAF P-38 Groups operating in North Africa, three in the fighter role (1st, 14th and 82nd) and two (ER's 3rd and 5th) on photo reconnaissance work. Initially things did not go well for the Lightnings and historian Jerry Scutts describes the situation at the end of January 1943 when the 14th FG was withdrawn from combat for a rest and retraining:

> The 14th FG's 48th FS had experienced a particularly gruelling period of combat since 18 November, having lost thirteen pilots and some twenty P-38s in that short time. Six aircraft went down

Elliott Roosevelt checking maps with Lt Col Frank L Dunn, CO of 3rd Photographic Gp, in North Africa in May 1943. (USAAF)

on 23 January, which was something of a last straw in terms of morale. Early experiences of the P-38 groups assigned to the 12th Air Force were much the same – universally depressing and morale-denting. It was obvious in the early days that the largely inexperienced Lightning pilots were up against some of the Luftwaffe's best, and if anyone doubted this, the 'Axis Sally' radio broadcasts constantly reminded them that it was so.

In fairness, these observations reflected the fortunes of the fighter groups; the P-38 fared somewhat better in the photo reconnaissance role.

Col George McDonald, responsible for intelligence tasking in North Africa, later recalled:

In the early part of 1943 the limited facilities of the RAF PRU in North Africa had almost been obliterated by bombing. The USAAF photo reconnaissance business, under command of Elliott Roosevelt, was exceptionally hard put due to a series of combat losses of PR planes and other aircraft grounded for lack of essential spare parts and insufficient numbers of special PRU aircraft …

Left: Elliott Roosevelt, as CO of the 3rd Recon Gp, receives the DFC in North Africa on 27 December 1942. Behind is the B-17 41-9045 *Stinky* of the 92nd Bomb Gp, which would crash land near Athenry, Ireland, less than three weeks later. (USAAF)

Below: Gen. Dwight Eisenhower is helped into the cockpit of a P-38/F-4 Lightning by Col Frank Dunn, CO of the 3rd Photo Gp, as Elliott Roosevelt looks on. North Africa, 1943. (USAAF)

Roosevelt had already had his eye on the Mosquito for some time, but now, deep into combat, the comparative merits of Lightnings, Spitfires and Mosquitoes in their specialist roles must have become interestingly obvious to him. In February 1943 he would take command of the North African Photographic Reconnaissance Wing, which would include 682 Sqn, RAF, with Spitfire PR.IVs and XIs, and 60 Sqn, South African AF, on Mosquitoes, British types even closer to home. Hansen, states that this instilled in him 'Mosquito Envy', and that the President's son 'went back to Washington harping to everyone about getting more Mosquitoes'. A brisk exchange of correspondence on this very subject would quite shortly be taking place between Washington and London (see Chronology), and it would make specific reference to ER's PR wing in North Africa.

If ER was sounding the virtues of the Mosquito, others close to him were less enthusiastic. In September 1943 Lt Col Alan Eldridge (ER's executive officer) and Lt Col Frank Dunn, commander of the 3rd Photo Gp, went into print saying that while the performance of the F-5A approached that of the Mosquito, its chances of surviving an interception were superior. In addition, they made the strange statement that: 'The Mosquito with low or medium-altitude engines is useless for our purposes. With the Merlin 6100 [sic] engine its usability has yet to be proven.' Higher up the USAAF

Elliott Roosevelt awarding a medal to Lt Silverman of the 90th Photo Recce Wg in North Africa on 10 March 1943. (USAAF)

Elliott Roosevelt and Gen. Dwight D Eisenhower study aerial photographs. North Africa, summer 1943. (Fold 3)

chain of command, Col Minton Kaye, USAAF Director of Photography, was similarly cool about the British aircraft, stating: 'The F-5 is superior to the Mosquito with the 6100 engine. It is faster, will climb faster, and is more manoeuvrable than the Mosquito. The latter, however, has greater range and carries a navigator; it can penetrate up to 1,000 miles, whereas the F-5 will only go 500 to 600.' This reference to the Merlin 6100 – they must mean Merlin 61 – seems at variance with reality since none of the marks of Mosquito destined for the Americans was powered by Merlin 61s.

No account of ER's part in the USAAF Mosquito story at this point would be complete without mention of his working relationship and friendship with Wg Cdr Adrian Warburton, probably the most highly regarded reconnaissance pilot in the RAF at that time. 'Warby', as he was known, took over command of 69 Sqn at Luqa, Malta, in August 1942. Ever since its formation in 1916, No. 69 had been a specialist reconnaissance unit and by the summer of 1942 it was flying a variety of types including Martin Baltimores for co-operation with Beaufort shipping strikes, Spitfire PR.IVs for high-altitude PR, together with Marylands and Wellingtons for night

Leon Gray with his F-4 Lightning when Operations Officer of the 3rd Photo Gp during Tunisian, Pantelleria and Sicilian campaigns in 1943. He would take over the 25th Bomb Gp in September 1944. (USAAF)

shipping strikes and special signals work. After a somewhat shaky start in the RAF, 'Warby' was in his element in the reconnaissance world.

It is not certain where ER and 'Warby' first met but it was probably Malta. Warburton's biographer, Tony Spooner, describes how ER had retained a 'personal' B-17 that brought 'much needed extras to Malta: not just welcome food and bottles of the right "stuff" but even items like refrigerators: very welcome during the hot summer but quite unknown in wartime Malta'. Spooner also relates the gift of a Jeep from ER to 'Warby'. The latter had never seen one before and thoroughly enjoyed driving it around Malta. 'Warby' was very much a 'press on' character and ER admired both his gung-ho attitude and his operational experience.

When the RAF's 683 Sqn was formed from 'B' Flt of 69 Sqn at Luqa in February 1943, Warburton was appointed its first CO. Using Spitfire Mk IVs, the new squadron immediately began flying PR sorties over Sicily and Italy in preparation for the coming invasion of the latter. Much later in the year the unit would move to El Aouina in Tunisia, but in the meantime, in October, 'Warby' was given command of 336 PR Wg at La Marsa, also in Tunisia. The wing comprised Nos 680, 682 and 683 RAF squadrons, plus 60 Sqn SAAF. In November, however, he suffered a bad car accident, which put him in hospital. From his hospital bed in Algiers he wrote to his father, and his letter throws an interesting light on his activities at the time and of his regard for ER. First, concerning an apparent accident in a Lightning: 'I just got away with it, trying to get photos of the first landings in Sicily, second P-38 cut out in front on me on take-off, I hadn't got my straps done up and got chucked out just before it exploded.' Then about ER: 'As you will have seen there has been a big change round among "the high paid help" and my boss Elliott Roosevelt is moving so maybe I will go along with him, I hope so as he is very nice to work with.'

However, 'Warby's' wish was not to be granted. A protracted recovery meant that he was replaced as OC 336 Wg by another RAF wing commander. The wing itself moved on to San Severo, Italy, in December 1943, and 'Warby' found himself posted back to England and to RAF Mount Farm, Oxfordshire, as liaison officer to the 7th Photo Gp (Recon). This was effective from 1 April. On 12 April he took off in an F-5 for a reconnaissance of southern Germany, failed to return, and was listed as MIA. The remains of pilot and aircraft were discovered at a crash site west of Munich in 2002. Bullet holes in one of the propellers suggest he was shot down. Thus began and ended a productive and mutually empathetic wartime relationship.

Meanwhile, ER became the first CO of the 90th Photo Wg (Recon), which was activated at La Marsa (Tunisia) on 22 November 1943. The following month the wing transferred to San Severo (Italy), remaining there for the rest of the war. The wing's groups, the 3rd and 5th, provided photo reconnaissance for the 12th and 15th Air Forces.

On 25 January 1944 Col Karl Polifka took over command of the 90th Wg from ER. A highly experienced reconnaissance pilot, Polifka had flown the F-8 Mosquito *Faintin' Floozie III* from the USA to North Africa. This change of command had come about because ER had been summoned back to England to provide a reconnaissance input to the planning for the invasion of France. That month ER took over the reins of the newly formed 8th Recon Wg (Prov), which the following August was redesignated the 325th Photo Wg (Recon). Based at High Wycombe, the wing controlled the 7th Photo Gp (Recon) (with the 13th, 14th, 22nd and 27th Recon Sqns) at Mount Farm, and the 25th Bomb Gp (652nd, 653rd, and 654th Bomb Sqns) at Watton. In the latter two squadrons ER had at last gained direct control of Mosquitoes. His photographic intelligence staff officer was Maj. Harvey Brown, who as a captain had been sent to the RAF's Central Interpretation Unit at Medmenham in September 1941 with the aim, he thought, of studying

Right: Karl Polifka in the cockpit of an F-4 Lightning of the 3rd Recon Gp at some point in 1943 in North Africa. (Author's collection)

Below: Elliott Roosevelt (left) and Leon Gray, CO of 25th Bomb Gp, in front of a Cessna Bobcat at Watton. (Author's collection)

Leon Gray's damaged F-5 Lightning at an airfield in Italy in June 1944. (USAAF)

the latest developments in British camera techniques. He would go on to learn much more, including the importance of photographic interpretation.

Chris Hansen avers that ER and other luminaries in the US intelligence world had been pushing for independence in aerial reconnaissance for some time, and: 'Colonel Roosevelt retained command when the provisional wing [ie, 8th PR Wg (Prov)] became the 325th Photo Recon Wg after D-day. By then he had already proved the concept of independent American operation, and his superiors were well pleased.'

The 325th's unit history neatly summarises the work of the wing:

From D-day -7 until D-day +11, reconnaissance and photographic work was carried in all kinds of weather, and at all hours of the day and night. Vital areas and installations of the German West Wall were photographed completely; enemy activity in all enemy defense zones was photographed; and complete oblique coverage of the entire coast from Antwerp to Bordeaux accomplished. However, the important work of damage assessment, and mapping of German and occupied territory was not curtailed, but was carried out even more extensively. At the same time, more weather information was necessary, and scheduling of more weather flights became mandatory. Many *Epicure* flights (weather recon over the ocean), *Allah* flights (weather recon over the UK) and *Bluestocking* flights (weather recon over the Continent) were carried out in all kinds of weather. Scout weather planes, a new phase in tactical air warfare, were also dispatched to precede the heavy bombers, and to radio the weather conditions existing over the scheduled targets …

USAAF independence in photographic reconnaissance was one thing but 'jointery' in photo interpretation was another matter altogether. To recognise Commonwealth and American co-operation in this science the title of the Central Interpretation Unit was changed to the Allied Central Interpretation Unit, in 1944, in preparation for the D-Day landings. The unit was jointly managed by the RAF's Wg Cdr Douglas Kendall and the USAAF's Lt Col William O'Connor.

ER flew back to the USA for his father's funeral on 14 April 1945 and did not return to Europe. (Although he lived in England temporarily

US/UK aerial reconnaissance summit meeting. L-R: Col John G Hall (Chief of Reconnaissance, USAAF), Sqn Ldr John Weaver (Chief Intelligence Officer, RAF Photo Reconnaissance Unit), unidentified RAF wing commander pilot (probably from RAF PRU), Elliott Roosevelt. (Mighty 8th AF Museum)

some years later). He was succeeded as CO of the 325th Wg by the experienced reconnaissance pilot Col Leon Gray. Brigadier General Elliott Roosevelt announced his retirement from the USAAF on 12 June 1945. Throughout his life he courted controversy and, from a research point of view, is a frustratingly difficult man to pin down. In his biography of the man, *Enfant Terrible*, Hansen frequently quotes ER's own description of events, only to add that, after checking the facts, ER is probably getting the occasions confused. Historian Jonathan Dimbleby has described him as 'a notoriously unreliable witness'. Beginning his military career as a navigator, he was not a rated Air Force pilot – until 1945. He did, however, fly combat missions, although accurate figures for his pilot-in-command hours are elusive.

One of the most balanced observations on ER comes from the Second World War photo interpreter Constance Babington-Smith, in her aviation classic *Evidence in Camera:*

It seems worthy of mention that Elliott Roosevelt, in his book *As He Saw It* (which is for the most part painfully anti-British), pays the following tribute to his RAF colleagues:

In view of the criticisms which I have expressed in regard to some of the British warmakers, I am anxious to set it down that these R.A.F officers with whom I worked from mid-January up until D-Day and thereafter until the final Nazi capitulation were a group of consummately knowledgeable officers, thoroughly familiar with their job and individually and severally as hardworking and as anxious to win the war as quickly as possible as any group of men it would have been possible to find. Not only were they a constant credit to their country, but they were in large part responsible for the small percentage of losses suffered in the invasion itself. I know I speak for all the American officers who worked with R.A.F reconnaissance experts in according them a considerable amount of the credit for the success of our arms in Europe.

Perhaps we should leave ER at that point.

Chapter 2

25th Bombardment Group

The First Seven Months: January–July 1944

In early 1944 the months of prodding by Elliott Roosevelt and horse trading between the USAAF and the UK Air Ministry finally led to American Mosquitoes becoming a reality.

As far as actual aircraft were concerned, transfer of an agreed quantity of 120 PR Mk XVIs began in February and initially involved deliveries to three USAAF bases as part of a wide-ranging modification programme. The very first delivery, on 2 February, was MM310, which went to Langford Lodge in Northern Ireland, location of the Lockheed Aircraft Modification Center and the USAAF's Base Air Depot (BAD) 3, for the installation of night photo equipment. Next off were MM337 and '338 flown to BAD 1 at Burtonwood, Lancashire, on 11 February for general modification with American equipment. Then, on 22 February, MM308 arrived at Alconbury, Huntingdonshire (now Cambridgeshire) to be fitted out with H2X radar together with the radar cameras so long championed by George Goddard. The relevance of Alconbury was that it was the home base of the 482nd BG, whose several roles (using both B-17s and B-24s) included the testing and development of radar equipment such as the British Gee, Oboe, H2S and its American equivalent, H2X. MM308 was modified with a new bulbous nose containing an American AN/APS-15 radar scanner and, fitted with H2X, was the prototype Mosquito for the so-called *Mickey* missions, in which the aircraft would fly ahead of bomber operations and take pre-attack radar photographs of planned targets.

While the delivery of Mosquitoes was gaining momentum, the provision of suitably experienced air and ground personnel was less straightforward. The 50th FS, based in Iceland with P-38 Lightnings, had been earmarked to provide an initial core of personnel for the build-up of the USAAF Mosquito force, and in February began the move down to the UK. The P-38s were ferried, initially, to Nuthampstead in Hertfordshire (at that point home to another P-38 unit, the 55th FG), some staging via Prestwick, and others through Stornoway (which had been the UK landfall for some of the

50th Fighter Sqn P-38s at a wintery Patterson Field, Iceland, in early 1944. The squadron would very soon provide personnel for the USAAF Mosquito squadrons in the UK. (USAAF)

Lt Clayton Hackman, a pilot with the 802nd Recon Gp and then the 654th Bomb Sqn. Prior to that he served with the 50th Fighter Sqn in Iceland, where he is pictured with one of the squadron's P-38 Lightnings. (C Hackman)

P-38F 42-12595 of 50th Fighter Sqn, flown by Lt Clayton Hackman, burnt out after its landing accident at Patterson Field (Keflavik), Iceland on 1 February 1944. Hackman would later serve with the 654th Bomb Sqn at Watton. (USAAF)

first Lightnings being ferried across 'the pond' to England in July 1942). Ground personnel travelled by sea and air.

Robert Howle, one of the pilots involved, takes up the story:

> I was in the 50th Fighter Sqn (P-38s) in Iceland from Aug 1942 until Feb 1944. There was very little German air activity in Iceland during our last year there, so they [the USAAF] decided to move us down to England. We flew our P-38s on 4 Feb and never flew them again as they were being phased out as a fighter in the ETO. So it seems that the RAF was doing all of the weather reconnaissance flights for the Allied forces and with the weather flying that the 50th had gained in Iceland they thought we could do the weather mission for the 8th AF in England, and also pass on weather information to the RAF.
>
> In mid-Feb 44 at Nuthampstead we received two Mk XVI 'Mozzys', no dual controls – and a US Flight Officer 'Ollie' Emmel who was formerly in the RAF and transferred back to the USAAF. Emmel was current on the 'Mozzy' so he proceeded to check us out as best as he could. Most of us survived the checkout

19

and in mid-March we got our first dual control 'Mozzy', the Mk III. 'The 'Mozzy' was chosen as the best aircraft for our mission due to its versatility. It was definitely a great aircraft. Speed, range, altitude, manoeuvrability, outstanding on instruments and I never experienced a build-up of ice to cause concern. I truly loved the 'Mozzy'.

MM364 being handed over to the USAAF at Mount Farm, Oxfordshire. It would become 'C' of the 654th Bomb Sqn. (USAAF)

Another view of MM364 at Mount Farm. (USAAF)

At Nuthampstead the 50th was attached to the 8th Recon Gp (Special) (Provisional), which, on 30 March and for administrative reasons, became the 802nd Recon Gp (Special)(P). Earlier that month a move was made to Cheddington, Buckinghamshire. Clearly aircrew training on the Mosquito was somewhat ad hoc at this time. Oxford T1066 was assigned to the 802nd Gp but was involved in a mid-air collision a mile south of King's Lynn, Norfolk, on 5 May, killing pilot Capt. Richard Thompson. Mosquito T.IIIs were becoming available and, for example, LR516 was delivered to Mount Farm in January but was written off in a take-off accident at Nuthampstead on 27 February when being flown by Maj. George Doherty. The American tyro Mosquito pilots were finding the powerful twin a handful on take-off and landing, as Lt Carl Satterlund found when he ground looped LR534 at Bury St Edmunds, Suffolk, on 27 April. Plane and pilot lived to fight another day. LR553 entered the USAAF inventory on 25 May and served without any major mishaps. During the Cheddington tenure a number

T.III LR534 of 8th Weather Recon Sqn, 802nd Recon Gp, pictured at Bury St Edmunds (home of the 94th Bomb Gp B-17s) after being ground looped in the hands of Carl Satterlund on 27 April 1944. The Mosquito is still in RAF markings. (Russell Zorn)

25th Bomb Gp aircraft over Tuddenham airfield in 1944–45, then an RAF Lancaster base some 23 miles (37km) south-west of Watton. (W Merriwether Jr Collection via 8th AF Research Center)

of American air and ground crews visited Hatfield and de Havilland's dispersal factories. The serial numbers of at least some of the Mk XVI aircraft in use at Cheddington in March can be found in the crash reports of the time; MM337, '344 and '385 all suffered minor damage in take-off and landing incidents. On 12 April the 802nd moved to Watton in Norfolk, to where direct deliveries of Mosquito PR.XVIs from Hatfield began, with the first, NS555, arriving on 19 May.

Although still only a provisional group at this stage, the 802nd's Light Weather Squadron Mosquitoes began daily meteorological reconnaissance missions over the Continent on 25 May, initially with one aircraft but rising to three by 7 June. The build-up of crews and aircraft enabled it to launch two Mosquitoes scouting for bombers attacking targets in France and Germany, plus seven on weather flights on 18 July.

Turning back to the delivery of MM308 to Alconbury in February for *Mickey* development, Tom Fields was closely involved in the work and describes his experiences on the project:

> In those days I was a Tech Sgt in photo reconnaissance. I helped develop a system of photographing a radar scope, enabling us to take recon photos at night, through cloud cover, without the use of light. My story begins with my arrival in England in January

Above: NS518, of 8th Light Weather Sqn, 802nd Recon Gp, still in RAF markings, after a take-off accident at North Pickenham on 3 June 1944. (G Scruggs)

Right: Tom Fields at Watton in October 1945. (Tom Fields)

1944 and initial assignment, in February, to the 13th Photo Recon Sqn, 7th Photo Recon Gp at Mount Farm. On 12 April I was transferred to 6th Combat Crew Replacement Centre at Watton, but reported directly for detached duty to the 8th Recon Sqn (Sp) at Alconbury [which was detached to Alconbury from Watton].

When I took over the [*Mickey*] project some of the primary decisions had been made. The type of camera had been selected – I believe it was the K-22. It used a long roll of film making square photos. We had to determine the best type of film to use, the best developer, and the length of developing time. One of my assistants, Staff Sgt Carl Wanka, was a camera technician and it was his job to make modifications to the camera – to determine the best way to mount it in the aircraft, and rig it to be operated by the navigator. The camera had to be positioned a certain distance from the radar scope which it photographed. Attached in front of the camera was a Rolex wristwatch to record on each photo the exact time it was taken. The end product was a photo (without flash bombs)

An anonymous PR.XVI from the 802nd Recon Gp (shortly to become the 25th Bomb Gp), pictured at Alconbury in 1944 for H2X conversion. (Tom Fields)

that looked something like a silhouette. It showed coastlines, entire cities, etc. The radar scope picked up certain objects that reflected its beam, like rocks, mountains, cities with their metal construction. Technical support was provided by the [resident] 482nd BG and we had the use of their photo lab to work out of. My duties included a trip to Warton [Base Air Depot No 2] to procure spares for our work. Mosquitoes ... flew the missions so that we could develop this project. Initially, they were only training missions over England while various problems were worked out. Later, they were combat recon missions deep into Germany. Also, we had the ground crews for the Mosquitoes.

I recall a tragic incident that stands out clearly [to Mosquito NS558 on 21 June]. One day when things were going rather slowly Capt. Richard Clounch got up from a game of cards and announced that he was going to fly his Mosquito down to

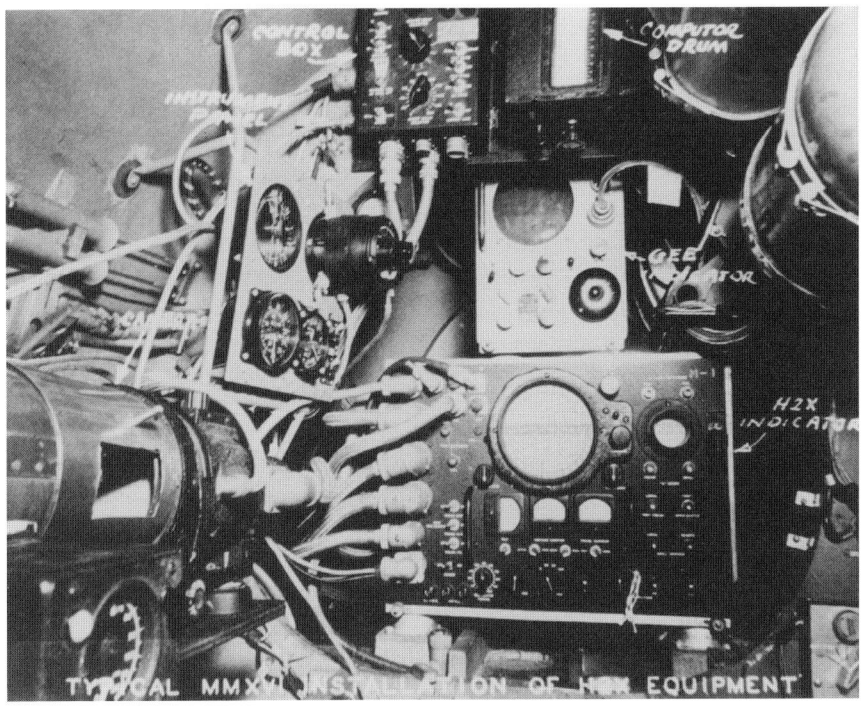

H2X radar equipment installed in *Mickey* Mosquitoes of the 654th Bomb Gp. (USAAF)

Left: Photo flash bombs loaded aboard a 25th Bomb Gp Mosquito. (NARA)

Below: Close-up of split vertical 12in camera installation in a USAAF Mosquito PR.XVI. (Dana Bell)

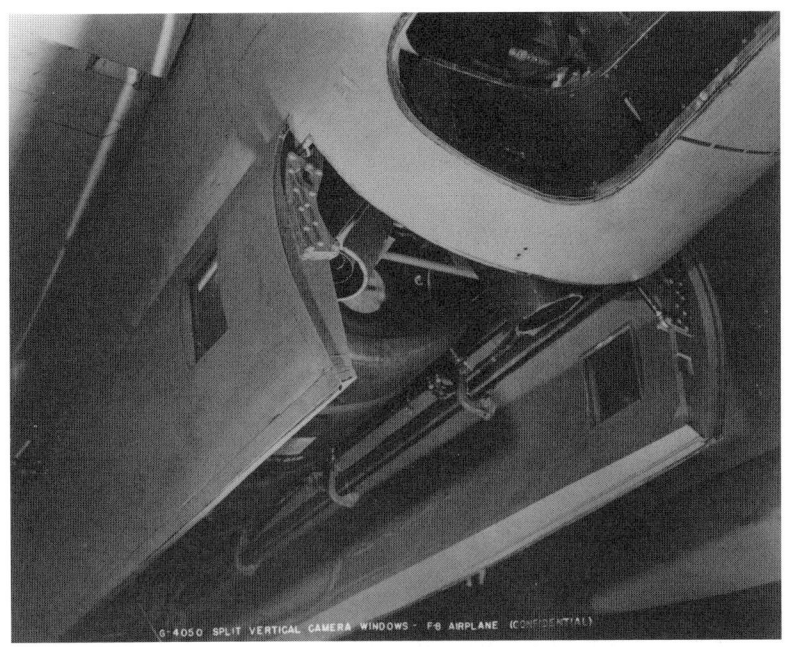

Mosquito bomb bay showing the installation of split vertical cameras. Note windows for cameras in the bomb bay doors. (Dana Bell)

Rear view of split vertical 12in cameras on USAAF Mosquito PR.XVIs. (Dana Bell)

25th Bomb Gp Mosquito pictured at Alconbury for H2X conversion in 1944. (Tom Fields)

Gravesend to visit some of his old RAF buddies with whom he had served. I drove him out to the plane in a jeep and he took off. That was the last time I saw him. As he approached his destination, the aircraft's wing was sliced off by a barrage balloon cable which was above the clouds by mistake. Naturally, the cable alone was hardly visible at that speed. Next day I flew down with someone in a small plane to Gravesend and took a camera to photograph the remains. Clounch [and his navigator, 1/Lt Connor O'Connor] had augured into a potato field. The two engines were buried far apart; otherwise there wasn't much but splinters widely scattered. Gravesend was an ironic implication. My detached duty at Alconbury ended on 25 July, when I moved back to Watton and the 802nd BG. There, at the end of August, I was placed on flying status.

Frank McKee was a ground maintenance man who joined the formative USAAF Mosquito fleet in April 1944 and recalls his experiences:

As an aircraft mechanic (Tech Sgt) I was assigned as a crew chief with one other mechanic to aircraft No NS559 (letter 'I').

My Squadron [which would become the 654th (SP)] received their 'Mossies' over a period of several months, starting, as best as I can remember, in March '44. These were the new high-altitude Mk XVI recon version with the 76/77 (I think) Merlin engines. About eight or ten of these were modified by the USAAF for night photography by installing bomb racks for photo flash bombs. The flash, 1M candle power, activated the cameras upon detonation. They were also painted gloss black over most of the fuselage and wings for night operations, in addition, of course, to the American insignia. I might add, all of the 'Mossies' had American comms equipment installed in lieu of the British Marconi sets. Also recall they were equipped with LORAN, GEE and OBOE equipment.

The two 'Mossie' squadrons had, in addition, about four [Airspeed] Oxfords that were used for twin-engine pilot training. There were also additional American aircraft in the Squadron which included several B-26 Marauders, one Havoc and one P-38 Droop Snoot. This P-38 was one of those that had been modified by lengthening the nose and making a kind of bombardier/ photographer compartment where the gun bay had been.

Loading photo flash bombs into a 654th Bomb Sqn Mosquito at Watton. (Robert Howle)

29

THE MOSQUITO IN THE USAAF

The first four months at Watton were spent primarily in training both the aircrew and the ground support personnel. At this time I would like to comment on the base facilities at Watton. The fact that they were of a permanent construction, steam heated, equipped with showers and bath tubs, a drying room and other niceties that I can't recall just now, didn't hurt one bit. When compared with the usual air stations with Nissen huts, potbelly stoves, usually cold water etc, the base at Watton was heaven.

Many of the maintenance personnel were sent to school to learn more about the Mosquito, with about half going to the de Havilland Factory School at Hatfield. The others, including myself, went to the Rolls-Royce Merlin engine School at Derby.

I do recall very vividly preparing my aircraft the day and night before the [D-Day] invasion. It was going to be used, as I remember, by the Group Commander. There was a need to swing the compass and this caused us some concern because we needed the aircraft to be in a level position on the compass rose. But we managed, and the 'Mossie' was ready with invasion stripes around midnight. [Author's note: USAAF Mosquito ops are recorded for 4 and 7 June, but not for the 5th or 6th]

Lack of proper recognition of these [Mosquito] aircraft by USAAF personnel, when painted black with American insignia, led to combat losses. I will quote the following example. As was customary at the time, the crew chief would accompany the pilot on many routine flights. On one such flight I flew with a pilot to Bassingbourn where the 91st BG (B-17s) was stationed. The pilot had planned to make some night landings there while our runway was being worked on. As was routine, he made a typical fighter type approach and buzzed the runway, then pulled up in a chandelle to the left to get into the pattern. This caused many of the personnel on the ground to notice the airplane and think our 'Mossie' was something other than what it was, perhaps a captured German Me 210 or 410. Upon landing, a large crowd gathered around the aircraft and waited until we climbed out of the cockpit. At that time numerous questions were put to us, such as what we were flying, where we came from etc. Many of the questions came from the B-17 combat crews who had not properly identified the 'Mossie'. Once they realized what it was, they seemed disappointed. Moreover, we had difficulty convincing a few that the USAAF was using this type of British aircraft.

As a crew chief it was standard procedure for me to taxi the aircraft for numerous reasons. Initially I found it difficult to get used to the air [pneumatic] braking system that was installed in the 'Mossie'. With its spring-loaded tail wheel it had to be brought round rather hard so you could get the tail wheel out of the take-off position. But eventually most of us became rather proficient. I might add that there were times when we taxied just to go for a ride. The small air compressor that ran off the starboard engine (as I remember) didn't seem to be large enough to maintain proper air pressure in the storage tank. This was especially true if frequent turns were required. Several close calls resulted from low air pressure, which caused us to be very cautious when taxiing.

We experienced one or two maintenance problems. For example, the bomb bay doors would sometimes creep open, either in the air or on the ground. Failure of the seals on the selection valves seemed to be the problem and we were always replacing them. The primer lines, constructed of copper tubing, for starting the engines were always cracking, resulting in leakage. The term 'boost', as opposed to 'manifold pressure' was unfamiliar to us, and we had to convert pounds of boost to inches of manifold pressure. Overall, though, the two Mosquito squadrons had a

Air and ground crew of the 8th Recon Gp pictured at Alconbury in 1944. (Tom Fields)

31

good serviceability rate. Generally speaking, maintenance was routine and spares were not too difficult to obtain. The fact that the Mosquitoes were brand new helped in this respect.

Activities at Watton in June inevitably focused on preparations for the air support of the D-Day Landings on the 6th. Although no Mosquito missions are officially recorded 'on the day', they followed soon after – and brought losses for the 802nd. After successfully carrying out a successful reconnaissance of the beachhead on 8 June, Mosquito NS555 returned to England and landed at Middle Wallop to refuel, and then took off for Watton. Witnesses reported that at about 1900 hrs they heard an aircraft in cloud flying in a northerly direction with the engines being opened up and then throttled back. The machine then suddenly broke out of the low cloud in a vertical dive with both engines flat out. It made a desperate half turn before crashing into a railway embankment in a ball of fire about a mile from High Wycombe. It was assumed that the pilot, Capt. Walter Gernand, had become disoriented and lost control, killing himself and his crewman, Sgt Ebbert Lynch.

Having joined the 802nd BG back in April, Capt. Jonah 'Gene' Goodbread had only six hours on the Mosquito when he flew his first operational mission on the type on D-Day + 5 – a two-hour forty-minute trip to Le Mans. He recalls:

25th Bomb Gp Mosquito with invasion stripes in 1944. (NARA)

Before flying Mosquitoes I had flown a tour in B-17s [twenty-five missions] from October 1943 to March 1944 with the 100th Bomb Group at Thorpe Abbotts. So flying over Europe did not bother me a lot, and that was an advantage. I was a flight commander in the 653rd Squadron and we flew missions such as weather reconnaissance both day and night for both ground and air forces, dropping chaff in front of the bomber streams, and flying the commanders of Bomb Groups to observe bombing results during raids. The weather recce missions were exciting at times when we would return to base in the late afternoon or night and the weather would be almost zero-zero. I recall taking off one day when I could see only one runway light. The summer of 1944 occurred in one afternoon and winter came early. We had very heavy snow at times and no snow removal equipment, so it stacked up on the runway and turned into ice as it was packed down. I recall spinning round three times on one landing, but fortunately without damage. We did not carry any guns or bombs, instead we had a gasoline tank in the bomb bay and two underwing tanks, which gave us considerable range. The best range was at about 22,000 ft in low 'blower' – but if you went into high 'blower' to get additional power for higher altitude the fuel consumption increased rapidly. I usually flew at 30,000 ft over the Continent on weather recon missions, and from 22,000 to 24,000 ft when working with the bombers.

Goodbread's longest trip was a six-hour, twenty-five-minute affair to Poltava, Ukraine, in the Soviet Union, on 11 September to support a *Frantic* force of B-17s and B-24s attacking oil and industrial targets in southern Germany on the 13th. He would go on to complete fifty-three missions and clock up more than 200 hours on the Mosquito. Of Leon Gray, Elliott Roosevelt et al, he says: '… they were all great guys during the war years and it was a pleasure to serve with them.' And of the Mosquito itself: 'In my opinion it was the finest propeller-driven aircraft ever built, and I have flown many other types. It did have its faults, such as a full swivel tail wheel, and tremendous torque which made take-offs exciting to say the least. This, of course, could have been corrected with a tricycle landing gear – but considering the times it was the greatest.'

Deliveries of Mosquitoes to Watton continued apace through June and July, with the result that on 9 August the 802nd was reconstituted as the

Gene Goodbread and Warren Barber escaped injury in this landing accident at North Pickenham, 7 miles north-west of Watton, on 25 July 1944. The Mosquito is NS510 'I' of the 802nd Recon Gp, predecessor of the 25th Bomb Gp. (W Barber)

MM364 was delivered to Burtonwood in March 1944, then went to Cheddington with the 802nd Recon Gp. It is shown here as 'C' with the 654th Bomb Sqn, post-D-Day. (Author's collection)

25th Bombardment Group (Reconnaissance), the first of the three permanent USAAF units to operate the Mosquito, with Lt Col Joseph Stenglein as CO. Its component squadrons, activated on the same date were:

652nd BS (Heavy, Weather Reconnaissance) – with B-17s and B-24s.

653rd BS (Light, Weather Reconnaissance) – with Mosquito PR.XVIs (plus B-17s and B-24s).

654th BS (Heavy, Reconnaissance, Special) – with Mosquito PR.XVIs (plus some B-25s, B-26s and P-38s).

For the following thirteen months of the Second World War the 25th BG would develop and refine the work begun by the 802nd and its tasks would include reconnaissance over the waters adjacent to the British Isles and

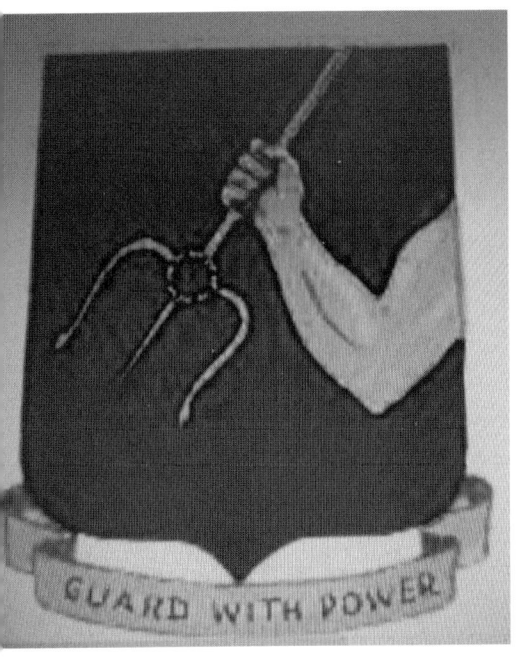

Above left: 25th Bomb Gp insignia. (Air Weather Recon Assn)

Above right: 653rd Bomb Sqn Ops sign, with the squadron badge, at Watton. (Norman Malayney)

Above left: 654th Bomb Sqn Ops sign, with the squadron badge, at Watton. (Norman Malayney)

Above right: Firing up the Rolls-Royce Merlin engines of a 25th Bomb Gp Mosquito at Watton. A group B-26 Marauder is in the background. (AAM)

occasionally the Azores to obtain meteorological data; sorties over the Continent to provide weather information for operational planning; night photographic flights to identify enemy activity; and mapping missions over the Continent. In addition, scout missions, already mentioned above, would occasionally be mounted to provide last-minute weather information for bomber formations already en route to the target, together with evaluation in the target area of attacks actually in progress, for the benefit of the participating bomber crews. Finally, chaff missions would be flown to confuse enemy radar during the course of Allied attacks. The missions flown on the 10 August provide a good example of a typical day's work for the Group's Mosquitoes: three on the scouting force; two on *Mickey* sorties to central Germany; one carrying out night photography in the Le Tréport area of France; and three on weather reconnaissance over south west England and the Brest peninsula.

During the Second World War the USAAF established sixteen Combat Camera Units (CCU) to provide still and motion pictures of military activity in all the theatres of operation. The material produced by the CCUs

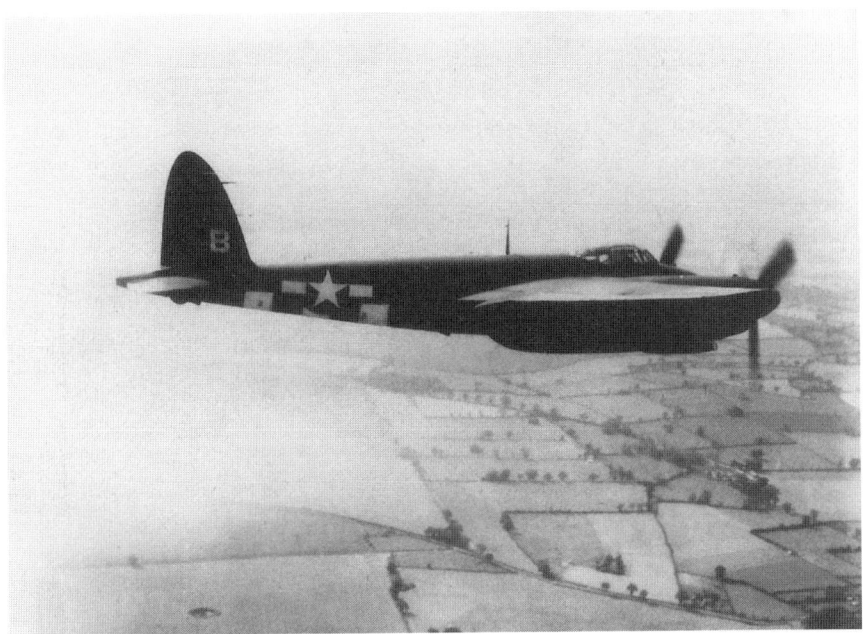

NS590 'B' of 654th Bomb Sqn captured by SSgt Bill Merriwether, base photographer at Watton. (W Merriwether)

MM388 'H' of 654th Bomb Sqn. Note unusual squadron lettering under the port wing.

was invaluable for operational analysis, training, public information and historical record. Typically, a unit comprised around twenty-three men, a large proportion of whom were assigned to flight duties. On the ground the units' photo technicians played a vital role in maintaining camera serviceability. With reconnaissance as the 25th BG's raison d'être it was logical to locate one of these units alongside the 25th BG at Watton, and this was the 8th CCU.

Above: 25th Bomb Gp Mosquito 'G' airborne over the English countryside. (Dana Bell)

Left: 25th Bomb Gp Mosquito 'H' undergoing servicing at Watton. (Eberly Family Spec Collections, Penn State University Libraries)

Operations in August 1944

A nominal change of title had not altered tasking in any way and the 25th BG started to play a significant part in operations in August. Up to this point the 653rd Sqn, and its antecedents, had been led by Maj. Hugh Bozarth, who had been with the 50th Fighter Sqn since January 1941. In 1977 he reflected, briefly, on his time on Mosquitoes.

I had 30 months in Iceland flying P-38 Lightnings, then two six-month tours in England as Squadron CO (653rd) and Assistant Group Operations Officer (25th BG). Weather recon, (not chaff nor night photo) was my outfit. I never touched down on the Continent, my time was all in England, February '44 to May '45. The 'Mossie' flew beautifully on wonderful Rolls-Royce Merlin engines and it sure was a big help to have the dual 'Mossie' for transition in checking out pilots. I modified the ship: bright white light aft to scan for vapor trails at night. (Weather recon pre-dawn for bomber information.) Installed the mike button to the starboard throttle lever so the right thumb could run the brake when taxiing. I also inserted a dummy plug in the external power source connection so as to disconnect the battery from all possible 'leaks' when parked away from home base. (We were often diverted to a FIDO base.) I once lost the overhead hatch on take-off, and on another occasion the landing gear folded on touchdown. I 'bellied-in' on a grass field. Following a rather uncomfortable fast descent for landing one night in a PR.XVI, I discovered ice on the leading edge of a wing. So I painted part of the leading edge, which enabled me to see rime or clear ice from the cabin. I also screened (with paint) a portion of the side windows so that exhaust flames wouldn't blind me as I approached for night landings. I jumped a bit when a double layer windscreen separated and fell onto the control column one night when crossing a coastal defense 'gate'. Apparently, the silica gel crystal vent tube was blocked. I made Berlin in one hour one night, which I guess was due to a jetstream. Another time I witnessed the results of a pilot trying to taxi without air brakes. The yaw increased and the tail swung round, hitting a mechanic's work stand. The tail broke off, aft of the wing, like a cracked egg.

Bozarth now moved on to the 7th Photo Gp and was replaced by Maj. Marshall Wayne, (with Robert Howle as Operations Officer).

25th Bomb Gp aircrew. L-R pilot Lt Handren with his navigator Lt Gordon. (Warren Borges via Dana Bell)

The 653rd described this month as:

> the most successful period for the Squadron since arrival [from Iceland] in the UK. During the month 74 weather scout missions were flown in support of the Heavy Bombardment Divisions and these covered practically all targets attacked by the 8th AF. These included the Operation *Frantic* targets covered by Allied bomber formations on the shuttle run to and from Russia. Two of the Sqn's aircraft crewed by Capt. Joe Baker and Maj. John Walsh, plus Lts Ronald Nichols and Elbert Harris mounted the shuttle run. The initial mission to Russia was successful, as was the second leg, an operation from Russian bases to Italy attacking targets in Bulgaria en route. However, on the last leg, from Italy to the UK flown on 12 August, the Sqn suffered the only loss of the month when Nichols and Harris flying NS533 were listed as

MIA. Bomber crews reported seeing the Mosquito going down in the target area from 29,000 ft, under control but with both engines stopped. No parachutes were seen.

It soon transpired that the loss was due to 'friendly fire'. At around 1145 hrs two P-51 Mustangs of the 357th FG climbed from 23,000ft to attack a twin-engine aircraft silhouetted against the sun. The attacking fighter pilot stated he saw neither air force markings nor invasion stripes on the victim. After the misidentified 'bogie' turned on to his six o'clock and tried to dive away he considered it to be hostile. Terminally damaged, the Mosquito crashed south-west of Toulouse, France, killing pilot Nichols. However, navigator Harris managed to bail out, evade capture and return to Watton on 6 September.

Following this incident the squadron history reports: 'As further identification aid for friendly aircraft, Mosquito Scouts are now marked with crimson tail planes and all organisations with which we might be allied on operations are notified of our presence by 8th Air Force field order.'

Throughout the month the 653rd flew seventy-one weather reconnaissance sorties of a pre-target selection type. Despite the fact that the Mosquito was a British design, constructed largely of wood and comparatively unfamiliar to American maintenance crews, the squadron managed a creditable

25th Bomb Gp cameramen about to install equipment aboard one of the group's Mosquitoes. (Author's collection)

NS557 after its landing accident on 6 August 1944 at Langford Lodge, Northern Ireland, when on the strength of 8th Special Sqn, 802nd Recon Gp. Three days later the 802nd would become the 25th Bomb Gp. The aircraft in the background appear to be Douglas A-20s or DB-7s. (James Matuska)

Another view of NS557 after its landing accident on 6 August 1944 at Langford Lodge, Northern Ireland. (USAAF)

85 per cent serviceability rate at this point. In this area MSgt Stanley McKuskie was commended for perfecting a hot air pipe designed to prevent Mosquito windscreens from icing up at high altitude.

The 654th BS began August with *Mickey* H2X missions to Emmerich, Manheim, Hamburg, Wesburg, and to Harburg, where the H2X equipment failed due to a blown fuse. The third day of the month also saw the launch of two *Joker* missions, which were night photo reconnaissance using photo flash bombs. Daylight recce sorties, termed 'PRU' missions, were also flown, such as the one on 6 August over 3rd Air Division targets to determine post-strike damage. Photos were taken of airfields, docks, railways and other objects of military importance. 'The mission was successful with no mishaps.' Using a Mosquito and a B-25, Gouremont, Gournay and Gace in France were photographed. A constant drive to improve the quality of photographs taken by such means as adjusting camera timings, modifications to photo flash bomb fuses, flying at different altitudes and even the introduction of fresh airframes was starting to give steadily pleasing results. On 7 August the *Mickey* Mosquito flown by 1/Lt Walter Thompson (P) and 2/Lt Carl Edgar (N) sent to Salzbergen, just over the Dutch border, and Magdeburg, deeper into Germany, was shot down by a Luftwaffe night fighter and the crew were not heard from again. They were later listed as KIA. The first mention of a *Dilly* mission occurs in the squadron records for 9 August. Dilly was the code word for the night photography of V-1 sites in France and two of these were flown on that date over Belle, Nogent and Alençon using a Mosquito and a B-25, both aircraft returning safely.

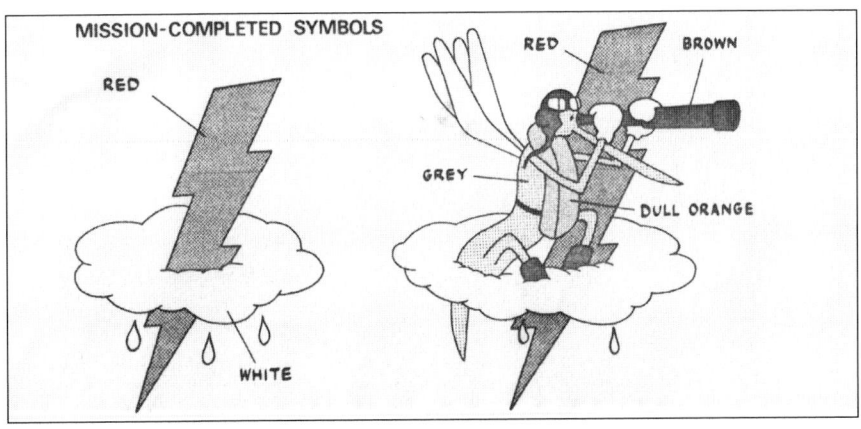

653rd Bomb Sqn 'Mission Completed' symbols. (Courtesy Ducimus Books)

25th Bomb Gp aircraft over the English countryside. Coded 'G', this makes it either NS508 or '552. (Author's collection)

At the same time as the new group and squadron designations came into force on 9 August, Maj. John Larkin assumed command of the 654th BS. The following day saw an interesting turn of events for the men of 8th CCU when one first sergeant and six photo technicians were removed from flying status. This was because the current regulations forbade personnel from flying in combat unless they were at least of sergeant rank. The month saw a marked improvement in aerial photographic techniques, especially in developing prints. There was a brisk crew room discussion on the relative merits of mechanical means versus airborne photographers. On one of the two *Dillys* flown on 11 August to the St Germain-Creux area, Col Elliott Roosevelt from the 325th Recon Wg HQ acted as co-pilot to Maj. Hoover. On the same day the crew of a *Mickey* over Bremerhaven and Politz obtained good results but complained of upset stomachs due to greasy food back at base!

A typical *Mickey* was mission 8/15, flown by F/O Russell Whitmer and his navigator, 1/Lt Bill Cannon, on the night of 12–13 August, to photograph Schweinfurt and Nürnburg. Taking off from Watton at 2238 hrs, NS584 made its way out over Southwold and crossed into enemy territory at Westhooft on the Dutch coast. Well into the mission the H2X definition proved to be

25th Bomb Gp Mosquito, serial number unknown, nicknamed *Ware*. (Dana Bell)

poor, and the camera created interference when on intervalometer (a device that controlled the number of exposures at set time intervals). Maximum brilliance was required on the remote scope, and the set was found to be noisy. Faced with these problems, the crew resorted to manual photography for the entire task. Flak was encountered over Westhooft, but fortunately this was low and behind the Mosquito. Over Nürnburg searchlights tried to cone the aircraft but Whitmer was able to slip away unscathed. Retracing its flightpath back to Watton, '584 touched down at 0238 hrs and the results of the mission were assessed as 'fairly good, despite the H2X kit performing poorly'.

Experience with the H2X equipment thus far prompted the following comment in the Squadron records: 'H2X is quite temperamental but easily understood. It consists of 17 different circuits, and you have to be careful what you say near to it! Avoid unnecessary roughness – use great skill during maintenance. Constant efforts are being made to remedy the present faulty [maintenance] conditions.' Reference is made to two *Seaweed* missions flown on 15 August that photographed Brest, Lannilis, Roscoff and Morlaix. *Seaweeds* were the photo reconnaissance of French coastal towns. The two *Joker* missions flown on 16 August are interesting in that one was flown by a Mosquito and the other by a B-26. Following the *Dilly* mission flown on the same day the crew suggested that the bomb release indicator in the Mosquito be replaced with a toggle switch because: 'At present the navigator cannot be sure the bombs have gone.'

The commissioning of two pilots, Vance Chipman and Richard Geary, as second lieutenants is recorded on 19 August, with the added comment: 'Both pilots are ex-RAF and are among the best in the business.' Chipman was one of the 25th's most colourful characters and his name crops up frequently in American Mosquito folklore. His navigator, Bill Cannon (who would later be shot down with him), remembers him vividly:

> He and several other pilots on the 25th were trained in the Mosquito as RAF and Canadian Air Force pilots. These were the 'Yanks'

An unidentified 25th Bomb Gp aircraft starting up engines at Watton. In the background are B-26 Marauders and Mosquitoes. (USAAF)

The 25th Bomb Gp's legendary pilot Vance 'Chip' Chipman (centre) with his navigator Bill Cannon (left) and crew chief TSgt Jordan. Behind is Chipman's personal Mosquito *Chip's Chariot*. (Bill Cannon)

that enlisted in the RAF and RCAF prior to the US entry into the war. When the 25th BG was formed these men were transferred to the USAAF to fly the Mosquito in the Group, with the result that they were experienced combat pilots. Vance was probably the finest (and he could tell you so) pilot of the Group. He took particular pride in making a smooth landing. As the navigator rode in the bomb bay of the plane Vance would talk to me over the intercom and give me a running report on the approach and attempt to make a landing which I could not detect at the first touchdown. The navigator didn't have a window so I could not see anything outside of the bomb bay, and it was close quarters. Vance flew whenever he could. He loved the 'Mossie' and had me make night flight plans for him to fly along on a practice mission around England. I stayed on the ground as often as I could.

An online forum check of Vance Chipman reveals that immediately before joining the 25th he was flying Mosquito FB.VIs with the RAF's 605 Sqn

Lts Vance Chipman (left – pilot) and Richard Clounch in front of a 654th Bomb Gp machine in mid-1944. (Author's collection)

at Bradwell Bay in Essex. On 20 February 1944, flying 'UP-G' (with nav Flt Sgt Hugh Morrison, RNZAF) he was credited with damaging a twin-engine enemy aircraft, possible an Me 110, over Munster. A similar claim followed on 2 March, when flying HJ784 'UP-F' north-east of Paris. And then on 26 April he destroyed a twin-engined enemy aircraft at Laon-Athies airfield in France. He was thus a well-qualified and timely addition to the group. He also made an impression on Tom Fields, who still remembered him some thirty-two years later:

> Probably the most distinctive character in our outfit was Lt Vance Chipman … and I DO mean 'character'. He was rather like an Errol Flynn type – handsome, dashing and wild – and he loved drinking and chasing women. He was also a fantastic pilot who seemed to fear nothing. Our outfit seemed to have an abundance of mascots – all sorts of animals. Chipman had a monkey – I have no idea where he got the critter. Once at a drinking party at the Officers' Club Chipman had the audacity to challenge Elliott

48

Roosevelt (son of the 'Great White Father') to a duel – with fire extinguishers! Being considerably outranked, Chipman naturally lost out – in more ways than one. Next day, for punishment, he was ordered to live for 30 days in a one-man pup tent on the grounds outside the Officers' Quarters at Watton. On this Station we had unusually nice quarters for both the officers and NCOs. This meant more of a sacrifice to vacate his room for a small tent. Therefore, Chipman let his monkey occupy his room while he served out his punishment. Chip took this bare-minimum accommodation very light heartedly and outside his tent he had a big sign made that read: 'These quarters occupied by 2nd Lt Vance F Chipman, the No 1 fire extinguisher fluid dispenser and buzz artist in the Group. Date of occupation: 26 July 1944'.

The 654th BS lost its second *Mickey* Mosquito on 20 August when NS625 went down on a mission to Bremen. Pilot 1/Lt Raymond Musgrove apparently lost control and was killed in the crash, navigator 1/Lt Harold Fordham surviving to become a PoW.

Alongside the daily *Mickey* and *Joker* missions, which were hazardous enough in themselves, August saw the group involved in more dramatic operations that would intrigue historians down the years – support

Vance Chipman's pup tent at Watton in 1944. The sign reads: 'These quarters occupied by Vance F Chipman, the No 1 fire extinguisher fluid dispenser and first in the Group. Date of occupation 26 July 1944'. (Bill Cannon)

Above: Capts Lionel Proulx (navigator, left) and Earl Muchway (pilot) leave 653rd Bomb Sqn Operations at Watton for another mission. (Author's collection)

Left: 653rd Bomb Sqn Capts Lionel Proulx and Earl Muchway pose for a publicity shot with Mosquito NS509 'H'. (Peter Frost)

for *Aphrodite*. This project involved stripped down B-17 Flying Fortresses and PB4Y-1 Liberators (referred to as 'babies'), filled to capacity with high explosives, being guided to Continental targets by a radio-controlling 'mother' ship. 'Babies' had a crew of two – pilot and radio man – who would perform a normal take-off, and then, once radio control had been established by the accompanying 'mother', would bail out over the English countryside. The crewless 'baby' would then continue towards the target under radio control. The role of the 25th BG (actually still the 802nd Gp at this point) would be to provide a camera ship and a weather scout for each launch.

The first such mission took place on 4 August 1944, the target concrete V-site structures near the French coast, of which the 654th operations record has this to say:

> Two Mosquitoes with movie cameras flown in support of 3rd Division for *Aphrodite*. Only 1 mission completed – both planes returned to base. The aircraft failing to complete the mission encountered heavy flak which necessitated evasive action. The cameraman took pictures of the flak and the aircraft returned to Watton. Mosquito NS559 also ran into flak over the target area, which resulted in return to base on one engine. Small damage to port wing where several flak holes found.

This somewhat understates the drama of what took place that day and Roger Freeman, in his *Mighty Eighth War Manual*, paints a fuller picture. Two 'babies' were flown out of Fersfield, Norfolk, in the early afternoon, five minutes apart. The first 'baby', a B-17, was successfully guided across the Channel towards its target, Watten, after the crew had successfully made their planned exit over Suffolk but control was lost at the last minute and it crashed in a spectacular explosion at Gravelines. The second 'baby' met disaster at an even earlier stage of the operation. Shortly after radio control was established, while still over England the Fort went into an uncontrollable spin and subsequently crashed near Sudbourne, Suffolk. Both crewmen bailed out but pilot Lt John Fisher left it too late and was killed. Later in the day two more 'babies' took off from Fersfield, bound for Wizernes and Mimoyecques respectively, but were no more successful. Just before noon, Mosquito NS516, crewed by Capts Willis Locke (P) and Lloyd Humphries (N), had taken off to weather scout the target area. Later on, at 1330 hrs, Lt Dean Sanner, with Sgt Marc Ortega from the 8th CCU as cameraman, flew NS581 to film and observe the missions, meeting heavy flak in the process.

In an October 1976 letter to the author, Gen. Earle Partridge described how, as commander of the 3rd Bomb Division (the controlling authority for *Aphrodite*) he had flown a P-38 to observe the first live mission on 4 August. Alongside him, in another P-38, was Gen. Jimmy Doolittle, commander of the 8th AF.

While the 8th CCU's Mark Ortega had filmed the initial *Aphrodite* missions from a Mosquito, other cameramen from the CCU, S/Sgt Augie Kurjack, Sgts Ralph Thiry and Joe Capicotto, flew in the 'mother' ships from Fersfield. A review of the quality of respective photographic material produced from Mosquito and 'mother' ship caused a rethink at the CCU, as recorded in the unit's combat report:

> After showing the film it was decided that the risks overshadowed the results of the mission. Moreover, too many cameramen were tied up in the assignment. Results were poor and the men were recalled from Fersfield. The Mosquito flights proved that good photo results could be obtained from a low altitude plane – so future ops covering APHRODITE were planned for the Mosquitoes.

A plaudit for the specialist PR.XVI.

The *Aphrodite* mission scheduled for 12 August marked a violent climax to the project. Early that evening eight-year-old Mick Muttitt was standing in the back garden of his house in Suffolk when he saw a mixed formation passing over. Already a keen aircraft spotter (he would eventually become a Master Air Electronics Operator in the RAF), he could pick out two B-17 Flying Fortresses, two P-38 Lightnings, two P-51 Mustangs, a Mosquito, what looked like two Hudsons (actually PV-1 Venturas), and, at the head of the formation, a B-24 Liberator. Suddenly, to his horror, the Liberator disappeared in a deafening explosion that rocked the formation and showered wreckage on the countryside below. What he didn't know was that the Liberator was actually a PB4Y-1, piloted by Lt Joe Kennedy Jr, US Naval Reserve, with Lt Wilford 'Bud' Willy as co-pilot/radio man, and that the bomber was part of Project Anvil, the US Navy equivalent, and operating alongside, the USAAF *Aphrodite* programme. The Venturas were acting as 'mother' ships and the target for the Liberator was the innovatory V-3 cannon, designed to fire high-explosive projectiles at London, located at Mimoyecques.

While young Muttitt had witnessed the Liberator's fiery demise from the ground, the observers in the airborne formation had gained a closer and more hair-raising view of the incident. Again, the records of the 8th CCU include a graphic description of events.

> *Aphrodite* again held the spotlight on 12 August. Lt McCarthy flew as cameraman with Lt Bob Tunnell of 654th BS as pilot. Although the flight was not considered a complete mission it was packed with action. [McCarthy stated from his hospital bed] 'We were flying over England and decided to close in on the "Baby". I was flying in the nose of the plane so I could get some good shots of the "Baby" in flight ahead of us. The "Baby" just exploded in mid-air as we neared it and I was knocked half way back to the cockpit. A few pieces of the "Baby" came through the plexiglass nose and I got hit in the head and caught a lot of fragments in my right arm. I crawled back to the cockpit and lowered the wheels so that Bob could make a quick emergency landing.'

Lt Tunnell added:

> I didn't get a scratch but I was near scared to death. As 'Mac' told you, we were coming in to take close-ups of the 'Baby' which was under control and flying level. We came in on the right side, high and then the damn thing exploded in mid-air. The Mosquito went up a few hundred feet and I didn't get any response from the controls. I was getting ready to reach for my parachute but decided to check the controls again. This time they responded. I decided to try to make a landing. One engine was cut and the other was smoking. We were near a field so I headed straight for it. We made a good landing and then the second motor cut out. I had just enough speed left to get the 'Mossy' off the runway, but I couldn't taxi into a hardstand. I'm sure glad that the pictures of our previous mission were good because I don't think we're going to get that close to the 'Baby' again.

The 8th CCU's report goes on to add a sad postscript to the tumultuous events of 12 August:

> Since Lt McCarthy was hospitalized, S/Sgt August 'Augie' Kurjack was selected to fly in the 'Mossy' on the following day. This was to be the last chapter of *Aphrodite* to be filmed during August. It was also

Above left: Ground crew examine damage to Lt Bob Tunnell's 654th Bomb Sqn NS569, sustained when an *Aphrodite* PB4Y-1 Liberator they were filming exploded prematurely on 12 August 1944. (USAAF)

Above right: Lts Bob Tunnel (pilot) and David McCarthy (cameraman) of 654th Bomb Sqn in front of Mosquito NS569, damaged when a PB4Y-1 Liberator exploded. (USAAF)

the last chapter of *Aphrodite* for Lt Sanner and S/Sgt Kurjack. One person was seen to parachute from the Mosquito before it crashed on the coast of France. It is believed that 'Augie' was the parachutist since the escape hatch was more readily accessible to the cameraman.

What had actually happened was that on 13 August the 654th BS's 1/Lt Dean Sanner (with Kurjack as cameraman)had been tasked with filming the first operational Batty mission. This centred around a standard 2,000lb bomb modified for television guidance and radio control, with small wings and moveable tail surfaces. Two of these weapons were carried on racks mounted under the wings of a B-17 'mother' ship. Target for the day was Le Havre. Straying too close to one of the weapons after its release, MM370 was struck by fragments when the bomb detonated and in the ensuing crash Kurjack was killed, Sanner surviving to become a PoW. Sanner recalls exactly what happened:

SSgt August 'Augie' Kurjack, cameraman with the 8th AAF Combat Camera Unit, who flew photo missions with the 25th Bomb Gp. He was killed in action in Mosquito MM370 on 13 August 1944. (Dana Bell)

On the way to the initial point I had 'Augie' take pictures of the stubby-winged glide bombs hung under the wings of the B-17. When the first bomb was released I followed it down until it neared the ground. I found it difficult to follow and keep in sight. It seemed erratic in horizontal and vertical flight. After either losing sight of the bomb or seeing that it wasn't going to hit anything, I broke off the pursuit and climbed back to follow the second glide bomb.

After all aircraft were again in position at the IP the second bomb was released and I followed it on its descent. I zigzagged back and forth considerably to hold the faster Mosquito behind the slower gliding bomb. Later I had a difficult time keeping within photographic range because of the final steep dive of the bomb. At low altitude I once again broke away to escape range of the explosion. It had fallen in the marsh.

Upon breaking off I remained low to the ground. Any effort to climb to altitude would slow the craft and leave it vulnerable to enemy activity. My intention was to head for open water between the banks of the Seine River, then climb back to altitude over the English Channel. As fate would have it, I flew over the bomb as it exploded. The immense blast blew me out of the aircraft. After the explosion I found myself in the air. My right arm was practically useless. I pulled the parachute ripcord ring with my left hand and made a swing or two before landing in the mud of the marsh. My right shirt sleeve and right pants leg were shredded and bloody. My right ankle was bent inward at quite an angle. I am afraid that my cameraman was not so fortunate. Only one parachute was seen to open.

In great pain and unable to walk, Sanner was soon picked up by German soldiers and moved first to hospital in Amiens and then ultimate incarceration in Stalag Luft 1, near Barth in Germany.

Before bringing the momentous events of August to a close it is irresistible to return for a moment to that formation of aircraft on the Kennedy mission of 12 August, and in particular the P-51 Mustangs noted by young Muttitt. Prompted by a statement in Jack Olsen's book, *Aphrodite: Desperate Mission*, implying that Generals Partridge and Doolittle were pilots in the formation – '… both were up in their own fighter planes …' – the author wrote to Gen. Doolittle in 1976 about his possible involvement on the day in question. He replied: 'I was flying in the vicinity – I think in a P-51 – and saw Joseph P Kennedy's aircraft crash. It crashed among some trees and I have a distinct recollection of the trees leaning away from the blast and then springing back.' It's just possible that, after thirty-two years, he was confusing missions. But if so, who was flying the Mustangs?

Capts Lionel Proulx (navigator, left) and Earl Muchway (pilot) at Watton in August 1944. (Author's collection)

Operations – September 1944

Significant events for the group as a whole began, on the 15th, with a lecture by 2/Lt Elbert Harris on escape and evasion in France. Harris was qualified in his subject for he was the navigator of Mosquito NS533 shot down over the country on 12 August. He was fortunate in being the first aircrew man to return to Watton after being listed as MIA. On 25th Lt Col Stenglein moved to the 325th Wg as deputy CO and his post as CO of the 25th BG was filled by Lt Col Leon Gray, who would remain as 'boss' for the duration of the war. The latter is described as an 'old hand at recon work [who] flew in N Africa and Italy for nearly two years'. During the month informal names were given to the constituent squadrons, the 652nd (with B-17s and B-24s) being known as the 'Heavy Weather Sqn', the 653rd as the 'Light Weather Sqn', and the 654th as the 'Special Sqn'. Two ex-RAF pilots joined the group at this point, John Noble and Roy Ellis-Brown. The latter was assigned to Group HQ in the rank of captain, the equivalent of his flight lieutenant RAF rank, and initially assumed duties as Assistant Ops Officer. With chance US citizenship, his background was interesting in that he had completed two tours on Short Stirlings, including a spell with 7 Sqn at Oakington, the first squadron to operate the first of the RAF's four-engined heavy bombers. No. 7 was among those selected to form the core of the RAF's Pathfinder Force.

Roy Ellis-Brown, ex-RAF
Stirling pilot, Group
Operations Officer with the
25th Bomb Gp at Watton.
(Roy Ellis-Brown)

Roy Ellis-Brown with parachute, all set for a trip in a Mosquito T.III. (Roy Ellis-Brown)

Maj. Roy Ellis-Brown, Ops Officer for the 25th Bomb Gp (and ex-RAF 7 Sqn Short Stirling pilot), at the controls of a Mosquito during a trip to Holland with *Flight* magazine photographer John Yoxall in early 1945. Note the British-issue flying helmet. (Flight)

As Assistant Ops Officer, and using his own extensive operational experience, Ellis-Brown tackled his new USAAF career with energy and enthusiasm. The workload and challenges of the time placed a heavy responsibility on the group's executives, as Ellis-Brown relates:

> So this fell on the Operations Office. In this I was aided very well by a Maj. James McNulty who was my Deputy Group Operations Officer. He was a very dedicated soul and performed his task very well: he did most of the leg work and left me the opportunity to do most of the planning. At about this time we had a visit from General Jimmy Doolittle, who came up to the base and spent a day with us. And he was very emphatic about the fact that we should get cracking and get fully operational, become more efficient. [He] let us know that he was depending on us and so were Generals Patton, Bradley and several of the other army ground commanders to provide [reconnaissance] information. The Group at this time was getting pretty efficient.

The weather forecasting for the group's operations was, felt Ellis-Brown, a weak area and so a new Met man was installed:

> There had been no co-operation at all with RAF Intelligence or even the Met Office, and I set about at this point to eliminating this particular road block. And from then on, we started getting some pretty good co-operation between the two branches of the Service.
>
> In connection with this, I made a visit to the famous [RAF] 100 Gp which was stationed not very far from us, and made myself known there and what I needed. Also, offered any information that we might have which would be useful to them. These people were flying Lend-Lease B-17s at high altitude and doing countermeasure experimental work as well as electronic surveillance, radio communication monitoring of the German Air Force. I met a very fine individual over there, a flight lieutenant, who helped me tremendously. He was right on top of his job and gave me a tremendous amount of information. I relied on RAF 100 Gp pretty heavily. [Author's note: 'E-B''s reference to nearby 100 Gp and B-17s suggests he visited Oulton, 23 miles further north in Norfolk, then home to 214 Sqn and its Boeing Fortresses.]

Lt Oliver Emmel in the cockpit and navigator Lt Iver Fischer in the nose of this 25th Bomb Gp Mosquito with four mission symbols under the cockpit. (USAAF)

According to the group's combat record, the most interesting operations of the month were the low-level reconnaissance sweeps over the battle areas performed by the 653rd Sqn for the 9th AF. These missions were often so numerous that the 654th Sqn had to help out. Since the 'Special' Sqn had more pilots experienced in night flying, it tended to undertake the night operations. These flights, made to identify the altitude of the base of low cloud, 'were often made at heights below the surrounding terrain and man-built structures'! The record further observed that: 'Becoming evident that, with the present planes and equipment, the "Special" Sqn's night photography with flash bombs is becoming impossible due to the distance to the battle fronts and limited radius of action with present equipment.'

For the 653rd Sqn, September brought an end to Scout missions for the bomb divisions after trials revealed that P-51 Mustangs were more suitable. The squadron could take pride in the pioneering work it had done for this type of operation, and the unit's record book took the opportunity to take a retrospective look at how Scout missions had been mounted:

> To trace the course of one of these missions [they] start at 8th AF
> HQ. The mission is 'built' by the joint planning of Group Ops,

25th Bomb Gp Mosquito named *Kitty* and crews. (Dana Bell)

Intelligence, Navigation, Weather and Communications, guided by a Master Field order. The aim of the SCOUT mission is to arrive at a prescribed target, despite obstacles/opposition, at a predetermined time and give target weather data to the 'heavies' who are, at this time, still some distance from the target. A lookout is also kept for possible smokescreens and enemy action. The numerous commendations sent down from various Divisions testify to the value of the SCOUT missions. Once the mission is 'built' the crew assemble for a thorough briefing by the various specialist departments.

SCOUT crews mainly consist of pilots who have completed tours on 'heavies' and observers who are meteorological experts as well as rated navigators. After briefing the crew is taken to their ship – a Mosquito XVI assigned to each crew for their sole use. Flights average four hours and vary from 'route' SCOUTS to 'target' SCOUTS, and from minor penetrations to flights clear to our Russian bases. On return, crews are debriefed by Group Intelligence and the information gained used at subsequent mission briefing.

The 379th Bomb Gp's B-17s are the backdrop to this shot of NS748 'A' from 653rd Bomb Sqn on a visit to Kimbolton. (379th BG Assn via 8th AF Research Center)

Three Mosquitoes flew the 653rd's last Scout missions on 22 September. (The Scouting Force concept had been originated early 1944 by Col Bud Peaslee, CO of the 384th BG. Three Scouting Forces were formed, the First being activated at Honington on 19 September and taking over the role first performed by the 25th BG's Mosquitoes. Peaslee's name will crop up again in the USAAF Mosquito story.)

The old saying that 'a good landing is one you can walk away from' was amply demonstrated on 9 September when Lt John Noble made an emergency, wheels-up landing in MM391 due to mechanical failure. He and his navigator, F/O Gorham, were unharmed but the aircraft was 'washed out'. It happened again five days later when Lts Porter and Davis crash-landed after a mission to the Continent. The Mosquito was acting as an observation aircraft for two B-17 drones being guided by two B-17 'mother' ships to the Hemmingstedt oil refinery. Porter experienced problems during flight, losing his airspeed indicator and one engine while over enemy territory. On return to base the u/s engine cut back in but caught fire on final approach, causing the pilot to land despite the knowledge that he was overshooting. Although the aircraft was a write-off the crewmen were uninjured.

On the ground a number of maintenance personnel attended UK training schools for instruction in a range of mostly Mosquito-related technical subjects. These included the de Havilland School at Hatfield for airframes; the Rolls-Royce Engine School at Derby to learn about the Merlin; RAF Melksham, Wiltshire, for servicing the Fluxgate compass; RAF Sutton-on-Hull (the RAF School of Fire Fighting and Rescue) for a course on crash tender maintenance; and even RAF Weeton, Lancashire, the RAF Police School.

Over at the 654th Sqn there was tragedy on 8 September when Mosquito NS538 exploded in mid-air during an air test, killing F/O Russell Whitmer and M/Sgt Raymond Armstrong. The cause was not known and an investigation was begun. Due to a decrease in the number of operational

NS538 'F' of 654th Bomb Sqn, an H2X conversion, was lost when it exploded in mid-air on 8 September 1944. (Dana Bell)

NS538 'F' of the 654th Bomb Sqn. (AAM)

missions, the squadron took on the task of weather reconnaissance and flew its first *Bluestocking* mission on the 19th. Flown by the CO, Maj. Larkin, this covered Holland and Belgium. The record states: 'Mission flown on the deck – shooting came from farmers ploughing fields, civilians in towns, and local talent driving along roads in carts. One superman became so incensed that he threw his pitchfork at the aircraft.' Later, apparently, even rocks were hurled at the low-flying Mosquitoes, though no damage was suffered! The two *Bluestocking* aircraft sent over northern France, Holland and Belgium on the 21st encountered flak over Calais. The aircraft flown by Lt Rhoades was hit and suffered damage to the port wing and gas tank, but returned safely. Lts Claybourne Vinyard (P) and John O'Mara (N), up in NS570 on another *Bluestocking* over the Continent on 25 September, were not so lucky and were shot down by an enemy fighter. Fortunately, both managed to bail out and survived to become PoWs, the aircraft crashing near Gerhardshofen in Germany.

Maj. Willis D Locke (right), CO of 654th Bomb Sqn, alongside air and ground crew with a photo flash bomb used by the squadron. (NARA)

The compiler of the 8th CCU's monthly report clearly relished his job and in the process provides an interestingly different perspective to Mosquito operations. Due to a reduction in combat tasking, the emphasis shifted to training and the report goes on to say:

Since the cameraman replaced the navigator in the Mosquito it was suggested that photographers study map reading and navigation. All flying personnel attended classes during the month in preparation for the dual role they are to assume in the Mosquito.

Capt. Emmett Bergholz completed his first mission in the ETO after flying 48 combat missions in the South Pacific. Bergholz flew in a Mosquito piloted by Lt Bob Tunnell and filmed the attack on Heligoland Island [the second and final *Anvil* Liberator drone operation mounted on 3 September to attack the island U-boat base]. 'I guess the toughest part of the mission was sweating out the three aborts before it finally came off' said Bergholz on his return. 'Bob Tunnell is the best pilot I have flown with on a photographic mission. He knows where the picture is and gets the Mossie in such a position that the cameraman has a swell view of the subject to be photographed.'

The report continues:

Ten days later Capt. Jack Blake pulled his first sortie over the Continent. Veteran of thirty-two missions in the SW Pacific while assigned to the 5th AF also flew with Bob Tunnell in the pilot's seat. [Blake goes on to describe what is probably the 13 September drone attack on Hemmingstedt]: 'We were following instruction to the "T" and were hovering over the target waiting for the strike. The "Baby" plane that we followed hit a target of opportunity about 10 miles away. By the time we got to the 'new' target all I could see was smoke … nothing that could make a good picture story.' On his return Blake commented: 'In the Pacific I always sweated out a forced landing in the jungle, or a ditching in the sea. Once that happened, "you'd had it." But today I wasn't worried about that. I thought about the enemy fighters and flak I have heard so much about. Luckily, I didn't meet up with either, so I can't judge which theater is the toughest.'

Although its entire career was with the USAAF before being struck off charge at war's end, MM388 oddly bears RAF tail markings. Vance Chipman crash landed her at her birthplace – Hatfield – on 2 September 1944. (S Goldstein Collection via 8th AF Research Center)

Tragedy struck the 8th CCU on 18 September when cameraman S/Sgt Johnny Cunney was alerted for his first mission in a Mosquito, his task being to photograph airborne troop activity in Holland. With the ubiquitous Bob Tunnell at the controls, NS593 took off for the Nijmegen – Eindhoven area but was shot down by ground fire near Plantlunne airfield in Germany. Both men were killed. On a more cheerful note, the movie showing at the base cinema was *Double Indemnity* starring Edward G. Robinson, Fred MacMurray and Barbara Stanwyck, and on 29th of the month Marlene Dietrich, together with other entertainers from the USA, made a personal appearance in Watton's hangar No. 3.

Camera controls at the navigator's station in USAAF Mosquito PR.XVIs. (Dana Bell)

Vertical camera installation in 25th Bomb Gp Mosquitoes. (USAAF via Dana Bell)

Another view of the vertical camera installation in 25th Bomb Gp Mosquitoes. (USAAF via Dana Bell)

Above left: Cockpit camera controls in a 25th Bomb Gp Mosquito PR.XVI. (Dana Bell)

Above right: On 29 September 1944 Marlene Dietrich and seven other entertainers from the USA gave a concert in Watton's No. 3 hangar at Watton. Here she is with Leon Gray. (Tom Fields)

Operations – October 1944

Having played a key role in getting Scout missions off the ground, the group now turned its attention to pioneering work in the field of long-range navigation – or, to use its acronym, LORAN. With the high priority placed on strategic bombing, LORAN was of particular interest to the UK. The RAF had an existing navigation system, GEE, but used for bombing operations on distant targets in Europe. After a briefing on GEE by the Tizard Mission (Henry Tizard was a British scientist and chairman of the Aeronautical Research Committee), Alfred Loomis of the US National Defense Research Committee designed a new type of system that would improve on GEE. Originally known as SCR-622, it became AN/APN-4 and thus was born LORAN. Under the title of *Skywave*, both squadrons began flying LORAN missions, the first of which was to Italy on 6 October, flown by John Larkin with Lt William Mishko in the navigator's seat. Lead navigators from 8th AF bomb divisions and combat wings, together with RAF personnel, began visiting the station to learn about the new equipment under the expert tutelage of Captain, Lionel Proulx, the Group Navigator. Lt Howard Kaplan, the Group Radar Officer, and some of his men visited Alconbury for a short course on LORAN equipment.

Flying training during the month consisted primarily of transition training on the P-38 with the possible prospect of using the Lightning for H2X missions. There was a theory that it might be more efficient for this

A still from the de Havilland company's official film about the Mosquito, which included footage of 25th Bomb Gp aircraft at Watton. Nearest is NS739 'F' of 653rd Bomb Sqn. (Author's collection)

Cpl Charles Austin, Sgt Herbert Caudle and Pvt Paul Sachs with a night camera for a 654th Bomb Sqn Mosquito. (NARA)

Ground crew load cameras aboard a 25th Bomb Gp Mosquito named *Suzanne*. Pictured are Herb Caudle, Charles Austin, Paul Sachs and Milron Greenberg. (USAAF/NARA)

type of mission. This conversion training claimed the life of 2/Lt Stanley Hazlett from the 654th BS when his Lightning crashed at Tollgate Farm, Scoulton, 5 miles east of Watton on 11 October.

For some time crews had been complaining that the British oxygen system gave an insufficient supply at high altitude. Tests conducted by medical officer Capt. Omer Snyker seemed to justify this criticism and US equipment was duly installed. The number of Mosquitoes available for ops fell while the work was carried out but 'No further squawks have been heard'. To try to minimise airframe down time, modifications to Mosquito wing leading edges, ordered by a directive from de Havilland, were carried out at the same time.

Lt Malcolm MacLeod and his navigator Lt Edward Fitzgerald of the 653rd BS had a narrow escape on 22 October when they were forced to cut all switches on take-off in NS514, apparently at RAF Tangmere, Sussex. They lost power on one engine before they were airborne and the aircraft ran off the runway while MacLeod was attempting to decelerate. The Mosquito was destroyed but the crew got away with it. MacLeod would not be so lucky the following month.

Photographing Emmen in Holland from 22,000ft through 5/10 cloud, Lts Richard Geary and William Mishko obtained fair results on 2 October.

Ground crew servicing NS554 'N' of the 25th Bomb Gp. (H J Caudle Jr collection via 8th AF Research Center)

The Photo Interpretation Section noted that pictures taken from above 18,000ft were generally difficult to interpret because the flash bombs used illuminated too small an area. Weather conditions were found to play a major part in this type of photography.

Throughout the month the 654th flew sorties over Allied-controlled towns on the Continent to photograph railway yards. Good results were achieved from 4,000ft, although some of the larger yards, such as those at Aachen and Brussels, required several runs. The towns of Zwolle, Bonn and Cologne were all photographed at night from 22,000ft, while by day the Mosquitoes ranged over French marshalling yards. A rough idea of the state of some of the German towns at this point can be gained from the 654th's comments on the mission of 28 October: 'Capt. Matusko and Lt Mann had a successful PR mission "over the remains of Aachen."' Not everything was going the Allied way though. On 25 October 1/Lt George Brooks and his navigator 2/Lt Richard Taylor from the 654th took off in NS582 on a night *Joker* mission to photograph Duisburg in Germany. While over Belgium there was an incident, which is not described in detail in the 25th's records, which led to the death of Brooks but from which Taylor was fortunate to survive. Many years later, in 1999, historians Norman Malayney and Dutchman Erwin Vanden Broecke, with help from Richard Taylor, pieced together what happened. This is the train of events:

Capt. Robert Lee of 653rd Bomb Sqn with NS632 'I'. (USAAF)

Above: NS552 'G' of 654th Bomb Sqn, showing its lines for the publicity cameraman. (Author's collection)

Right: NS590 'B' of 654th Bomb Sqn. (Dana Bell)

Brooks and Taylor took off from Watton at 0215 hours on 25 October. Shortly after take-off Brooks corrected a swing to port, straightened the plane and climbed into the night. Taylor gave Brooks the first course to be steered as soon as they crossed the English coast at Clacton at about 15,000 feet. When Taylor asked Brooks how the plane was behaving, he answered 'OK'.

While crossing over the English Channel Brooks remarked that something was wrong with the supercharger. The altimeter was reading 18,000ft but the crew agreed that the supercharger only cut in at 21,000ft. Brooks continued the climb and the supercharger duly started to function at 21,000ft.

They crossed the Belgian coast at 22,000ft, at which point Brooks encountered difficulty in keeping the Mosquito on course, and the artificial horizon indicated that the starboard wing was lower. Brooks surmised that a landing wheel was hanging down and stated he was returning to an area over the Channel where he would attempt to retract the supposedly errant wheel. Taylor gave Brooks a course of 309 degrees to steer.

Then Taylor felt the plane begin to slide – actually it hit a stall, and Taylor immediately said 'Get ready to jump.' Taylor clapped his table, stood up straight and pulled the handle of the canopy which immediately flew away. Then the plane went into a steep spin. Due to the centrifugal forces the crew found it difficult to move around in the narrow confines of the cockpit. Taylor reached for his chest parachute but it seemed as though he had been nailed to the floor of the Mosquito. However, he managed to snap one side of his parachute to his harness. Then, he crawled from his position over the floor and managed to open the nose hatch. He looked back and saw Brooks climbing through the top hatch, his face looking towards the aircraft's nose.

Taylor wriggled through the hatch, his face towards the rear of the aircraft. The next thing he remembered was falling through the air. As he did so, he managed to clip the other side of his parachute to his harness. After pulling his parachute D-ring he blacked out momentarily, but recovered moments before reaching the ground. Once on the ground he made his way to a farmhouse some 2 miles distant, where the residents informed the police in the town of Diksmuide (in West Flanders). Shortly afterwards, the police arrived saying that pilot Brooks had been found about a mile away and that he was dead with an unopened parachute. It was surmised that on bailing out he had hit the tail fin and had either been killed immediately or knocked unconscious.

The Belgian police took Taylor to Ypres, where he was put in touch with a Canadian police unit. The Canadians took Taylor for a brief visit to the crash site to find that the photo flash bombs had all exploded and that the Mosquito was completely destroyed. Making his way to Melsbroek, he was returned to the UK on a B-17 and was soon back at Watton to relate his story.

Taylor described Brooks as a capable and conscientious pilot.

Having already made a name for himself as originator of the Scouting Force concept, Col Bud J Peaslee now reappears as champion of another type of operation – chaff dispensing. In 1979 he responded to a request from the author and recorded his involvement in the work:

In the summer of 1944 the Germans were being pushed further back and bombing targets were being more and more heavily defended by anti-aircraft guns. It became known that the enemy had found that radar gun-laying was far more effective than optical sighting, even in clear weather. As the guns became more and more dense and their effectiveness increased, our leading bomber crews became more and more reluctant to fly in the front formations. This was because the initial bursts of flak were usually in, or very near, the leading aircraft, after which a dense box barrage was initiated, forcing the following bombers to be subject to very heavy and accurate fire.

As commander and founder of the Bomber Command Scouting Force flying P-51 Mustangs, I had experimented dropping large concentrations of chaff contained in the British-made paper wing tanks. These had been sawn in half and bound back together with steel bands. The tanks were filled with chaff and released in front of the bombers during the bombing run. We usually carried one tank of fuel and one of chaff, which caused the Scouting aircraft to fly in an unbalanced manner until both tanks were released. This was not particularly successful and severely limited the Scout's range of operation.

In October 1944 I was assigned the duty of adapting the British Mosquito to be used for dispensing chaff in front of the bomber stream and to develop the tactics and techniques of operation. For this job I was assigned a Mosquito aircraft from the 25th Bomb Group commanded by Col Leon Gray. I was also furnished a British-designed, electrically operated machine into which was fed twin fabric ribbons to which were attached bundles of triangular shaped packages of chaff at frequent intervals of about 12 inches. Each, when released, was to represent the same radar reflection as one American bomber.

With the aid of Col Cecil West of the Air Depot we constructed a plywood box of suitable dimension to fit in the bomb bay of a

Mosquito. On installation of the dispensing equipment it seemed logical to mount the dispensing machine in the rear of the bomb bay. After many failures and the loss of a Mosquito when I struck a flock of birds at about 400 mph over the airfield runway and the birds penetrated the plywood wings. At my suggestion we reversed the dispenser to function from the forward end of the bomb bay. This solved our major problem and I decided to fly the first mission alone as we only had one Mosquito operational with the special equipment installed at that time.

My records indicate that on 25 November 1944 I flew the first screening mission alone in a chaff-loaded Mosquito. I took off at a time long after the bombers had departed, calculated to intercept the leading elements at the Initial Point prior to their bombing run on the synthetic oil plant at Merseburg. I overtook the bomber stream as planned and passed them with my excess speed. They were easily identified as they were drawing heavy contrails and I intercepted them as they started their bomb run. We had encountered a solid undercast making it necessary that bombing be done with radar. As we proceeded along the bomb run I flew my Mosquito just ahead of them, then turned on a divergent course of about 20 degrees to their left and turned on the chaff dispensing equipment. As the bombers approached the bomb release point a heavy flak barrage appeared in my vicinity at least two miles to the left of the formation, and never at any time during my period of observation did any bursts appear near the bombers. Needless to say, I was delighted with this outcome and felt confident that the misleading chaff pattern had paid great dividends. My return to base was uneventful with the exception that both Rolls-Royce engines stopped dead when I was several miles out over the North Sea, even though the main tanks had lots of fuel remaining. In fear that I was about to have a dead stick landing I turned toward the coast of Holland and switched the tanks to reserve. The engines again picked up and began to function properly, but every time I switched back to main they would run for about four to five minutes and stop again. Juggling the use of main and reserve fuel, I followed the coast to the English Channel and back to base without further incident. I never did learn what had caused the malfunction of the fuel system.

On 29 November my records indicate I flew a mission to Misburg without incident, this time over a smoke screen, followed by trips to Kassel on 4 December, and Frankfurt on the 11th with three Mosquitoes. Then it was back to Merseburg for the last time on 12 December. On 15 December, with four chaff-equipped Mosquitoes, I turned command over to Col Leon Gray, the 25th BG commander and returned to the USA. Assigned to the Pentagon, I became Chief of the All-Weather Program.

My evaluation of the Mosquito is that on the ground it was a tricky and unusual aircraft to handle, particularly for American pilots. Many had trouble, both on take-off and landing, preventing ground looping. This occurred if the pilot raised the tailwheel off the runway under 100 mph, due to the torque of the two great engines, and many times it was necessary to use the delicate application of the brakes with the thumb control. This was also true on landing which required great skill and early, delicate braking. In the air, with the large [landing] gear retracted, it was one of the finest aircraft I have ever flown, and that includes practically all the American operational aircraft developed at

MM345 'Z' of 653rd Bomb Sqn. (USAAF)

that time. I am particularly proud of my experiences with the British Mosquito on either one or two engine operation, as well as its handling in mock combat that I engaged in with that great American fighter, the P-51 Mustang, which was my first love.

I regret that I cannot include the ultimate destiny of the Screening Force, which was turned over to Col Leon Gray when I returned to the USA. I should include the fact that he and his 25th Bomb Group were most helpful and co-operative in the initial phases of the chaff project.

Operations – November 1944

This month the group was tasked with pioneering a new type of mission titled *Redtail*, the visual observation of raids by the three bomb divisions 'heavies' already described by Gene Goodbread. All four missions during November were flown by Goodbread himself.

A record-breaking 126 *Bluestocking* missions were flown, of which 120 were successful. Due to the seasonal weather conditions in Europe, these meteorological flights were standardised in terms of time and frequency.

The prime task for the Group Navigation Section was LORAN training. Two officers and three enlisted men, specialists in LORAN, were flown in by C-54 from Boca Raton Field, Florida, the USAAF's radar training base. Navigators from the all three bomb divisions descended on Watton for instruction in the

MM345 'Z' of 653rd Bomb Sqn landing at Watton. (Dana Bell)

equipment. Capt. Lionel Proulx, the Group Navigator, not only supervised operational missions but also planned a LORAN training programme. Held in high regard by the 8th AF, the Section was tasked with many of the experimental flights involved in getting the radar into smooth operation.

With six months operational flying under its belt, the Group's Training Flight, under Maj. Hugh Bozarth, now began a formal training course for newly assigned Mosquito aircrew. Subjects covered on the course included foul weather procedures, instrument flying, navigation, and specialist meteorology topics. The navigators' programme was supervised by the Group Navigation Section, while pilots were checked out by ex-RAF Lt Oliver Emmel before being sent off on operations. Local and cross-country flying, both day and night, was carried out in both PR.XVI and T.III Mosquitoes.

The group record reports that on 1 November 'the eccentric, but popular, Lt Vance Chipman, pilot, and Lt William Cannon, navigator, failed to return from a *Mickey* mission and were officially reported as MIA.' Flying NS677, they had been shot down over Schweinfurt, and Cannon recalls what happened:

> When we were shot down I don't know whether it was by anti-aircraft fire or a night fighter as I couldn't see any activity from my bomb bay home. If a night fighter did hit us it probably wasn't Vance's fault since we had to maintain this straight course which was approximately 120 degrees and then we turned for home at about 300 degrees. As soon as he completed the turn we were hit. I was hit badly in the leg and my headset was shot off, which cut off contact with Vance. I released the side emergency door to look out at the motors and then decided to leave the plane. I had heard [later] that Vance held the plane as steady as possible to give me time to get out and then he too abandoned the Mosquito. He didn't arrive at the same hospital as I did so I imagine he was several miles from Schweinfurt. I landed in the city and was immediately picked up, fortunately, because I had a massive wound above my right ankle, approximately one inch from losing the foot. I thought we were hit by anti-aircraft guns because it sounded like one large explosion.

As Cannon confirms, Chipman survived his bail out and even made his way back to Watton, but efforts to trace this colourful personality post-war have proved fruitless.

The 653rd Sqn suffered two losses on 6 November. While attempting a landing at North Pickenham after a *Joker* night mission to Cologne, NS568, flown by Lt Otto Kaellner, crashed 2 miles west of the station, killing the pilot and seriously injuring navigator Lt Edwin Cerruti. Strong crosswinds at Watton had forced Kaellner to divert to North Pickenham and Lt Robert Grimes in MM386 found himself in the same position after a *Bluestocking*. Short of fuel, he had shut down his port engine prior to making an emergency landing. On the approach contact was lost with air traffic control and the Mosquito flew into a row of trees. This sheared off 6ft of the left wing, causing the aircraft to roll over on its back and crash into a field near Wendling School, killing pilot and navigator Lt Clarence Jodar instantly.

Worse was to follow. On 22 November pilot Lts Russell Harry and Milford Hopkins climbed into NS515 for *Bluestocking* 11/92, a weather reconnaissance of the Continent. Just after take-off the Mosquito was seen to catch fire and then crash fatally at Great Cressingham, 5 miles west of Watton. A second crew, comprising Lts Malcolm MacLeod and Edward

1/Lt Clarence Jodar, navigator on 653rd Bomb Sqn, KIA on 6 November 1944 in the crash of MM386. (L Proulx)

NS568 of 654th Bomb Sqn undergoing maintenance at Watton. (USAAF)

Fitzgerald, were then tasked with flying the uncompleted mission. They took off safely in NS630 and carried out the operation as briefed, but on their return the English weather gremlins struck again. Both men were killed when the Mosquito 'crashed in attempting to land in very adverse weather ...' The Mosquito had hit trees at the village of Thompson, some 3 miles south of Watton.

An odd name slides into the group's November narrative – that of Lt Col Marshall Wayne. A noted American swimming and diving star, he caught fame through his success at the 1936 Olympics, where he put Hitler's nose out of joint by winning the 10m Platform event, thus displacing the dictator's favourite competitor, Hermann Stork, who was predicted to take gold. Wayne and his navigator, Lt Richard Wright, failed to return from a Mosquito mission over the Continent. Word came back that they had bailed out safely over Italy, Wayne landing in a tree and severely damaging his leg. The pair were taken in by an Italian family and later smuggled back to England, Wright to duty at Watton and Wayne to the USA nursing his injuries. The narrative notes that: 'The imperturbable Wright found time to stuff his "hot shot charlie" cap into his flying suit and to note the time of bail out before "hitting the silk".' Wayne was a reconnaissance pilot, had flown with the 7th Photo Gp over at Mount Farm, and was probably a staff officer in the reconnaissance hierarchy at this point.

Lt Gen. Doolittle visited Watton on 13 November on an inspection of the group. Accompanied by Elliott Roosevelt, CO of the 325th Wing, the pair took a special interest in the Radar Sect, headed by Lt Howard Kaplan. There they viewed LORAN and tail warning equipment and seemed impressed. The latter kit was probably AN/APS-13, a tail search radar for fighter and reconnaissance aircraft, which gave visual and audio warning to the pilot of the approach of another aircraft from the rear within about 4 miles. The first installation was made in Mosquito NS709 with assistance of RAF personnel from Upwood air base. Two test flights of the tail warning system were made during the month 'with partial success', and the first dual installations of GEE and LORAN were made in Lt Col Gray's aircraft.

There was a reduction in the number of missions flown by the 654th Sqn this month. This was due to the planned transfer of part of the squadron to the Continent (but also because the front lines were now beyond the range of the Watton-based B-26s). The transfer duly took place on the last day of the month and involved six officers plus twenty-nine enlisted men who were detached to the 27th Photo Recce Sqn, 7th Photo Gp, then based at Denain/Prouvy in France. A damage assessment photo recce sortie flown in ideal weather on 4 November to Charleroi and Haine St Pierre, in Belgium, produced high-quality pictures from 4,000ft. More fine photos were produced on 6 November from the two *Jokers* flown over targets in the Ruhr. These were taken from 22,000ft and were a nod to the possibilities of high-altitude photography. 'Test after test was flown from 23,000 ft.'

Due to the implementation of a reorganisation plan, *Mickey* missions were inactive during the month. However, in the short time that the 654th had been flying them exceptional results had been obtained and the H2X equipment was rapidly gaining a laudable reputation, both for its day-to-day effectiveness and for its potential.

Over in the 8th CCU camp discussion centred on the use of the P-38 versus the Mosquito for combat camera work, and during the month a conference, with representatives from HQ 8th AF, 325th Recon Wg and 8th CCU, was held to discuss the subject. Col Todd from the 8th AF Ops Staff recommended that the CCU fly most of their missions at a lower altitude in P-38 'Droop Snoots'. All agreed that the modified P-38 was more adaptable to the needs of the combat cameramen than the Mosquito flown previously. The Lightning had more space for the photographer, with wider photo angles and better visibility. Todd estimated that he could have five 'Droop Snoots' available for the exclusive use of the CCU. Col Stenglein (the 25th's first 'boss' and now acting CO of the 325th Wg) suggested the

CCU move to Mount Farm [home of the 7th Photo Gp with various models of the F-5 Lightning] so that the P-38s could be serviced properly. They would also be closer to the fighter coverage [P-51s] that would escort the camera planes. The Mosquito was bowing out of combat camera work.

November witnessed another new innovatory development, the so-called *Redstocking* mission, and it is interesting to look at how this operation and its specialist equipment evolved. Beginning in 1942 the British developed the S-Phone, a UHF duplex radio-telephone system that enabled Special Operations Executive (SOE) agents working behind enemy lines to communicate with overflying friendly aircraft, and thus exchange information on the locations of, and timings for, drop zones (DZs), all in a reasonably secure manner. The American equivalent of the SOE, the Office of Strategic Services (OSS, and predecessor of the Central Intelligence Agency), performed essentially similar activities as SOE in the Second World War – collecting intelligence by spying, acts of sabotage, waging propaganda war, and organising and co-ordinating ant-Nazi resistance groups. Of this the CIA would later diplomatically comment: 'Despite a mutual desire to co-operate, however, relative harmony between OSS and its British counterparts [SOE] took time to achieve.' Quite understandably, OSS wished to, and was quite capable of, producing its own independent form of secure communications between its agents on the ground and USAAF aircraft in the air.

The OSS set about doing this in late 1942, with the initial design work being performed at RCA's laboratories in Riverhead, New York. The equipment itself would be known in the OSS as Joan Eleanor (or 'JE') and two key figures were drivers in its development – Lt Cdr Steve Simpson and DeWitt Goddard. Pre-war Simpson had been an RCA scientist with a long-standing interest in radio-transmission technology, but with America's entry to the Second World War found himself commissioned in the US Navy and attached to OSS, London. Goddard was an RCA engineer who worked alongside Simpson on 'JE'. The latter code name derived from a combination of Joan, a WAC acquaintance of Simpson's, and Eleanor, Goddard's wife.

The equipment itself involved two transmitter/receivers, one for use by an agent on the ground, and the other mounted in an aircraft flying overhead. The system was in the UHF band since it was known that the Germans could not monitor those frequencies effectively. The agent would make his report in plain speech and the receiving aircraft would record the transmission on a wire recorder. Since Morse code was not needed the agent's training time was much reduced. Finally, the aircraft could seek immediate and secure clarification and expansion of any points, as required. Agents in the field

Distinguished visitors to the 25th Bomb Gp in November 1944. From left: Maj. Albert Straff (25th BG Air Exec) Col Elliott Roosevelt, Gen. James Doolittle and Col Leon Gray (CO, 25th BG), Unknown. (Author's collection)

would be equipped with a hand-held SSTC-502 transceiver, while aircraft would be fitted with an SSTR-6 transceiver. The HQ 8th AF considered the B-24 for the Joan-Eleanor missions, but decided it was less than ideal and opted, instead for the Mosquito, with its high speed and manoeuvrability.

In an unfortunate incident on 27 November, Lts Wallace Rouse (P) and Allen Morrow (N) from the 654th BS took off in NS596 for a high-altitude, cross-country training sortie. They somehow strayed off course, ran short of fuel and crash-landed a few miles north-east of Paris. Both walked away from the wreck.

The 654th BS was assigned the 'JE' missions, the first of which was launched on 16 November and recorded at the time as a 'special flight over Holland'. Because of the classified nature of the work, the 25th BG records contain scant mention of the missions flown. Moreover, the JE baton would shortly be handed over to the 492nd BG. The work-up and subsequent operation of this type of mission, which fell naturally under the Carpetbagger (or special operations mantle) was recorded at the time in the so-called Joan Eleanor Log and for convenience this is dealt with under the 492nd BG activities.

Operations – December 1944

Trials carried out in November had confirmed the Mosquito's suitability for dropping chaff, now referred to as Window, and on 4 December the first 'live' mission took place. Code-named *Graypea* (an acronym for Gray and Peaslee), the mission was flown by the CO, Lt Col Gray, with Lt Richard Davies in the navigator's seat. Fitted with specially designed Window dispensing gear, the crew rendezvoused with 1st Division bombers over the Continent and then flew ahead to drop their tinsel countermeasures. So promising were the results of this inaugural sortie that 'practically every 1st Division raid was accompanied by a *Graypea* from this Group'. In all, thirteen *Graypeas* were flown during the month. Experience showed that the best results were achieved when three Window Mosquitoes flew in support of the raiding bombers. Mosquito crews were encouraged to suggest methods of improving the Window dropping operation. Some initial difficulty was experienced with the release mechanism due to securing straps breaking, but improved versions were soon sourced, resulting in an immediate improvement in results. Crews were enthusiastic about the all-round success of the operation, resulting in a plan to extend it to support all three bomb divisions. All the Window missions were flown by the 653rd Sqn.

The group's expertise and success in its assigned role of reconnaissance attracted interest from beyond UK shores and prompted a visit from a Soviet Air Force party on 8 December. Consisting of Gen. A Shavopov,

NS585 'D' of 653rd Bomb Sqn. (Author's collection)

Resplendent in D-Day stripes and red tail, NS591 'S' of 653rd Bomb Sqn lands at Watton. (Flight via Peter Frost)

Lt Col N Roudoi and Maj. Samarin, the delegation were primarily interested in the night photography programme. They made an extensive tour of the station and spent a considerable time in the S-2 combat library examining the results of night photo missions.

Fog resulted in an approximate 25 per cent decrease in the number of *Bluestocking* weather recon missions flown by the 653rd Sqn during the month. Of ninety-one launched, eighty-eight were successful.

On 13 December the group received a letter from Lt Gen. Doolittle commending Lts Robert Walker and Roy Conyers of the 654th Sqn for successfully completing a highly important *Bluestocking* mission, 'under unusually trying and hazardous conditions' back on 25 November. Despite a faulty oxygen system that at times rendered the navigator unconscious and the pilot groggy, the pair refused to abandon the mission and, with the aid of the emergency oxygen system, completed their vital weather observations. The mission involved a round trip of 1,150 miles, of which 500 were over enemy territory, frequently at 10,000ft.

Up to now, *Mickey* missions had been flown by unescorted Mosquitoes at night. This had resulted in a comparatively high loss rate, which had resulted in the virtual cessation of this type of mission during November. However, from now on, *Mickeys* would be flown in daylight with an escort of four fighters per Mosquito. The results soon justified the change of policy – no losses were sustained, photo coverage was just as effective as night missions, and deeper penetration of enemy territory was possible.

While there were no operational losses during the month, unfortunately the same could not be said for non-combat flying. At approximately 1140 hrs on 23 December, F/O James Spear and his navigator Lt Carroll Bryan took off in NS638 for a local test flight. About an hour later witnesses reported hearing the Mosquito's engines misfiring and the aircraft crashed in a wooded area at Breakheart Hill, some 2 miles south-west of Dursley in Gloucestershire. There was no radio contact after take-off and the cause of the crash remained a mystery. A local man, Gordon Thompson, actually witnessed the crash and in 1979 recalled what happened:

> In the extremely cold winter of 1944/45, during the very early days of December at about 1100 hours, a Mosquito was travelling at about 400mph across a fog-filled valley above the town of Dursley, Gloucestershire, when it flew into a wooded hillside at about 500–600ft above sea level. At the time, I was 17 years old and taking a stroll in adjacent woods prior to going to bed as I was on night shift in a local factory. I heard the aircraft approaching in thick fog, then a tremendous crash as it ploughed into trees and carved a path nearly 800 yards through the ice-covered foliage. On arrival at the scene, I noted that the remains of the aircraft were a Mosquito bearing USAAF insignia. Unfortunately, both crew members perished in the crash.

The tail warning radar, originally intended for H2X-equipped aircraft flying unprotected at night, and championed so enthusiastically the previous month, was now dispensed with. The reason – *Mickey* missions would now be flown, with fighter escort, by day, so there was no need for it. The first *Mickey* mission from Watton with a fighter escort was flown on 23 December by Leon Gray with Lt Toth navigating. This was to Politz in Germany and good pictures were taken from 23,000ft.

December saw the 2,000th mission of the 25th BG as a whole (actually flown by Mosquito crew Capt. Robert Lee (P) and Lt Wendell Biggers (N)) and on 16 December suitably lavish celebrations were arranged in all corners of the base to mark the achievement of this hard-fought milestone. Of the event Leon Gray wrote: 'I congratulate each and every one of you for a job magnificently done, and I can only point with pride to my association with you. I know that in the ensuing months we will keep up the splendid effort until the enemy goes down in final utter defeat.'

A creditable waypoint in the 25th's Second World War journey, the 2,000th mission also prompted the group to reflect warmly on the sturdy and reliable service of the Mosquito. 'Mosquito MM387 has completed 56 consecutive missions without an abort of any kind. This is largely due to crew chief TSgt Sherman Housman. He has looked after this aircraft since it was assigned to the [653rd] Squadron, and it has flown 293 hrs 10 mins of operational time. NS508 has completed 52 missions (SSgt Hatton), and NS516 (TSgt Henderson) 53 missions.' Two other Mosquitoes received 'Excellent' ratings from the Group Inspector during the month: NS585 (SSgt Hull) and NS509 (TSgt Cabaz).

The 653rd Sqn summarised its December operations thus: thirteen *Graypeas*, six *Redtails*, and ninety-one *Bluestockings*. This was a reduction from the previous month's figures, due mainly to fog. Icy conditions caused Mosquitoes to slide off the runway, one of which, flown by Lt Hunt, caught fire but was extinguished before becoming a write-off.

Typical of the 654th Sqn's work at this point was the 12 December mission to Augsburg. Excellent H2X pictures were taken of the town from 22,000ft using 24in focal length cameras, which gave an overall photographic scale of 1:11,000, within the scope for reasonable damage assessment.

TSgt Sherman L Housman, from Paducah, Kentucky, crew chief of Mosquito MM387, the first 25th Bomb Gp Mosquito to complete fifty missions over occupied Europe. Alongside Housman's name under the cockpit is that of pilot Lt Oliver Emmel. (NARA)

Right: There is no clue to the identity of this 25th Group PR.XVI but the photo is worth including because of the nose art and name *Jo*. (L Erickson)

Below: An immaculately turned out and carefully maintained 25th Group aircraft, there is no clue to its identity or location, but the scene is probably Watton. (Bernard R Silver via 8th AF Research Center)

Air and ground crews pose in front of this 25th Bomb Gp aircraft. The eight mission symbols on the nose of the Mosquito give no clue to its actual identity. (Dana Bell)

While the 8th CCU had drifted away to the P-38 for operational work, they now turned their attention back to the Mosquito temporarily – for publicity reasons. Work was begun on a film entitled *The Mosquito Story* framed around a script submitted by Capt. Bergholz and approved by Leon Gray. The purpose of this production was to 'record the efforts of weather scouting Mosquitoes in co-ordinating and effecting better results on

Air-to-air view of what is probably NS590 from the 654th Squadron. (Authors' collection)

8th AF bombing missions'. The group's Mosquitoes also featured briefly in a film, made about this time, by de Havilland. Entitled simply *The Mosquito*, it describes the design, development and operation of the aircraft and includes a tantalizingly short and rare sequence of a 25th machine taxiing to its hardstand at Watton, surrounded by other Mosquitoes from the group.

Christmas Day, 1944, the group's first at Watton, dusted the base in a festive frost, prompting personnel to capture the scene on camera. A fine party was laid on for local children.

NS519 'P' of 653rd Bomb Sqn comes to grief after take-off at Watton on 27 December 1944 with Lt Morton Hunt at the controls. (W Borges)

NS519 'P' served with the 8th Light Weather, 653rd and 654th Squadrons. (Dana Bell)

Operations – January 1945

Mickey operations, flown by 654th Sqn, were resumed in January but showed disappointing results. Thirty-six missions were flown, the greatest number in one month thus far, but only four were successful and one partially successful. The reasons advanced for this included: meteorological conditions adversely affecting the operation of H2X sets, fluctuating power supply resulting in temperamental electrical systems, lack of space in Mosquitoes for the necessary equipment and the consequent inability of the navigator to operate H2X sets efficiently. Less apparent, but equally important, was the lack of thorough training for the air crew handling this highly complicated 'gadget-ridden machinery'. A high degree of concentration was required of navigators in carrying out their primary role and also operating the H2X sets in order that missions were not jeopardised. In an attempt to remedy matters, a rigorous training programme was planned covering the use of H2X. Training sorties would be flown over the UK.

The 654th Sqn's *Redstocking* missions increased to seven at the turn of the year, six flown by Mosquitoes, the seventh by an A-26 Invader. In connection with this highly classified activity, a letter was received from OSS Detachment HQ commending the work of Capt. Victor Doroski, and Lts William Mishko and Robert Walker 'for flying an experimental mission of great significance involving a certain new secret communications system, with little preparation and in adverse weather conditions'.

On 21 January 2/Lt Jerry Roberts and 1/Lt Ralph Fisher of 653rd BS were listed as MIA after being briefed to fly a *Bluestocking* weather mission

Capt. Robert Hastie in front of Mosquito T.III LR556 at Watton in early 1945. (Robert Hastie)

Lt Col Leon Gray, CO of the 25th Bomb Gp, with his personal Mosquito at Watton in early 1945. (Flight)

NS509 'H' of 653rd Bomb Sqn. (C Hackman)

over the Danish peninsula and northern Germany. The pair took off in NS509 at 1422 hrs and a German account, taken from the *Kriegstagbucher* [War Diary] of the Kiel Marineflak-Brigade provides graphic details of what happened over the Continent. At around 1600 hrs navigator Fisher called a warning of tracer fire past the Mosquito and shouted 'Yellow nose Mustang.' As Roberts put the aircraft in a steep left turn and looked back to try to locate the 'Mustang' he felt hammer blows against the back of his seat. With the port wing and engine on fire and forward visibility difficult, Roberts put on full power on the starboard engine and shouted for Fisher to bail out. Fisher, however, had been badly injured by shrapnel, was unresponsive and was blocking access to the exit hatch. Roberts worked feverishly to open the hatch and push Fisher out, eventually succeeding, pulling the latter's parachute 'D'-Ring (to open the 'chute) and kicking him into space. Now close to the critical height for a safe parachute drop, Roberts bailed out himself, hitting the ground hard seconds after his canopy opened. Some local farmers had observed the crash and, using a makeshift stretcher, transported Roberts to a nearby fire department house. The badly wounded Fisher was taken on a cart to the fire department house but died before medical assistance arrived. Roberts survived to become a PoW.

The 654th Sqn's *Mickey* capabilities were given a boost by the arrival from the USA of six radar mechanics, specialists in H2X equipment. The Radar Section was now able to work round the clock. Capt. Omer Snyker was awarded the group's first Bronze Star medal for the valuable work he had performed the previous July and August on the testing and installation of the American Demand oxygen system, preferred by the aircrew, which replaced the British equipment in the US Mosquitoes.

NS569 'N' of 653rd Bomb Sqn framed by a B-17 at Watton. (de Havilland Aircraft Museum)

T.III LR566 at Watton in early 1945. (Robert Hastie)

Navigator's station on a USAAF Mosquito PR.XVI. (Dana Bell)

The Mosquito's notoriously challenging handling during take-off and landing were made no easier in the wintry conditions at Watton in January. Returning from a weather recon mission in NS594 on the 28th, Lt Robert James lost control of the aircraft on the icy runway and slid into a snow bank, breaking off the tail section. He and his navigator walked away unscathed. On the other hand, the harsh weather didn't prevent crew chief Ralph Hatton's NS508 from completing its sixtieth mission for the 653rd BS without an abort.

For its part the 654th BS was flying up to four *Mickeys* on most days of the month to such destinations as Kassel, Berlin, Freiburg (marshalling yards) – and a place named Brux, in the Sudetenland, which, up until September 1938, when it was annexed by Hitler, had been part of Czechoslovakia. In 1944 Brux was the largest of the detached sites of nearby Stalag IV-C (at Wistritz, and a main Nazi PoW camp,) and was the location of *Sudetenlandische Treibstoffwerke* ('Sudetenland Fuel Works), part of the state-owned industrial conglomerate *Reichswerke Hermann Goring* plant, designed to process oil from coal. It was bombed several times by the Allies between July 1944 and April 1945.

One of a series of publicity photos of cameras being loaded aboard a 25th Bomb Gp Mosquito named *Suzanne*. (USAAF)

Brux does not feature on modern-day maps because it is now Most, in the Czech Republic. Two Mosquitoes were sent to photograph Kassel on 3 January. The town had been a target for Allied bombing raids since RAF Wellingtons and Stirlings had first attacked it in February 1942. An important centre in the Nazi war effort, it was home to the Fieseler aircraft plant, the Henschel company, which manufactured the Tiger tanks, as well as busy road and rail transport facilities. Friedberg, an important German army barracks since 1914, was covered on the 16th, while six days later the first PR mission was flown to the industrial town of Merseburg, where excellent pictures of the chemical works were taken using a 36in focal length camera.

Overall, January was an encouraging month for the 654th Sq. The thirty-six *Mickey* missions flown produced an average acceptance rate of 12 per cent of the photos taken. In view of the intricacy of the H2X equipment involved this was considered 'good'. Much of this success was due to the fighter escort – crews could concentrate on the mission itself.

Among the pilots to join the 654th BS at this time was twenty-one-year-old 1/Lt Robert Hastie, who takes up his story:

> My navigator and I transferred to the 25th BG at Watton in January 1945 after completing a tour in B-17s with the 95th BG at Horham. Early on I attended the Rolls-Royce School at Derby to learn the operation of the Merlin engine. Quite a different power plant from the Wright radials we had in the B-17. After 2 hrs 30 mins in the right-hand seat, and 45 mins in the left-hand seat of the Mosquito T.III, I soloed on 24 February. More solo continuation training in the Mk III followed in March. The 'Mossy' was a dream to fly after four engines. The Mk III was very manoeuvrable, I can remember out-turning a P-47 and easily staying with P-51s in a rat race.

Among the memorabilia Hastie kept from his Mosquito days was the Rolls-Royce Aero Engine Instruction School brochure, issued to him for his course. The brochure gives a cheery, informal description of the courses run and, for example, includes the following advice: 'Wherever pilots congregate, the conversation invariably turns to their own professional "shop", so you will find the hangar doors wide open and everybody pleased to hear what you have to say, even if you bring up the hackneyed topics of air-cooled versus liquid-cooled, or radial versus in-line engines.' Also well worth quoting is the little ditty included in the notes:

Engine Handling – The 'Gen'
If you …Fly at night
Either fast or slow
With your revs too high
And your boost too low,
You'll run out of juice
With a long way to go,
And you won't get home in
The morning.

The 654th BS's operational report states that between 16 and 22 January '10 *Mickeys* were flown – with only two aborts due to H2X unserviceability. Germersheim, Freiburg, Speyer and Rastatt were photographed through the *Mickey* scope.' It is interesting to look for a moment at why these locations, all in south-west Germany, were selected. Germersheim gained the increasing attention of the Allied bomber commands when fighting on the ground moved relentlessly eastwards towards the German border. It was attacked by 1st Air Divn B-17s on 13 January 1945 as part of an overall raid on marshalling yards and Rhine rail bridges. Freiburg, on the other hand, was not an industrial town and was not bombed by the RAF until 27–28 November 1944 because it was a minor railway centre and because large numbers of German troops were believed to be in the town. American and French ground units were advancing in the Vosges, a mere 35 miles to the west. A total of 1,900 tons of bombs were dropped on Freiburg in twenty-five minutes by 341 Lancasters and ten Mosquitoes, missing the rail targets but flattening some 2,000 nearby houses. On 13 January 1945 eight B-24s of the USAAF's 2nd Bomb Divn visited the town as a 'Last Resort', marshalling yards, target, dropping 19.4 tons of bombs. Finally, the marshalling yards at Speyer were raided as a 'Primary Target' on 8 January 1945 by 1st Air Divn B-17s, which released 198 tons of bombs on the hapless town. Rastatt was another Rhine crossing point. Later, on 16–17 March, when 225 Lancasters and eleven Mosquitoes of RAF Bomber Command delivered a devastating raid on Wurzburg, 101 miles (160km) to the north-east, they used Rastatt as a navigation point to avoid German defences.

The county of Norfolk was, at this point, home to the RAF's 100 Gp and Watton was surrounded by the group's airfields, which on many occasions provided emergency landing grounds for aircraft in trouble. One of these

After Lt Robert James ground looped her at Watton on 28 January 1945, NS594 'U' of 653rd Bomb Sqn was written off the following month. (USAAF)

was Foulsham, about 17 miles to the north-east, where, on 31 January, 654th Sqn Mosquito pilot 2/Lt Richard Geary found sanctuary when his Mosquito suffered 'one engine burned out and landing gear frozen before landing'. At the time a small detachment of P-38Js from the 7th Photo Gp at Mount Farm was attached to the RAF's 192 Sqn at Foulsham, specialising in electronic intelligence. Whether this had any bearing on Geary's choice of bolt hole is not known.

Operations – February 1945

One of the features of actual warfare is how quickly new ideas, systems and equipment can be brought into service, and how equally quickly they can prove unsuitable and be abandoned. The shadow of this tenet now fell on the Mosquito's suggested replacement in the *Mickey* role, the P-38. The 25th BG report for February records the thinking that prevailed at this point:

> After a number of flights, both experimental and operational, it was obvious that the Mosquito, while ideal in speed, altitude and range, was unsuitable. The electrical system proved unequal to the task of operating the additional load imposed by the H2X

equipment. Under conditions of low temperature at high altitude, when the scanner was switched on, the intense cold congealed the oil in the engines and the resultant current surge blew fuses and, in some cases, burned cables. Lack of space hampered the navigator, preventing the efficient operation of equipment. As an experiment, the P-38 was modified and put into operational use. While it solved the problem of power supply, it did so only at the cost of reducing navigational efficiency, as it was necessary for the navigator to sit in an extended nose to operate the H2X equipment and camera. Lack of space prevented him from even keeping a navigation log, and cramped him on long missions.

It was therefore apparent that neither aircraft was suitable for H2X reconnaissance. The ideal plane would combine speed, range and altitude, sufficient space to house equipment and enable the operator to make adjustments to the set in flight, and [be equipped with] a power supply capable of providing smooth current and regulation.

The conclusion reached on the use of the P-38 for *Mickey* perhaps provides some mitigation for the Mosquito on which, perhaps surprisingly, the same verdict was arrived at earlier. And these thoughts were still at the 'reflective' stage.

NS569 'N' of 654th Bomb Sqn at Watton in early 1945. (Flight)

NS569 'N' of 654th Bomb Sqn at Watton in early 1945. (Flight)

An interesting development of the *Mickey* programme was suggested by SSgt Edward Corcoran of the Group's Radar Intelligence Section. This consisted of an H2X remote reception system. Accordingly, experiments were carried out by Lts Donald Winters and David Anthony of the Radar Section to prove that it was possible for information presented to the operator of an H2X set in flight to be similarly and simultaneously presented to an observer on the ground. The idea was code-named *Janie*. The theory advanced was that an aircraft flying several thousand feet above the bomber stream could transmit a continuous picture of the formation together with the terrain over which it was flying. Faults and breaks of formation could be noted instantly and navigation could be checked. Moreover, radio-controlled aircraft could be navigated from the control base by observing the remote indicator. The report goes on to speculate that: 'Remote sea search, night photography, bombing and reconnaissance are only a few of the possible uses. Work on this was discontinued in February due to operational necessity, but it is understood that work continued at Wright Field, Ohio.' For sure, a shape of things to come!

To get an accurate idea of the scale of 25th BG operations at this point in the war it is worth examining February's effort – a typical month. The total numbers of sorties flown, under three broad headings, was as follows: Photo recce (including *Mickeys* and *Jokers*) – fifty-seven; weather recon

25th Bomb Gp Mosquitoes at an unidentified location. Nearest is *Patty*, while beyond her is almost certainly NR709 'R' of 654th Bomb Sqn. (Author's collection)

(*Bluestockings*) – 103; special ops – (*Redstockings* and *Graypeas* (chaff dispensing)) – seventy-three. Looking at each in turn, the photo recon sorties covered Freiburg, Speyer Rastatt, Kassel, Hamburg, Brux, Giessen and Misburg. USAAF B-17s and B-24s had raided Giessen on several occasions in November and December 1944. On 6–7 December a force of 255 RAF Lancasters and ten Mosquitoes hit the town centre and railway yards. And then on 6 February 1945 it became a target of opportunity for B-17s when cloud obscured the primary target. On the same date, a *Mickey* mission was flown over the English town of Rugby, primarily for test purposes.' Misburg, about 5 miles east of Hannover, was the site of an important German oil refinery and was attacked by 8th AF bombers in November and December 1944, and more recently by RAF Mosquitoes on 13–14 February 1945. The 654th sent three *Joker* Mosquitoes to the town to assess bomb damage on 3 February. The Krupps Wanne-Eickel synthetic oil plant in western Germany, received the attention of three *Jokers* on 14 February. The plant had first been attacked by RAF Mosquitoes back in August 1944 and received another pounding by Lancasters this February. Interestingly, the three *Mickeys* flown on the 1st of the month comprised two Mosquitoes and one P-38, with 'poor and good' results respectively.

On the weather recon front, the group report records that the 653rd Sqn flew 115 *Bluestockings*, five *Redtails* and six *Skywaves*. Turning lastly to special operations, eleven *Redstocking* missions were flown in support of OSS agents on the Continent by 654th Sqn. The Group total of fifteen *Graypea* chaff-dropping missions were shared by the two squadrons, flying a standard three-ship launch – eleven by the 6563rd and four by the 654th, occasionally with a fourth Mosquito being airborne as a 'reserve', which then returned to base when it was established there were no aborts. Additional Mosquitoes were being modified for chaff dispensing in anticipation of increased support for the 8th AF's bombers. Not a day went by in February when the 25th BG's Mosquitoes were not out on one task or another.

The group suffered its only loss of the month on the 8th. On that day two 654th Sqn *Joker* Mosquitoes were launched just before 0200 hrs for night photography of Hamburg and the Deurog Synthetic Oil refinery at Misburg. Cloud obscured Hamburg and so Hanover was selected as a target of opportunity, with poor photographic quality results. In the Misburg ship were Capts Victor Doroski (P) and Jacob Hochman (N). A contemporary report of events by the group's Statistical Officer, Capt. George Sesler, states the following:

> Scheduled radio silence was maintained with Mosquito NS583 by Flying Control of this station until ETR 0526 hours. At 0600 hours, after unsuccessful efforts were made to establish radio contact with the Mosquito, RAF 12 Group was telephoned and a plotting requested. 12 Group had had no plot on this aircraft. 325th Photographic Wing Reconnaissance, A-3, reported that contact was established with this Mosquito by the Continental ground station, Nuthouse, at 0235 hours, but no further transmissions were reported. The plane crashed on fire at 0315 hours at Oberschonhagen, 6km east of Detmold in north eastern Germany. The two crew members were initially buried at Leistrup-Meiersfeld on 9 February. At that time Capt. Doroski could not be identified because he was burned.

Fire reportedly destroyed 99 per cent of the aircraft and there was speculation that the flash bomb had ignited and caused the crash.

In his 25th Group history, George Sesler describes a *Redtail* mission involving a very famous celebrity performing the role of Command Observer this month. On 27th of the month the 653rd's Lt John Green was tasked to fly first to a nearby USAAF base to pick up the senior officer, who would be acting as 'command pilot' for a B-17 raid on Leipzig. When he arrived at the base (which was possibly Hethel, home for the B-24s of the 389th BG and a stone's throw from the 2nd Air Divn HQ at Ketteringham Hall) he reported to Operations, where he was introduced to the distinctive figure of Col Jimmy Stewart, the famous film star and at that point chief of staff of the 2nd Combat Wing, 2nd Air Divn, who would be occupying the second seat in the Mosquito. This was Green's first daylight mission in a Mosquito; he had previously flown only *Bluestocking* weather missions at night. The general opinion was that the Command Observer role was a very popular one among senior officers. As Green says:

> After all, the Mosquito had acquired a reputation of being a very hot aircraft. One would only have to see it in flight, presenting an image of a rapidly darting, stinging object. And then hear the distinctive roar and popping of its engines on a final approach, landing with its power pulled off completely (as we Yanks were fond of doing). The noise, I suspect, could be heard from miles around, and of course it drew attention. We who flew the 'Mossie' were extremely proud that we had been so privileged to fly this unique craft.

With a celebrated crewman and an airframe fresh out of hangar maintenance, Green was keen for the mission to go well, but events seemed to conspire against this. When he pressed the engine starter buttons nothing happened. He tried again. 'Still only the silent turning of the blades. No engine roar. Not even a sputter.' Eventually a starter trolley was produced and this brought the Merlins to life, but time was slipping by and before an RV [rendezvous] with the bombers, Green first had to catch up with his escort of P-51s. 'Fortunately, that would not be much of a problem with the "Mossie".' The bombers were met as planned and the raid observed, but it was a poignant moment for Green who, in his previous tour, had flown B-17s with a group that had suffered grievous losses while bombing Leipzig. With the task completed it was time for a speedy return home independently of the Mustangs and Green asked Stewart if he would like to navigate. 'Of course.' replied the star. But between them there was a breakdown in navigation planning; flying above cloud and with unknown wind speeds, they were soon lost. After an agonising interval, Green realised they were out over the Atlantic and visualised the spectre of newspaper headlines screaming 'Jimmy Stewart Missing in Action: Presumed Lost at Sea'. Eventually, after numerous unsuccessful attempts, contact was made with RAF Manston, the most south-easterly point in England for a vector and the Mosquito was soon overhead the base. A too-rapid descent into the airfield brought a cry of agony from Stewart, whose ears had not adjusted to the manoeuvre. After a flight of five and a half hours they touched down in silence and Green reflected on a mission that had seemed jinxed from the start. 'A flight that I was sure Col Stewart would not remember with satisfaction or fond memories. And I hoped only that our paths would never cross by chance.'

Aside from the loss of the Doroski-Hochman crew, minor mishaps nagged at the group during February. On 1st of the month the 654th's Lt Allen Bateman, returning from a diversion base in the UK in NS559, attempted to land too closely behind another aircraft. To avoid a collision he pulled to one side, but after rolling some distance on the shoulder of the runway, the left landing gear collapsed. Lt Roger Gilbert's arrival at Alconbury on 19 February, similarly resulted in a collapsed landing gear. Flying RF985 (654th BS), he experienced difficulty lining the Mosquito up with the runway, and on his third approach he landed well down the track, running off the end and through a barbed wire fence. The following day, Lt Warren Davis (653rd) suffered the ignominious experience of cracking up a Mosquito in the morning and then duplicating the performance in the afternoon! On each occasion the aircraft veered to the left as it landed

The scene at Alconbury on 20 February 1945. RF985 from 654th Bomb Sqn sits forlornly after its take-off accident the previous day. (USAAF)

at Watton and in both incidents Davis over-compensated, charged off to the right and left the runway. Both machines (one of which was MM345) suffered major damage. Exeter airfield in Devon was the scene of an unusual occurrence. Lt Wallace Rouse, also from the 653rd, had earlier diverted to the base due to bad weather and was due to depart in NS730 on the 4th to return to Watton. The (UK) Accident Investigation Board report, quoted in the group history, describes what happened: 'Take-off was normal 700 yards of its run, at which point there was a black puff of smoke from the left engine. From this point on, the aircraft did not have enough power to become airborne and was travelling too fast to pull up on the remaining runway. The aircraft bounced over a fence at the end of the runway, where the pilot found himself among a group of houses. By skilful handling of the aircraft the pilot was able to avoid the houses and to keep the aircraft in the street until it stopped.' The group historian quips: 'The pilot was not invited in for tea by any of the neighbours.'

A final note in the group report for February records that aircraft markings (emblem) for the 654th BS received official approval from HQ AAF in Washington, as follows:

Aircraft Markings
Over and through an ultramarine blue disc with border equally divided white and dark red, a stylized black bat with red mouth and eyes, affronte, holding a black aerial camera with the right foot and a black flash bomb with the left foot, all outlined white.

Significance
The black bat carrying the camera and flash bomb symbolize the Sqn's primary mission of night photographic reconnaissance.

The 653rd's emblem would be approved the following month and would consist of the following:

Over and through a light yellow green disc, a caricatured gray mosquito [insect] wearing brown aviator's helmet and flight boots, tan flak vest, and white goggles and gloves, kneeling on small, white cloud formation, edged black, shadowed gray, and peering toward sinister through crooked, brown telescope held to right eye, all in front of a large, jagged, grayed light red lightning flash piercing cloud.

Operations – March 1945

The *Graypea* chaff missions, which had begun on an experimental basis with the 1st Air Division (AD) only, had by now become virtually SOP for all three air divisions. During this month thirty-three missions, comprising 134 sorties, totalling 530 hours twenty-two minutes were flown by the 654th Sqn. This broke down into twenty missions in support of the 1st AD, eight for the 2nd AD and five for the 3rd AD. The primary purpose of these Mosquito missions was to act as a screening force for the lead units of bomber formations on heavily flak defended targets when cloud cover had been forecast as 4/10ths or more. Division Field Orders usually indicated the RV point, screening manoeuvre and points at which to start and stop chaff dispensing. Generally, the screening force made RV with the lead combat wings thirty minutes before the Initial Point (IP). Normal screening procedure was then for the Mosquito to fly along the side of the bomber stream to the IP and then pull ahead to a point two minutes before release of chaff, 'S'-ing across a line parallel to the actual run. At the start of chaff dispensing, a slow climb was usually begun to reduce airspeed and maintain the correct distance from the bombers.

It was in this month, after many *Graypea* missions had been flown, that the three-ship formation of Mosquitoes was devised, an arrangement that

NS651 'F' of 654th Bomb Sqn after the undercarriage collapsed on take-off at Watton on 5 March 1945. (USAAF)

NS651 'F' *Woodpecker's Delight* after its accident on 5 March 1945 piloted by James Evans of the 654th Bomb Sqn. (W Borges)

NS651 'F' named *Woodpecker's Delight* was on the strength of both 25th Bomb Gp squadrons. (Dana Bell)

Another view of *Woodpecker's Delight*. (Dana Bell)

would provide lead bomb groups with the maximum amount of screening cover. Immediately prior to dispensing, the Mosquitoes formed into line abreast, separated by up to 300yd. In order for all three Mosquitoes to synchronise their 'S'-ing manoeuvre during the run to the IP, the screening leader called out the headings every fifteen seconds or so. Not all screening missions were successful; failure to make contact, visually or by VHF at the appointed time or place, occurred more than once. Occasionally confusion resulted from the failure of the bomber leader to respond to radio calls from the screening force. On the whole, however, missions were successful.

During the month it was decided to equip some of the *Graypea* Mosquitoes with cameras. Weather permitting, photos were taken of the target area before and after bombing. Back on the ground the photographs were immediately despatched under armed guard to HQ 325th Photo Wing.

The group report highlights 'danger from enemy aircraft, notably jets, but also from our own bombers. Four missions were fired on by the "heavies"' gunners. Fortunately, there were no casualties, although Lt Luse returned from one mission with bullet holes in his tail and fuselage. This could affect crew morale and operational efficiency. Appropriate quotation: 'Oh Lord, save me from my friends, from my enemies I can protect myself.'

Recording the sixteen *Jokers*, two PRU missions and six *Redstockings* flown by the 654th Sqn, the group report mentions an interesting organisational change in operations. 'The latter mission [*Redstocking*] is still highly secret. Since 13 March these missions have been flown from another base, though our flying personnel are still being utilized.' That 'other' base was Harrington in Northamptonshire.

Meanwhile, the 653rd was labouring away at its less highly classified but still vital *Bluestocking* missions (137 this month), *Skywave* long-range navigation sorties (nine), and, last but not least, *Redtails* (thirty-six). In the performance of this latter mission the squadron was justifiably moved to record their satisfaction with a job well done:

> This is so highly regarded that the 2nd Air Division has issued an SOP to cover it. Under the SOP the Combat Wing leading the Air Division in bombing operations provides an Air Commander of Division lead calibre to fly in the command Mosquito as adviser to the Air Division Commander. It is the responsibility of the Mosquito Air Commander to give as much aid as will enable the Division and Combat Wing air commanders to successfully execute the briefed plan. This responsibility consists of striving

for integrity and proper order of Combat Wing and Division formation throughout the mission, and orderly manoeuvre in the target area. The Mosquito piloted by our personnel picks up the Command Observer at a station designated in the Field Order. Normal procedure is for the Mosquito to take off after the bombers and RV with them as they leave the coast or some point en route if a long mission is involved.

NS739 'F' named *Pamelia* of the 653rd Bomb Sqn. (Dana Bell)

Another view of NS739, showing letters 'WXF' under port wing. (Dana Bell)

NS710 'L' of 653rd Bomb Sqn, pictured outside one of Watton's hangars on 17 March 1945. (IWM)

Another view of NS710. (USAAF)

A notable 8th AF personality to perform the role of Command Observer around this time was Brig. Gen. Leon W Johnson, the famed commander of the 44th BG, leader of the August 1943 attack on the Ploesti oil fields and now CO of the 14th Combat Wing. In March the 25th was delighted to receive a letter of appreciation from Johnson in which he wrote: 'I flew with a pilot of the 25th BG (Rcn), First Lt Robert D Shoenhair, as Command Observer on the attack on Nurnberg, 21 February 1945, in a Mosquito aircraft. The manner of performance of the mission by the pilot, his flying skill, his willingness to co-operate and his general overall efficiency were commendable. Should I perform a similar mission in the future, I ask for no better qualified pilot than this man.'

The 653rd Sqn's increasing experience in *Skywave* missions prompted some reflection within the 25th Gp on LORAN progress thus far. The missions had been flown at both low and high altitude with a measure of success that established the system as an efficient and practical navigation aid in the ETO. One RAF crew had flown a *Skywave* sortie to confirm the results of earlier test flights. However, it was felt that LORAN was of more use in the Pacific theatre. The Loran Training Unit established within the group in November to train navigators in the systems had met with results that were not, initially, encouraging. The instruction, which utilised a manually operated trainer only, proved monotonous and failed to provide navigators with a clear and realistic picture of LORAN as it would function in flight. In an effort to rectify the situation the training team (comprising Lts Taub and Sparks, together with Cpls Neudeck, Holler and Malone) went into a huddle with the current Group Navigator, Maj. Walch, and set out to design a training system that would replicate the operation of LORAN in actual flight more dynamically. The outcome was a standard LORAN trainer married to a Link recorder that enabled continuously moving signals to be sent from a transmitter. This simulated moving symbols appearing in the LORAN scope in an aircraft in flight. Thus, practical instruction in LORAN equipment could be given on the ground. In simple, non-technical terms, a special map was devised across which the Link Recorder moved. The map was marked off with 'hyperbolas' (arcs) representing LORAN stations. Readings were taken from two LORAN stations at any time and superimposed on a Mercator projection, on which the navigator marked his 'fixes' and determined the position of his aircraft. A comparison of the navigator's map with the Link recorder provided a ready assessment of the accuracy of his work. The effectiveness of this new system was soon recognised by all the navigators and was formally introduced during the month. Regular in-house LORAN classes were arranged, which were also attended by navigation and radar men from other groups and divisions. The training was believed to be unique in the ETO, and possibly worldwide.

The suitability of the Mosquito for LORAN operations remained a topic for discussion and development in the monthly report. 'The Loran Section also devised an additional aid for navigators. Because of inadequate space in the Mosquito cockpit, the navigator has to operate the Loran equipment over his left shoulder, often in complete darkness. To overcome this handicap, the Section improvised a blacked-out booth simulating the exact conditions confronting the navigator while in flight. Using this, the nav is able to determine for himself the easiest manner of operating the equipment.'

At first glance, the operation of chaff dropping might seem routine, but the missions frequently brought drama, as the report graphically describes.

> *Graypea* mission 3/21 on 20 March 1945 proved quite eventful. In the target area from high at 6 o'clock at 1606 hrs there suddenly whizzed by an Me 262 which made a pass at aircraft [RF] 992 piloted by Lt Gilbert of the 654th Sqn. Strikes tore off about three inches of the port wing, disabled the aileron and peppered the canopy. Inexplicably the jet job pulled up and broke off, though our 'Mossie' was a virtual 'sitting duck'. Neither crew member was hit and by a superlative job of piloting, Lt Gilbert managed to make his way home. Shortly after this attack, aircraft [NS] 996, piloted by Lt Joseph Polovick and with Lt Blaum as navigator, was heard calling 'Mayday – one engine out, other rough'. A few minutes later it reported both engines out. The plane went into a

Caught by an Me 262 jet on 20 March 1945, Lt Roger Gilbert had the wing tip of RF992 shot off. (USAAF)

constant glide over Fohr Island [one of the North Frisian Islands on the German coast of the North Sea]. The accompanying aircraft observed one 'chute out over the west edge of the Island, the other billow midway on the Island where the ship [Mosquito] was seen to hit and burst into flames. Both crew members have been listed as MIA.

The pair became PoWs.

Another loss followed a few days later. 'On 24 March Lt Carroll "Stubby" Stubblefield, pilot, and Lt James Richmond, crew of Mosquito NS711, 654th BS, were officially reported as MIA. They took off on an operational mission of unknown nature with another command. At 1700 hrs, approximately 20 miles west of Kassel, the plane was attacked by friendly aircraft. Both engines were shot out and one member of the crew was seen to parachute safely.' The Mosquito was on a 'special reconnaissance' mission with an escort of P-51s and was mistakenly attacked by a 9th AF P-47. Sadly, Stubblefield was killed, though Richmond survived to become a PoW. Again, P-47s from the 5th ERS were out that day looking for downed aircrew.

The run of bad luck continued with the loss of another crew on 25 March. The monthly report traces the sequence of events:

NS619 'U' of 654th Bomb Sqn seen here in better days. She suffered terminal damage when Lt Kenneth McGriffin misjudged his landing at Watton on 22 March 1945. (P Breen Collection via 8th AF Research Center)

This shot highlights the distinctive red tail markings of what is probably NS774 'M' of the 653rd Bomb Sqn. (USAAF)

At 1448 hrs BLUESTOCKING 3/109 took off [in NS752]. The crew comprised pilot, Lt Bernard Boucher and navigator, Lt Louis Pessirilo (who had recently returned from the States for a second tour of duty). Their task was to report on the weather over Denmark and Central Germany. Forty-five minutes after the scheduled time of return, Flying Control at Watton requested plots of the aircraft from the RAF's 11 and 12 Groups. Unfortunately, there was none. Radio silence, as briefed, had been maintained after take-off and no further information on the crew or aircraft had been received. They were therefore reported as MIA.

The individual squadrons could look back with satisfaction on a busy and successful month. The 653rd had been out on every day of the month, flying a total of 137 weather recon missions over a hostile Continent, with occasionally up to six aircraft a day. The squadron score board for individual Mosquitoes without aborts continued unabated among the crew chiefs. T/Sgt Palmer, with a single machine in his care, led the field with sixty-three missions. T/Sgt Cousineau, with three aircraft under his wing, could boast eighty-three missions, followed by T/Sgt Housman (for two aircraft) on eighty missions. A good barometer of healthy serviceability on the line.

The 654th, meanwhile, had put up 147 sorties, the majority of which were chaff missions for all three bomb divisions. These had been highly successful and widely appreciated. For example, between 26 and 31 March thirty-one *Graypeas* were flown over Plauen, Berlin, Hanover and Bremen, producing some excellent strike attack photos. In addition to the chaff missions, *Joker* night photo runs had been made to a wide range of synthetic oil plants and railway viaducts deep in industrial Germany. On this squadron again, there was a buoyant feeling about current airframe serviceability. A dedicated crew was assigned to handle nothing but engine changes, leaving crew chiefs free to maintain their individual aircraft. Of the thirty-five Mosquitoes on the squadron, which included three trainers, 90 per cent had been in operational condition at all times.

The strike attack photos taken by the 654th chaff Mosquitoes produced a steady workload for the photo lab. A standard formation of four aircraft equipped with one or two 36in FL cameras could take as many as 500 exposures during a day's work. The film had to be processed and then viewed to discard the poor-quality shots that resulted from cloud cover. Each exposure was then numbered and printed, with distribution consisting of three sets for the intelligence staff plus two sets of target pictures for pilots and navigators. From 2,905ft of film handled, 7,921 prints were produced.

Back on the 8th of the month, the 653rd's Lt Robert James (P) and Lt Terrence Hall (N) had a close call when attempting to land NS782 on return from an op. In the circuit, James noticed that the left landing gear would not lock down. He therefore decided to try a 'wheels down' landing, but as the Mosquito touched down the left landing gear started to collapse. Thinking quickly, James maintained sufficient speed to take off again. After circling several times to try to shake the gear down, he noticed that he was getting low on fuel, and so opted for another shot at a wheels-down landing. This time, as the left landing gear started to collapse again, he tried to retract the right gear, but the result was a ground loop 'completely demolishing the aircraft'. Pilot and nav walked away unscathed.

Since taking over as 25th BG CO in September 1944, Leon Gray had rarely made the headlines, but now his efforts were recognised in the award of the Silver Star. The citation read:

> For gallantry in action while piloting an unarmed and unescorted aircraft on a hazardous mission over Germany, 23 December

1944. On this day Col Gray voluntarily performed a daring new type of photographic operation which, up to that time, had been attempted only once, and then without success. He experienced an uneventful journey to the initial point, turned onto the target run, and in the face of terrific anti-aircraft fire, flew a straight and level course to the objective. Fully aware that the entire area was now alerted and he would be justified in taking a devious route back, he turned, and with utter disregard for personal safety, retraced his flight plan to ensure thorough photographic coverage. Intercepted by two Me 109s on the return journey, he skilfully eluded them and arrived at base with excellent photographs. As a direct result of Col Gray's heroic exploit, a complete change in technique used in this type of operation was established, which has substantially increased the ratio of successful missions.

Gray's navigator on the mission was 1/Lt Louis Toth Jr from the 654th BS, who was awarded the DFC. In an impressive ceremony at Watton on 30 March, Elliott Roosevelt, as CO of the 325th Photo Wg, Recon, presented the awards to the Gray crew, and to other recipients, including the DFC to Lt Warren Barber (653rd Sqn) for 'extraordinary achievement participating in a large number of successful flights over Continental Europe'.

NS552 'G' of 654th Bomb Sqn, airborne shortly before a take-off accident on 23 March 1944 in hands of Lt Morton Hunt. (USAAF)

Left: 654th Squadron pilot Warren Borges in 'the office'. He first flew thirty-five missions on B-17s with the 306th Bomb Gp before joining the 25th at Watton in December 1944. (Dana Bell)

Below: Warren Borges escaped major injury when his take-off went wrong on 25 March 1945. His 654th Bomb Gp Mosquito NS774 'M' sustained rather more damage. (Dana Bell)

Operations – April 1945

'With the disintegration of Hitler's *Fortress Europe* there was a great reduction in bombing ops and hence a reduction in 25th BG ops. The only squadron unaffected was the 652nd which continued its long-range meteorological flights.' Thus, stated an early paragraph in the group's monthly report. This was certainly true for the end of the month, but during the opening days of April operational activity was still at full throttle. On 3 April 752 B-17s of the 1st and 3rd ADs, escorted by 691 P-51s, were despatched to bomb the Kiel U-boat yards and the airfield at Flensburg. Providing the customary chaff dispensing service for this force were six Mosquitoes from the 654th flying in two elements of three aircraft. The first element was led by Lt Col Alvin Podwojski, deputy 25th BG commander, and Capt. Lionel Proulx, Group Navigator, the second element by Capt. James McNulty and his navigator Lt Claude Moore. During the approach to the target, Podwojski's aircraft, NS650, developed engine trouble, but he decided to press on. After chaff had been dropped the engine problems worsened and the pilot decided to make for Sweden. Three Me 109s then appeared on the Mosquito's tail but by diving into cloud, Podwojski managed to lose them. The 25th BG historian George Sesler talked to both crew members after the war and found out what happened. First, Podwojski:

> The oil temperature gauge on the starboard engine was reflecting the heat; the radiator temperature was high; the oil pressure was down to fifteen pounds and the port engine started running rough. There was a direct head-wind of one hundred miles per hour above 25,000 feet over the North Sea. I asked Proulx for the time to England and received the answer of two hours and ten minutes. He estimated that it would take one hour and fifty minutes to reach friendly lines at low altitude and with two engines.
>
> In answer to my further inquiry, Proulx reckoned that, with the wind in our favour, it would take 40 minutes to reach Sweden. He added, 'You fly the damn plane – I'll do the praying.' So saying, he pulled out his rosary beads. The decision was thus left to me. I called McNulty and instructed our flight to proceed without us. We were due west of Flensburg when we turned east towards Sweden. Meanwhile, Proulx sorted his maps out and gave me compass directions.

Proulx next recalls:

I was carrying maps that listed escape routes to Sweden and Switzerland. The route to Sweden was mostly over Denmark and its islands which, though it was enemy air space, was not as heavily patrolled or defended as were German cities and industrial areas. 'Pod' attempted to call assistance from fighters attending our mission but with our flawed VHF no contact was made. With the starboard engine smoking and steaming and the oil pressure down to 10 lbs from the normal 70 lbs, 'Pod' turned off the starboard engine and feathered the prop. Though our port engine was turning 2,650 rpm, our airspeed was only 160 mph. 'Pod' tried to jettison the drop tanks on the wings but only one dropped. The port tank wouldn't jettison. It broke loose later, when we were in a banking curve while checking for enemy aircraft.

Keeping close watch to the rear, I observed over Svendborg, Denmark, German fighters either pursuing or shadowing us. We were yet a full 30 minutes from Sweden. With our slow descent through broken clouds, the German fighters lost interest. Flying by instruments, we came down out of cloud cover over the Swedish coast at approximately 9,000 feet. We were immediately intercepted by Swedish Air Force fighters, flying Seversky P-35 aircraft. Their insignia, three gold crowns on a blue background, was distinct. They escorted us to an airfield outside of Malmo called Bultofta. 'Pod' landed the Mosquito on the southwest runway. Immediately upon touchdown, Swedish fire trucks with their American equipment were in motion to flank our landing. They raced parallel to the runway with their nozzles trained on our aircraft in case we burst into flames. They were speeding at 80 to 85 mph and chancing a mishap to themselves in order to cut our risks.

Under international agreement we were considered as prisoners, yet for several weeks we were provided with accommodation at the Stockholm City Hotel. We reported daily to the embassy for duties where we were issued all the money we requested from the finance officer. On off-duty hours we visited tourist attractions and an occasional night club.

Proulx goes on to claim that he and Podwojski were repatriated after the end of hostilities by a 'black B-24', but there is photographic evidence that Roy Ellis-Brown collected them from Sweden in an Airspeed Oxford:

> [Eventually] a limousine arrived at our hotel and took us to the back of Bromma [Stockholm] Airport where we waited in the darkness. A black B-24 landed and stopped near us with engines running. We boarded the bomber and took off on our return flight to England.

In marked contrast to countless downed aircrew before them, and with Allied victory imminent, Podwojski and Proulx didn't have to wait long for repatriation. With Podwojski incarcerated in Sweden, Roy Ellis-Brown stepped into his post as Deputy Group Commander, with the rank of major.

Roy Ellis-Brown (second from left) collecting Lt Col Alvin Podwojski and Capt. Lionel Proulx from Sweden in an Airspeed Oxford at the end of the Second World War. (Roy Ellis-Brown)

Of the eleven *Redtails* flown by the 653rd all but one were uneventful. On 4 April Lt Theodore Smith took off from Watton in NS635 as *Redtail* 4/4 and made the short hop to Bungay in Suffolk, home base for the 446th BG and their B-24s. There he picked up Col Troy Crawford, CO of the 446th, who that day would be acting as Command Observer for a 2nd Air Divn raid by B-24s on Parchim airfield, some 75 miles east of Hamburg in north-east Germany, from which Me 262 jets were harassing Allied intruders. The 25th Group report describes the subsequent events.

> The Mosquito was jumped by two Me 262s and one engine was knocked out. In order to seek protection Smith swung under the bombers with the jets still on his tail. Heavy fire poured from the bombers' guns, presumably at the jets. Unfortunately, the Mosquito caught the brunt of the fire and a second engine was knocked out. The plane was last seen spiralling towards the ground. Not long after the Mosquito crew was officially reported MIA Col Crawford telephoned Group S-2 to report that both he and Lt Smith had parachuted safely to earth but had been captured by Krauts and were PoWs. The camp had been liberated by doughboys [infantrymen] in their swift rush east, but Lt Smith had been moved to another Stalag. He was still officially MIA.

The crewless Mosquito crashed between Parchim and Wesendorf.

Gunfire from 'friendly' aircraft was not limited to bolts from the bombers. On 9 April, a force of 1st Air Divn B-17s set out to attack Oberpfaffenhofen airfield, just outside Munich. Four Mosquitoes making up *Graypea* 4/10 provided chaff screening for the bombers. Returning from the mission, 1/Lts John Pruis (pilot) and Claude Moore (nav) found their aircraft developing engine trouble at the same time as a flight of P-51s with what were identified as French markings were spotted ahead of them. The P-51s peeled off to the left and about two minutes later a sudden explosion rocked the Mosquito. Black smoke and flame streamed from the starboard engine. Whether the damage had resulted from an attack by the Mustangs, or was simply a technical failure in the Merlin, was unclear. Moore grabbed his chest pack, which had been lying on the GEE box, but had difficulty putting it on. At about 1,000ft he managed to worm his way up through the top hatch and bailed out of the doomed ship. Only half in the parachute, and swinging in violent 360 degree turns, he nevertheless managed to make a safe descent, landing in a tree in which he dangled, some 40ft above the

Above: Named *Patches*, NS635 of the 653rd Bomb Sqn was lost on 4 April 1945. (Dana Bell)

Right: NS635 *Patches* served with both the 653rd and 654th Squadrons. She is marked up with twenty-three mission symbols and the legend on the nose states 'Pilot Capt. T R L Lee; Nav Lt W A Biggers; Crew Chief TSgt J D Kendrick'. (USAAF)

ground. He believed he blacked out several times before falling to the ground, where he was found by infantrymen of the US 7th Army. He was passed back to a dressing station and eventually evacuated to a general hospital in England, where he was treated for first degree burns to his arms and head, severe back injuries, and a damaged ankle. Pruis was found dead near the crashed Mosquito. The group report reflected that:

> This crew were living on borrowed time. Two days before they 'pranged', while taking off on *Graypea* 4/8, the right engine of their aircraft conked out and burst into flames. The pilot continued on to the bombing range near the airfield where he jettisoned his drop tanks and then returned to the field. Because of poor visibility he landed too far down the runway and, to avoid overshooting, he applied heavy braking, causing the craft to ground loop. Both landing gears collapsed. Although the plane was a total loss, the crew escaped injury.

After dropping chaff for a 1st AD Fortress raid on Regensburg on 16 April, the five Mosquitoes of the screening force were fired on by P-47s at 4,000ft, but, states the group report, '… with their superior speed they soon outdistanced the pestiferous Thunderbolts. No hits were scored.' The 56th FG was the only unit flying the P-47 at this stage of the war …

Although the serial number is obscured, this probably shows the 654th's RF988. (Flight)

Piloted by Lt Morton Hunt, NS552 suffered a take-off accident on 23 March 1945.
(W Borges)

With victory just round the corner it was especially cruel when losses occurred, but occur they still did. When 1/Lt Robert James took NS757 up for a routine training flight on the same day that John Pruis was killed he could reasonably expect things to go without incident. This was not to be. He took off from Watton at approximately 1500 hrs and at around 1525 hrs his Mosquito appeared in the vicinity of RAF Shepherd's Grove airfield, some 17 miles to the south of Watton (and home to two RAF Short Stirling transport squadrons, on SOE supply dropping duties). Fg Off A Watson was a flying control officer at Shepherd's Grove and saw what happened:

I was on the front balcony of the Watch Office – not on duty but simply watching flying generally. I noticed the Mosquito when it was in our circuit flying at approximately 1,500 feet in a north westerly direction at normal cruising speed. When the aircraft was just short of No 2 hangar it put on 90 degrees of port bank, the nose dropped almost immediately and it started diving vertically towards the ground. In the course of the dive it did a quarter spiral to port and on impact was facing south east. There was another Mosquito in the vicinity at the same time which was seen to be approaching from the same direction as the other one. My impression of the final stage of the dive was that control was recovered and if the pilot had had sufficient height, he would have been able to pull out. The engines were running normally all the time but during the dive they sounded as if the pilot had opened the throttles. I was on the Control Tower balcony for 15 minutes before the accident occurred and did not see any Mosquito doing a beat-up. I did not see any part of the aircraft fall off prior to it hitting the ground.

Sqn Ldr R Ponting, Shepherd's Grove's Senior Flying Control Officer, was on the tower balcony with Fg Off Watson, and corroborated his evidence, except that '… when I first saw the aircraft, it was already diving. My attention was drawn to it by the sudden increase in engine noise. As it dived, it oscillated from side to side about its longitudinal axis. I should say it did quite two or three oscillations before it struck the ground.'

As 25th BG Operations Officer, Roy Ellis-Brown was called as another witness to the crash investigation and his remarks provide an interesting insight into USAAF Mosquito operations at that time:

From my personal observation 1/Lt James was an excellent pilot, and completed 28 missions with the Group, during which time he showed no signs of physical fatigue due to operational flying. When Lt James came to the Group he went through the usual difficult period of transition which has been experienced with all our pilots. Due to the fact that we had no suitable aircraft for transition of bomber pilots into Mosquito pilots, he had two crashes, one of which was caused by a mechanical failure, and the other due to icy conditions of the runway. The latter accident possibly could have been avoided if he [had] had sufficient experience, which we were unable to give him due to lack of training aircraft.

Less serious (there were no casualties) were a crop of eight accidents throughout the month, nearly all of which involved hard landings, with the resultant collapse of the landing gear, at both Watton and other diversion bases. Despite twelve months of operational experience with the 25th BG, the Mosquito could still be a tricky beast to get down in one piece.

The twin challenges of the powerful Mosquito with its British equipment, and the enormous strides made by the USAAF in the development of navigation and bombing systems (NBS), meant that the Americans had to cast their net as widely as possible to recruit suitable aircrew for the 25th BG's two Mosquito squadrons. On the aircraft side, previous tours on B-17s and B-24s mainly met the requirement. Experienced radar men, on the other hand, were perhaps not so easy to source. One man who filled the bill admirably, however, was Lucien Peters, who recalls his experience:

I was a radar navigation-bombardier instructor at Langley Air Force Base before my assignment overseas to the 8th Air Force. From my first mission to my last in B-17s I was always in the lead ship position. I was assigned to many air bases and very seldom flew with the same crew. The command pilot varied from lieutenant colonel to general.

All my flights were above 40,000 feet altitude, were all day flights and were always above cloud. I was never on a mission in which the target was visible. Also, I never made a second run on a target. My accuracy, according to the established records at the time, was within one-half mile of the actual target. At that altitude, I was told, visual bombing was no more accurate. The radar picture in the B-17 was a full 360-degree picture, covering territory determined by the operator, and a good picture always had features which a radar operator could identify. The operator would inform the navigator of the aircraft's position above the cloud cover, and then alert the bombardier for the start of the bomb run.

After finishing a tour of duty I elected not to return to the United States for thirty days leave but, because of my specialization, volunteered to join the 654th Bombardment Squadron. This was very close to the end of the war so I did not become very familiar with everything that went on at Watton. I was warned that the assignment might be a dangerous one. Prior to my arrival at the base, I was told that the Germans had learned how to identify the unarmed 'radar planes', home in on them and eliminate them from the air. When I joined the Squadron, I represented the second active radar operator on the unit's roster.

The radar equipment in the Mosquito airplane displayed a 180-degree picture on the radar screen. This was more difficult to operate and interpret compared to operating the full screen of the

B-17; however, I was given an adequate training period. My crew position for operating the radar was in the centre of the plane. No windows were provided and my only means of contact with the pilot was by phone. To avoid the radar Mosquitoes from becoming an easy target for the Germans during my missions, we were provided with an escort of P-38s [sic – P-51s?] to our objective. Once the mission was achieved, all planes scrambled on their own to return home. In all my B-17 missions I never once had the radar equipment fail on me. However, in my experience, the Mosquito radar had a track record for failure. When the power went out it was exciting sitting in a 'black space' in the centre of the plane. On one mission, with all the electrical power out, the pilot had to fly from the Alps to England as close to the ground as he could. We were expecting the British to greet us with anti-aircraft guns! When the war ended, radar operators were considered extremely important and were to be reassigned without delay to the Pacific theatre. I was directed to leave the 654th Squadron immediately and went back to the US on a British aircraft carrier.

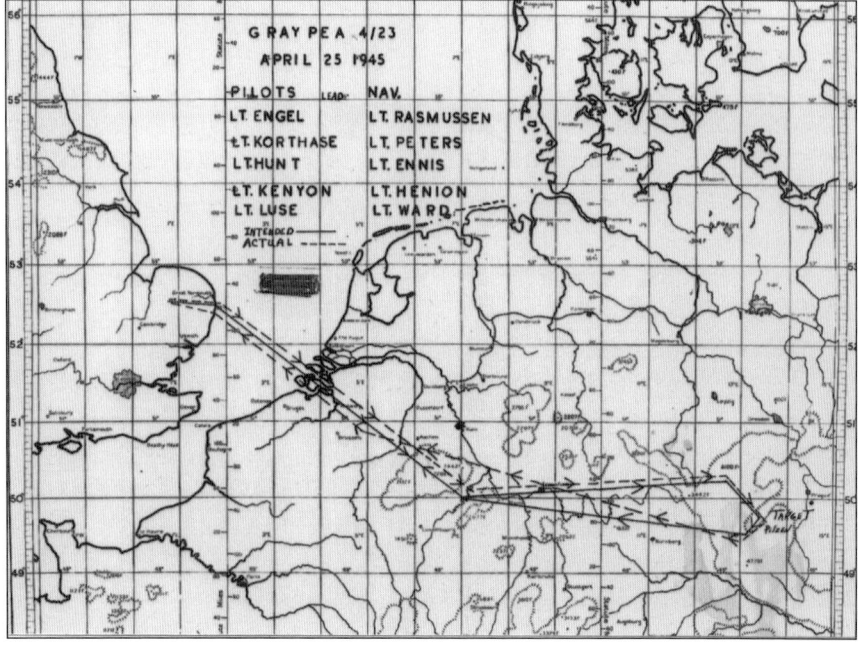

Graypea mission 4-23 flown to Pilsen on 25 April 1945 by five Mosquitoes, one of which aborted due to engine failure. (USAAF)

NS512 'J' of 653rd Bomb Sqn, possibly taken at the 453rd Bomb Gp's base, Old Buckenham. (USAAF)

This, the penultimate month of the war, saw moves and milestones for the group and the wing. With Elliott Roosevelt away in the USA attending his father's funeral, Leon Gray assumed command of the 325th Wing. Lt Col John Hoover moved in from the Wing HQ to take over the group on 14 April, and with Podwojski incarcerated in Sweden, Roy Ellis-Brown stepped into his post as Deputy Group Commander, with the rank of major. On the 12th, a party was held to celebrate one full year of occupancy of Watton. One of the hangars was cleared of all equipment and stages were installed at each end for two bands: Frank Rosato's Base Band, and The Century Bombers from the 100th Bomb Gp over at Thorpe Abbotts. Continuous music was provided for an enthusiastic crowd, with extra entertainment from the United Services Organisation (USO) show 'Yanks Abroad'.

Operations End – May 1945

VE Day – 8 May, brought a cessation of operational missions, and practically all other activities at Watton. Up to that point the 653rd Sqn flew nineteen *Bluestockings* plus one *Skywave*. The group's very last Mosquito mission of the war was a *Bluestocking* weather recon over the UK on 6 May by Lt Harry Flook. For its part, the 654th flew only four operational missions in May, all of them *Skywaves*, the last on the 4th. In their monthly report, the 654th reflected briefly on the success of the Mosquito in meeting its task. 'Prior to the invasion of the Continent, and until the Front was beyond range, B-25 and B-26 medium bombers were used [for night *Jokers*]. These aircraft carried 24 flash bombs with camera technicians operating the camera. They

Pilot Harry Flok got away with minimum damage during this landing on 28 May 1945. The Mosquito is NS758 'T' *Southern Belle* of the 653rd Bomb Sqn. (USAAF)

usually operated from 12,000 feet and proved successful ... Range soon became too great for the 'mediums' and the Mosquito was used. The results from the Mosquito constantly improved.'

In an 18 May letter to the 325th Photo Wg, the Joint Photographic Reconnaissance Committee at Benson praised the work of both the 7th Photo Gp and the 25th BG. During the period 1 June 1944–30 April 1945 the two groups flew 4,085 reconnaissance missions, day, night and H2X, involving approximately 11,000 operational flying hours. Around 72 per cent of these missions were successful. 'Nowhere else has the spirit of inter-Allied co-operation been so prevalent as that which exists in reconnaissance. It is this spirit of co-operation that has made reconnaissance such a success in this theater and a great deal of this is due to you and your staff and to the units of your command.'

NS559 'K' of 25th Bomb Gp pictured at Valenciennes-Denain, France, in 1945. This aircraft flew several Joan Eleanor missions. (AAM)

NS590 'B' suffered three reportable accidents during its time with the 654th Bomb Sqn at Watton, the last of which was in May 1945. It probably went into storage at 10 MU Hullavington before being struck off charge in September 1947. (Norman Malayney)

Another view of NS590. (USAAF)

Air-to-air view of starboard side of NS590. (USAAF)

Closing the Hangar Doors – June 1945

Early in the month, Vance Chipman, who had been shot down in November 1944, turned up and described how his ship had been riddled by flak, a piece of which had cut through his oxygen mask and knocked out one of his teeth. But otherwise he had been uninjured. Clayborne Vinyard and John O'Mara, downed in September while on *Bluestocking* 9/92, also returned from confinement as PoWs, along with Joseph Polovick, missing since March. The latter's navigator, Bernard Blaum, was known to be safe but exact whereabouts uncertain.

With mission completed, the job of disposing of the Mosquitoes began. Besides maintaining flight currency with some routine training flights, 653rd Sqn crews ferried a total of twenty-six Mk XVIs and three Mk IIIs to various bases in the UK on behalf of the group as a whole. The residual fleet, comprising six Mosquito XVIs, two Oxfords and one Noorduyn C-64 Norseman, would remain with the squadron for training and communications duties until movement orders from the UK were

Dusk shot of a 25th Bomb Gp Mosquito at Watton. (Author's collection)

received. These orders began to come in from HQ 8th AF in mid-month, indicating that elements of the group would return to the US by sea, on one of the 'Queens' (*Mary* or *Elizabeth*) and that Watton was scheduled to be closed by 15 July. *Mickey* navigators were a valuable asset and HQ AAF requested that they be returned to the USA immediately. Responsibility for preparing the 25th's fleet of aircraft for disposal, the American types back to the USA and the British machines to the RAF, fell to the 828th Air Engineering Sqn at Watton. Before work ceased on 21 June, all shops and sections of the squadron worked long hours and at top speed to complete all engine changes, modifications and aircraft woodwork on the Mosquitoes, in preparation for the long-awaited trip home. The squadron's historian, WO Ervin Malcolm, succinctly summed up the general feeling at this point: 'Now it looks as if the former members of the FBI (Forgotten Bastards of Iceland) ... will have their tours of duty in Iceland ... and England as long memories. Most of them are overjoyed with the thought of returning to their own country, but some have expressed strong desires to stay on duty in the United Kingdom, which goes to prove that England wasn't so bad after all.'

Chapter 3

416th Night Fighter Squadron

The Mosquito's career as a USAAF night fighter was tantalisingly brief and to explain why it was chosen, why it entered US service when it did, and why it served for such a short time it is well worth looking briefly at US night fighter development as a whole. Effective night fighter operations in the Second World War demanded two things – a reliable airborne radar, and a suitable aircraft to put it in. In the lead up to the war the Americans had neither of these, although development work on both was jogging along in a leisurely fashion without the impetus of actual hostilities. As Stephen L McFarland says in his 1997 [US] Air Force History and Museums Program study on the USAAF in the Second World War *Conquering the Night*: 'In the United States, air doctrine reinforced a disregard for night operations.'

The Birth and Introduction of Air Interception (AI) Radar

Looking first at radar, this was developed in parallel in the UK and the US in the years leading up to the Second World War. In the US it was developed in parallel between the Navy and the Army, with the Navy, ironically, leading the way initially. Experiments on the transmission of very high frequency (VHF) electromagnetic waves were begun at the US Naval Aircraft Laboratory's Radio Division at Naval Air Station (NAS) Anacostia in September 1922. Although the initial results were encouraging, further research was stunted due to a lack of government interest. An important milestone was reached when, in 1921, Albert Hull, of the General Electric Company, capitalising on work carried out by Swiss physicist Heinrich Greinrich, invented a device he called a magnetron. In essence this was a high-powered vacuum tube that works as a self-excited microwave oscillator. Crossed electron and magnetic fields are used to produce the high-power output required in radar. The development of the magnetron has been described as a 'simultaneous invention in different nations' and testament to this was the work of John Randall and Henry Boot of Birmingham University in England, who are credited with the first high-power version of the device suitable for mass

134

production in early 1940. In mid-1940 Sir Henry Tizzard, chairman of the British Aeronautical Research Committee, suggested sharing the magnetron technology with the US to capitalise on the latter's enormous production capacity. This resulted in the 'Tizzard Mission' to the USA in August–October 1940. Meanwhile, back in the USA, the Army had started to take an interest in the development of radar and in 1936 the Amy Signal Corps staff visited the Naval Research Laboratory to be briefed on pulse radar development – prior to this there had been little if any co-operation between the two US services. This eventually led to the production of the SCR 268 equipment, although this was a ground-based early warning system rather than an airborne radar.

Back in England the world's first early warning radar network had been developed in the Chain Home system – designed to provide warning of attacking enemy aircraft. Five sites covering the approaches to London began full-time operation in 1938. A major step forward though this was, it did not solve the problem of detecting and destroying enemy bombers over the UK at night. The solution was to mount a small radar on an intercepting aircraft, but the sheer bulk of the equipment in its current form and the associated aerials made this a considerable challenge. In 1935 George 'Taffy' Bowen, a talented member of Robert Watson-Watt's Radar Development Team volunteered to take on the task of installing radar in an aircraft. Work continued at Bawdsey, Norfolk, initially using Handley Page Heyford K6902 from the Royal Aircraft Establishment, Farnborough. The lumbering Heyford biplane had its limitations in work over the sea and Bowen was equipped with two more modern Avro Ansons, K6260 and K8758 based at Martlesham Heath (then home to the Aeroplane & Armament Experimental Establishment (A&AEE)). The first airborne radar transmitter was tested and in 1937 Bowen was able to demonstrate the use of radar in detecting ships of the British Fleet in the North Sea. There were now two strands to the work – air to surface vessel (ASV), and airborne interception (AI). The latter was much more problematic to perfect.

But perfected it was and the first operational AI, the Mk III version, was installed in the Bristol Blenheim IFs of the RAF's Nos 23, 25, 29, 219, 600 and 604 Squadrons, carrying out night patrols, in May 1940. The first AI score of the war occurred on the night of 22–23 July 1940 when a Blenheim of the Fighter Interception Unit downed what was thought to be a Dornier 17 off the Sussex coast. But at this early stage there were two shortcomings: the comparatively slow performance of the Blenheim and the limited range of the radar. This prompted the C-in-C of RAF Fighter

Command, Air Chief Marshal Sir Hugh Dowding, to rule that the role of night fighter was to be filled by the Bristol Beaufighter, which had the required performance and firepower. This in turn spurred on 'Taffy' Bowen and his team at what was now the Air Ministry Research Establishment (AMRE) at Bawdsey, together with assistance from the EMI Company, to produce the first really effective version of AI, the much-improved Mk IV. So began the Beaufighter/AI night fighter combination, which entered RAF service in September 1940 and which recorded its first success on the night of 19–20 November, when a 'Beau' piloted by Sqn Ldr John Cunningham of 604 Squadron destroyed a Ju 88 near Chichester, Sussex. It was a combination that would quite understandably catch the eye of the USAAF.

Another imaginative, but in retrospect somewhat desperate, British project to provide a night fighter solution lay in the so-called Turbinlite Havoc. In September 1940 Frederick Sidney Cotton, an Australian inventor and pioneer in the fields of aviation and photography (he was a key figure in the development of photographic reconnaissance), began work on the concept of airborne searchlights for night fighters. He termed the idea 'Aerial Target Illumination' and enlisted the help of serving RAF engineering officer William Helmore. Together they developed what became known as 'Turbinlite'. This involved the installation of a powerful searchlight in the nose of a Douglas Havoc with which to illuminate night-time raiding enemy aircraft, which could then be shot down by accompanying fighters. The scheme gained momentum with the first operational unit, 1422 (Night Fighter) Flt, forming on 12 April 1941, followed by a surprising ten squadrons earmarked for this specialist role. However, in practice, the idea proved a resounding failure and was formally abandoned in January 1943. Interestingly, though, it centred on the Douglas A-20 Havoc, which the Americans were actively working on as a possible night fighter at the same time.

The Birth and Introduction of the US Night Fighter

As with AI radar, the development of an effective US night fighter had, prior to the Second World War, been desultory but with the entry of the US into the Second World War events moved into another gear altogether, both in terms of actual aircraft types and the units to operate them. Quite sensibly the USAAF took an interest in how the RAF, with seven months of combat experience behind it, was going about things.

In May 1940 Lt Gen. Henry Arnold, Chief of the Army Air Corps, sent his Chief of Plans, Col Carl Spaatz, to England to observe how the UK was conducting the war against Germany. Spaatz's official assignment was as Assistant Military Attache (Air) to Britain, or 'high class spy' as he termed himself. In August he visited RAF Fighter Command's HQ 12 Group, at RAF Hucknall, Nottinghamshire, where he spent a day in the operations room observing day and night activity. Spaatz was part of a small team that included Lt Col Frank Hunter, an experienced fighter pilot who had originally been sent to France as an observer but moved over to England after the French defeat in June. Later in the year Hunter returned to Orlando AB, Florida, as CO of the 23rd Composite Gp responsible for testing and evaluating new equipment, techniques and tactical principles.

The next significant step towards the production of an indigenous, dedicated US night fighter was the offer by the American company Northrop, in response to a general Army requirement, of a twin-engine, twin-boom aircraft large enough to carry the newly developed radar equipment, a radar operator, and a gunner to operate the planned 0.5in guns and 20mm cannon. This would be the P-61 Black Widow, which first flew in its XP-61 form on 26 May 1942. However, the beefy new fighter would not reach operational units until early 1944 (outside the scope of this book) and in the meantime there were urgent requirements to be met.

An interim, but, as events would prove, not wholly satisfactory solution was found in the Douglas A-20 Havoc. To take advantage of the British AI radar, then being energetically developed in the UK, the first Army Air Corps A-20 was modified as a night fighter prototype in 1942 and redesignated the XP-70. The conversion work included a 'solid' nose containing the radar, and, under the fuselage, a gun pack armament comprising four 20mm cannon. A further fifty-nine A-20s were similarly modified to P-70 configuration to serve as operational trainers in radar-directed night fighting. Additional versions of the P-70 followed in 1943 with 0.5in guns in the ventral bay and AI radar (P-70A-1), and then with the armament in the nose (P-70A-2). The P-70B-1 was the first version to feature the American SCR-720 centimetric radar together with six-gun armament in blisters on each side of the fuselage. Finally, the P-70B-2 combined US radar with ventral armament. The P-70 saw limited use with US night fighter squadrons over Guadalcanal and New Guinea in 1943–44.

The USAAF Turns its Attention to British Night Fighter Types

With no ideal home-grown night fighter (or reconnaissance aircraft for that matter) available, in 1943 the Americans began lobbying the British for Mosquitoes that year, confident in their case that they were supplying American types to the Brits under Lend-Lease. Under the Arnold-Courtney Agreement (between Gen. Henry Arnold, Commanding General of the US Army Air Forces, and Air Chief Marshal Sir Christopher Courtney, the RAF's Air Member for Supply and Organisation), Britain was provisionally due to provide 120 Mosquitoes to the USAAF. Of these, twenty were to be AI-equipped Mk XIII night fighters. Discussions between Whitehall and Washington rumbled on throughout the rest of 1943 and into 1944, the Americans very keen to get their hands on the versatile Mosquito, and the British anxious to maintain the strength of their own front-line squadrons. The eventual outcome of this prolonged horse-trading was that the USAAF would be allocated a small number of NF.XXX Mosquitoes but receive an interim delivery of Bristol Beaufighters for night fighter work in the Mediterranean. Exactly how the decision to provide Beaufighters to the USAAF was reached is not as well documented as the Mosquito saga.

The First USAAF Night Fighter Units

So much for aircraft for the night fighter role, what about specialist USAAF units to operate those aircraft? The origins of formal US night fighter organisations go back to the 81st FS, which was activated in January 1942 with the role of providing air defence training as part of the AAF School of Applied Tactics. The squadron provided men and equipment for the formation, in October 1942, of the 348th NFS, the AAF's first dedicated NF operational training squadron. Douglas A-20/British-designated DB-7s and P-70s formed the squadron's equipment. Between July and November 1943 additional night fighter squadrons, the 349th, 420th and 424th, were activated and these, together with the original 348th, became the component squadrons of the 481st Night Fighter Operational Training Group, activated on 15 July 1943. Douglas B-18 Bolos (the standard US bomber in 1938–40) and P-70 Havocs were used to meet the group's mission of training new graduates of Training Command advanced flying schools, and converting experienced pilots on to the P-61, though production delays at Northrop meant that Black Widows were not delivered until early 1944. The 481st would go on to train the many NF squadrons and crews destined for both the ETO and the Pacific.

Four USAAF night fighter squadrons would be equipped with Beaufighters for service in the ETO. They would all conform to a broadly similar pattern: train in the US (Orlando) on the P-70 in early 1943; move to the UK in Spring 1943 to train on and receive Beaufighters; ferry the Beaus to N Africa in summer 1943; move to southern Europe in late 1943 or early 1944, following the Allied invasion of Sicily (Operation HUSKY) in July 1943. The squadrons concerned and their equipment were as follows:

a. **414th NFS**: Activated Orlando Feb 43; UK Mar 43; North Africa May 43; Sardinia Nov 43. Aircraft: P-70; Beaufighter; P-38; P-51; P-61.

b. **415th NFS**: Activated Orlando Feb 43; UK Mar 43; North Africa May 43; Sicily Nov 43. Aircraft: P-70; Beaufighter; P-61.

c. **416th NFS**: Activated Orlando Feb 43; UK May 43; North Africa Aug 43; Sicily Sep 43. Aircraft: P-70; Beaufighter; Mosquito; P-61.

d. **417th NFS**: Activated Orlando Aug 43; UK Mar 43; North Africa Aug 43; Corsica Apr 44. Aircraft: P-70; Beaufighter; P-61.

From this table it can be seen that only the 416th operated the Mosquito.

416th NFS Narrative

The 416th NFS was activated at Orlando, Florida, on 20 February 1943, and training of air and ground crews began soon afterwards at the Army Air Forces School of Applied Tactics. Night flying training was carried out using the Douglas P-70, a modified version of the Douglas A-20 attack bomber (known in the RAF as the Boston/Havoc), a rugged design with good handling qualities, but which the 416th was not planned to take into combat. On 5 May the squadron left for overseas service in the UK, where it would hone its skills and receive the tools of the job. On English soil it was based initially at RAF Honiley in Warwickshire, (sister squadron, the 417th, was similarly headquartered at Ayr in Scotland), but with detachments to a number of RAF airfields for various elements of night fighter training. This was all part of a carefully prepared plan, the aptly named Operation Cousin, promulgated by HQ RAF Fighter Command and designed to give maximum support to the Americans during their short stay in their UK. The principal detachment was to Cranfield in Bedfordshire, where No. 51 Operational Training Unit (OTU) provided training on AI Mk VIII radar to both 416th and 417th crews. Op Cousin stipulated that the Cranfield detachment should comprise a maximum of 56 officers and 170 enlisted men (EM), divided equally between the two USAAF squadrons. The detached EMs consisted of both technical and admin specialisations. In addition, eighteen observers were to be sent to RAF Fighter Command's HQ 10 Gp, while four Ground Controlled Interception (GCI) controllers from the 416th were to go to HQ 11 Gp.

Other detachments went to Usworth in north-east England, where No. 62 OTU also provided AI training, using Avro Ansons. Each Anson was fitted with two cathode ray tubes so that the instructor could monitor the pupils' interpretation of what was being seen on the screen, while a second pupil watched the target's behaviour visually from the front seat as he listened to the commentary over the intercom. Another detachment went to Charmy Down near Bath (a night fighter station that between September 1942 and January 1943 had hosted the RAF's No. 533 Sqn and its Turbinlite Havocs. The station was also earmarked for USAAF P-61 Black Widow units later on, in 1944); 'Bristol' is listed and this probably refers to Filton, where the Bristol Aeroplane Company manufactured the Beaufighter and USAAF crews could be familiarised with the aircraft (they hadn't yet received their 'Beaus' at this point).

In early June the 416th's HQ and its various detachments assembled at RAF Acklington in Northumberland for a short period of consolidation and to receive, at last, its planned Beaufighters. The station diary provides an interesting record of the squadron's activities during its remaining time in England.

June 1943 – RAF Acklington

7 Jun 43: Lt Bray, Liaison Off with 416th arrived on prelim visit preparatory to the arrival of the Sqn. Domestic & training matters discussed and much useful info gleaned.

8 Jun 43: Lt Ratz plus small advance party of 416th arrived to prepare the way for his unit.

10 Jun 43: Main dets of 416th arrived from Cranfield – 20 officers and approx. 160 EMs.

12 Jun 43: Maj. Davies, OC 416th arrived and took over command of the Sqn. Discip, org and training matters were discussed with the Stn Cdr. So far, only four of the Sqn's new Beau VIs have arrived and flying has not yet commenced. Col Towle and Col Briggs (US Army) arrived to by air to discuss the org and training of the 416th.

14 Jun 43: A training conference was held in the Stn Cdr's office to discuss the coordination of the training programme for the 416th. This covered sqn orgn, tech ground training, maintenance, and intelligence. A specimen schedule was drawn up to record the training progress of each individual aircrew member.

15 Jun 43: The AOC of the RAF's No 13 Gp, together with Wg Cdr Braithwaite (Org) and Sqn Ldr MacMillan (Trg) visited to discuss training and orgn with the 416th. S/Ldr Emmett (Liaison Off) 416th Sqn was there.

21 Jun 43: At approx. 1100 hrs an ac [aircraft] accident occurred near Hermitage Farm, Warkworth, Northumberland involving a Beau VI, V8769, of the 416th with Lt Leggett piloting. He was killed and the ac completely destroyed. Preliminary reports indicate that both engines failed due to fuel shortage. [Leggett was returning from a cross country exercise to RAF Hendon, on the northern fringe of London when the accident occurred. In his attempted forced landing he hit the bank of the River Coquet.]

26 June 43: Maj. Davies left on relinquishing command, 'S/Ldr (sic) Emmett (Trg Liaison) assumed temp command. During afternoon AOC 13 Gp plus Brig. Gen. Frank Hunter [now commanding general of the US VIII Fighter Command] and Col Towle (US Army HQ) visited to discuss the orgn and training of the 416th. [In his talk to the 416th Brig. Gen. Hunter announced that the squadron's new commanding officer would be Capt. – soon to be Maj. – Amberse Banks – replacing Maj. Davis, who had relinquished command on 25 June.]

At this point the 416th's operational diary enthusiastically records the arrival of their new CO on 27 July:

> Capt. Banks, who had been flying since 1924, is regarded as one of the best pilots in the Army Air Force. He entered the Air Corps in 1923 and at one time had flown every type of plane the Army had. On his present tour of duty he has flown 12 different types and has completed over 5,000 hours of night flying. His energy and efficiency have already made a good impression and we anticipate a smoothly running organisation under his command. Capt. Banks brought with him his own observer Flt Off Moody, Capt. Rulon Blake as our new Operations Officer (together with his observer, and Flt Off Plain who becomes the new Senior Observer.) All these individuals came over from the 415th NFS.

The Acklington diary continues:

> 1 Jul 43: Lt Col Frank Carroll, Inspector General of the 8th Fighter Command arrived by air to inspect the 416th. During the brief visit training and orgn was discussed with the station commander (Wg Cdr E Graham) and the 416th CO Capt Banks.

> 4 Jul 43: The unit is now settling well down to a steady and well-ordered scheme of training and appears to have overcome the initial disorganisation.

> 5 Jul 43: The application of the US custom of the Orderly Officer taking all meals with 'Other Ranks' was raised/considered. Complaints re food from the 416th have been few and small in nature, which is gratifying in view of the fact that few of their personnel have been in this country for long. A friendly and co-operative spirit appears to prevail in this unit. Sqn Ldr Goodman (HQ Fighter Command, Night Training) arrived by air to discuss Operation COUSIN. Purpose of the visit was to sort out operational and training problems – the chief of these being equipment matters. As a result, the Stn Equipment Off (Flt Lt F W Rayner) is going to 'Ajax' ('US HQs') to endeavour to smooth these out. High altitude training was also discussed.

(13 Jul 43: S/Ldr W A C Emmett, Liaison Off with the 416th Sqn …)

15 Jul 43: At 1630 hrs Beaufighter VI, FK905, flown by 2/Lt Kelly with Cpl Simpson as passenger, crashed on the airfield through a very heavy landing, which caused the port u/c to collapse. Neither of the two Americans were injured but ac sustained damage to engine, fuselage and propeller.

20 Jul 43: Sqn Ldr Dickinson, Equipment Liaison Off at the Air Ministry for USAAF units in this country visited to discuss the 416th's continuing supply problems. Demanding and delivering spares was not going smoothly. It was agreed that, rather than going through the RAF Group orgn, the 416th should demand equipment. This solved the problem.

21 Jul 43: Signal received from HQ 44 [Ferry Service] Gp stating the projected move of 416th to Portreath and thence to fly to Ras El Ma in Morocco. Mve dated for 31 Jul. This follows the signalled announcement from HQ FC of the completion of training of 416th and 417th Sqns. In this connection, HQFC asked HQ Coastal Command to provide experienced crews with Beau VIs to lead formations during overseas flights. Accordingly, HQ 44 Gp was tasked with transferring four Beaus and crews from RAF Lyneham to RAF Acklington to take place on 24th to act as leaders. Endurance test flights at 8000 ft to be carried out to ensure they are fit for purpose. 'The 416th arrived at this station on 10 Jun with little previous training – in fact, most of its personnel had been in this country only a very short time – and the fact that in the space of approx. 7 weeks it is considered to be operationally fit for overseas speaks exceedingly well for the energy and enthusiasm with which training in all branches has gone forward under the able leadership of the CO, Maj. Banks.'

22 Jul 43: Sqn Ldr Phillips, Gp Equip Off from HQ 12 Gp, visited Stn Equip Off (Flt Lt Rayner) visit to sort out a few remaining supply probs. 'Visit characterised by the 416th usual helpfulness'.

24 Jul 43: At 1900 the 416th gave a dinner in the Airmen's Dining Hall to mark their impending departure. Maj. Banks presided and the Stn Cdr and officers were invited. Dinner followed by a successful all ranks dance.

1 Aug 43: Beau V8816 crashed on take-off at approx 1430 hrs in a field adjoining the airfield belonging to Mr Bell, farmer. Ac written off. Pilot escaped injury but radio observer sustained spinal injuries and was admitted to Ashington hospital. Condition not grave. Incident caused by failure of the governing unit on the starboard variable pitch propeller. Engine went into fine pitch as ac became airborne. The Beau went down and through a wire fence and hedge. RAF Regiment guard placed on it.

2 Aug 43: Signal received from RAF HQFC saying 416th's move would be delayed due to congestion at Portreath, the point of departure from the UK. Movt of ground echelons fixed for 8th Aug.

3 Aug 43: HQFC signalled requesting immediate move of 416th's air echelon to Portreath and stating that spare crews would remain at Acklington to fly out replacement aircraft as they became available.

The squadron responded with commendable promptness to this order and the diary describes subsequent events:

4 August – The planes took off in heavy overcast (ceiling 600 feet) for Gibraltar and Africa. The planes were escorted by three RAF Coastal Command Beaufighters. It was a stirring spectacle; Acklington had never seen such an exhibition of mass buzzing. Sadly the occasion was marred by the loss of KV904 flown by F/O Brewer (P) and F/O Lawniski (RO) which suffered an engine fire and crash-landed at Bywell Farm near Morpeth in Northumberland. The Beau was destroyed by fire and the crew taken to hospital suffering from burns, lacerations and shock. Their lives were saved by the prompt action of Police Constable Laudie of the Northumberland Constabulary who was quickly on the scene. The planes took off as follows:

	Aircraft	Crew
1315 hours:	V8746	Brake/Gander
	KV912	Banks/Moody
	KV903	Morrison/Kiml
	V8828	Fors/Gaudette
	V8809	Cargill/Kight
	V8678	Morgan/Veslany
	V8693	Kelley/Quinn
	KV903	Killian/Robinson
1530 hours:	KV914	Blake/Plain

The ground echelon and the remainder of the aircrew commanded by Lt Monroe await further notice.

This would come a few days later when the rear party went by rail to Prestwick to be flown out to North Africa by C-54.

From Acklington the Beaufighters made for RAF Portreath but on arrival at the West Country airfield only one aircraft was able to land because of extremely unfavourable weather conditions, the remaining aircraft diverting to other airfields in south-west England. By 6 August all aircraft had arrived at Portreath despite continuing bad weather and after checking were found to be serviceable, apart from one piloted by 1st Lt Frank Killian. The following morning at 0300 hrs crews were called for breakfast and a final briefing, and then at 0517 hrs the first aircraft, piloted by the squadron commander, took off, followed by the remaining crews at approximately thirty-second intervals, with the exception of Lt Killian, whose Beaufighter was still unserviceable.

A refuelling stop was made at Gibraltar, which was reached at 1055 hrs, where the weather was found to be much too hot for the heavy flying clothing donned on departure from England. After lunch on 'The Rock', the Beaus took off and headed for Ras el Ma. However, working and domestic accommodation on the base was in such short supply that Maj. Banks decided to head on to Oran in Algeria, which was reached at 1805 hrs. A sudden and severe dust storm delayed the departure of three aircraft, a new experience for the American crews. On 8 August the squadron moved from Oran to Algiers in Algeria, where it was soon joined by the 'stragglers' left behind at Portreath and Ras el Ma. Here it was assigned to the Northwest African Coastal Air Force, whose responsibilities comprised the air defence of North Africa, air protection of Allied shipping, offensive action against enemy shipping, anti-submarine operations, and air-sea reconnaissance. Mobility was keynote at this point and on 17 August yet another move was made, this time to Bone, some 260 miles (418km) miles to the east. At Bone air crews were joined by supporting elements of the squadron and 'a temporary camp was pitched between the airdrome and the beach'.

The 416th had arrived in North Africa at a pivotal time. Operation Torch was the Allies' plan to take control of Morocco, Algeria and Tunisia. A combined Anglo-American amphibious operation, the landings had taken place back on 8 November 1942. Then, for six months the Germans and Italian forces slugged it out with American, and British and Commonwealth forces. But the Allied build-up had been unceasing and they gained control of numerous airfields. Starved of fuel and armaments, and without proper communications, the Axis forces were gradually worn down and by May 1943 it was all over. Col-Gen. Jurgen von Arnim and his 5th Panzerarmee surrendered on the 12th, while Gen. Giovanni Messe, commander of the German–Italian 1st Army, followed suit a day later.

How the Allies would continue to prosecute hostilities generally following victory in North Africa had already been decided when Churchill, Roosevelt and their Chiefs of Staff met at the Casablanca Conference in January 1943. The question of which point on the coast of Europe should be earmarked for invasion was discussed. It was too early to consider a cross-Channel attack from England on the west coast of France, but an advance up Italy, the 'soft underbelly' of the Axis, was a comparatively attractive proposition. With a large number of Allied forces now available in North Africa, Sicily would present a convenient stepping stone between Africa and Italy. This was agreed and the invasion of the island, Operation Husky, took place between 10 July and 17 August. The 416th thus found itself caught up in the general exodus from Africa and into Italy.

The squadron moved first to Catania in Sicily on 21 September as an interim base but then on 26 September the ground echelon went by sea to Taranto, with the Beaufighters, led by Maj. Banks, providing an escort for the ship. Docking at the Italian port in the mid-afternoon, the men had bivouacked in a nearby vineyard by 1900 hrs. Their arrival marked the presence of the first USAAF night fighter squadron on the continent of Europe (the 414th, 415th and 417th would follow later on.) On the morning of 27 September the squadron left Taranto by rail and road and made for Lecce aerodrome on the south-east heel of Italy. The following day the Beaufighters arrived from Bizerte (and one of the pilots, a Lt Kelley, is reported to have soloed in a Macchi 202 fighter.) The accommodation at

Lecce seemed 'luxurious after Bizerte and Catania', though the base was yet another waypoint in the drive north, and the squadron was soon issued with orders to move to Grottaglie (some 35 miles to the north-west) on the 30th.

Throughout the rest of 1943 the 416th flew patrols over the Straits of Taranto and the Adriatic Sea. On 29 December Lt King brought in the first AI Mk VIII-equipped Beaufighter for an acceptance check.

Beaufighter *Honeychile* of 416th Night Fighter Sqn at Grottaglie, Italy, in November 1943. (USAF)

Beaufighter KV912 *Fluff* of 416th Night Fighter Sqn at Grottaglie, Italy, in November 1943, (USAF)

Operations – January 1944

A move from the east coast to Pomigliano d'Arco, near Naples, on the country's west coast took place on 28 January 1944. Here the 416th immediately became involved in the Battle of Anzio (Operation Shingle), which had begun on the 22nd of the month.

Operations – February 1944

A significant milestone was reached on 8 February when the 416th notched up its first victory. On that date the squadron put up twelve patrols, seven over the Anzio beach and five above Naples. Among these was a Beau flown by 2/Lt James Urso and his observer F/O Daniel Powell (who had transferred from the 414th Sqn), which was patrolling an area on the coast between San Felice and Gaeta (about 60 miles/97km south of Rome). As they orbited at around 0500 hrs they spotted an enemy aircraft, which they identified as an Me 210. They followed it inland for about 45 miles to a point between Capistrello and Avezzano and at 0529 hrs Urso opened fire. The Messerschmitt broke in two and as it fell the burning wreckage was observed by another Beau crew, Capt. Morrison (P) and F/O Quinn (O). The event was recorded with delight: 'Enthusiasm is high in the squadron, for this is the first tangible result of our work. Until now we have had the satisfaction of knowing that we have defended various areas, but now we have the greater satisfaction of bringing down an enemy plane.'

Patrols over the Anzio beach continued unabated and on the 10th Capt. Cargill was fired on by flak. The 416th diary reports, on 12 February, that: 'Those whose duties bring them to the line at night wait with fear and trembling for the inevitable challenge by the many airbase security troops "Who Goes There?" There is a legend that a transport pilot once answered "257 Herman Goering Panzer Squadron" and was told to "Carry on".'

Pilots new to the 416th were beginning to fly the Beaus and on 13 February Lt King 'was fired on by flak and altogether had a busy time chasing Wellingtons and A-20s'. The following night Lt Killian was fired on 'by the eager tail gunner of a bogey which proved to be a Wellington. Our other ships were also plagued by Wellingtons.' On 17th of the month the restriction on flying over enemy territory with the Mk VIII AI equipment was reimposed for security reasons. 'The skies seem full of bogies, all of which were A-20s.'

A most welcome second victory was scored on 24 February, the details of which provide a graphic description of a typical successful interception. Capt. Darwin Brake and his RO, F/O Alfred Gander, in Beau VIF ND178, were patrolling over the Anzio beachhead just after 2000 hrs under the guidance of a ground controller coded *Virtue*. Flying south, the fighter was given a vector of 330 degrees and informed that a bandit was 4 miles to port, going north-east. Brake checked with Virtue for any friendly aircraft in the area, was told there was none and that this was definitely a hostile. The heading was held and the enemy aircraft, 5 miles ahead, was pursued through hard evasive action down to 1,200ft, where visual contact was made. The bandit's evasive action became less pronounced but continued. There was good radio contact with the controller, who advised Brake, now doing 220mph at 10,000ft, that the bandit was off to port at 4 miles, going north-east at about the same altitude. Over Rome, Gander got an AI contact as the bandit crossed in front, 3 miles away at 9,500ft and doing about 180mph. The Beau closed to 1,200ft and made a visual contact with an aircraft at twelve o'clock high. The night was moonless and very black but clear, and although there was some ground haze visibility was good. Evasive action by, and distance of, the target aircraft in the darkness made it difficult to identify and contact was momentarily lost when it dived and was lost in the radar ground return. However, visual contact was almost immediately regained when it pulled up. The Beau followed for around eight minutes of evasive action, and on closing to about 100ft the crew clearly made out the distinctive features of a Heinkel 111.

Throttling back to 170mph, Brake let the Heinkel pull ahead to a range of 150yd and then opened fire. It was 2125 hrs and they were some 60 miles north of Rome. The first burst hit the Heinkel's tail assembly, tearing off two large chunks, which flew over the top of the Beaufighter's cockpit. Other, smaller fragments flashed by to starboard. No return fire was seen and, aware that he was striking the Heinkel squarely on the tail, Brake gave the Beau some left rudder to nudge his cannon fire on to the enemy's port wing root. This was instantly effective, the German seeming to stop in mid-air and then falling straight down, below and out of sight of the Beaufighter. Although Brake orbited for some time to try to confirm the victory, there was no sign of the victim and the Beau crew deduced that it must have crashed into the mountains. The obvious damage wrought by sixty rounds of 20mm cannon and 300 rounds of .303 ammo was, they later reasoned, worth one He 111 confirmed destroyed.

Operations – March 1944

The next level up in 416th NFS's chain of command at this point was the 62nd Fighter Wing (FW) and the first inkling at a local level of the planned operation of Mosquito night fighters by the USAAF appears in a letter dated 7 March 1944, from the wing's Naples-based HQ to the CO, 416th NFS. Entitled, *Operation of Mosquitoe* [sic] *Type Aircraft Attached to 416th Night Fighter Squadron,* it advised the following:

1. It is the desire of higher headquarters to service test subject aircraft under conditions as now exist over the beachhead. Therefore, wherever possible, these aircraft will be used for that purpose.
2. The secondary purpose of attaching subject aircraft is to reinforce the 416th Night Fighter Squadron and as such they will be placed on the regular operations schedule.
3. As yet no special reports have been requested on the operation of these aircraft, however, aircrew, control, operations and maintenance personnel are enjoined to pay particular attention to both favourable and unfavourable operational features. A record will be kept of these details in the event this Headquarters is called on to furnish same.

Another addressee on the letter was the CO of the RAF's 256 Sqn, itself a night fighter unit operating a mixture of Mk XII and XIII Mosquitoes at Luqa, Malta, on convoy patrols and night defence of the island. With a relatively slack period in operations, 256 was assigned the task of helping the 416th to convert to Mosquitoes. To do this they would detach aircraft to Italy, where they would also take part in operations.

On the same date as the letter, the 416th's war diary announced that:

> A detachment of four Mosquitoes of 256 (RAF) Squadron has arrived from Malta to assist in our heavy commitment over the Anzio beachhead and in the Naples Sector. They have been placed on our operations schedule and their flying will be dovetailed with ours. Our Intelligence Officer will provide 'gen' for them and make their reports.

The 'Pomigliano Detachment', as it was known, duly consisted of eight aircrew and twenty-nine ground crew and would last until 17 February. The Mosquitoes themselves were all Mk XIIs and over the period of the detachment included HK125, '184, '187, '188, '399 and '400.

The RAF Mosquitoes were immediately in action, flying GCI-controlled nightly patrols of three aircraft over the Anzio beachhead and the Naples Sector. Initially, trade was lean with only fleeting contact made with distant and fast-fleeing bogeys. 'Free-lance' patrols brought no greater success. But then on 14 March things changed. Just before midnight Fg Off N Binks and his navigator, Fg Off D Brewer, took off in HK400 for a patrol of the Naples Sector at 4,000–15,000ft. They soon made contact with five 'bogeys' – which proved to be friendly. At 0135 hrs, when 10 miles north-west of Naples and at 4,000ft, they were instructed to free-lance. With the Mosquito orbiting, Brewer obtained an AI contact with a bandit at 7,000ft flying north-west. Binks closed the distance to 2 miles, at which point numerous other blips appeared at the same range as the target. Window was suspected. Not to be distracted, the navigator clung to his original target and the range was shaved to 300ft. There the hostile was identified as a Ju 88. Binks opened accurate fire, destroying the intruder, from which no return fire had been experienced and no parachutes were seen. Another 256 Sqn crew, Fg Offs E Harrington and W Cox in HK125, observed the flaming '88 crash into the sea 10 miles south of Castel Volturno.

Alongside the 416th, the RAF Mosquito detachment continued its nightly trio patrols over the Anzio Bridgehead and Naples, but encountered nothing more hostile than Allied Bostons and Beaufighters. The last such missions were flown on the 18th.

A third victory for the 416th was notched up on 17 March by a Beau flown by Lt Fors and F/O Gaudette. 'At 0335 hrs, while they were on patrol ten miles south east of the Anzio beachhead, they were vectored onto a bandit. They closed in and obtained a visual, but then lost it. They obtained another visual at 1,000 ft and identified the bandit as a Ju 88. The enemy aircraft was destroyed. Six patrols were flown, two of the Anzio beachhead, two of Naples and two convoy patrols.'

The 416th presence in Italy at this point coincided with the eruption of the country's famous volcano and attracted the following 18 February diary entry: 'Mt Vesuvius has begun to put on a magnificent and terrifying show, the greatest eruption since 1872. The spectacle is clearly visible from camp.'

Operations – April 1944

An upbeat diary records the following flurry of activity in April:

> Major Blake and Lt Moody had an exciting patrol of the Anzio beachhead [on 10 April]. After a long chase, they destroyed one

Heinkel 177 near Cape Linaro, north of Anzio, then obtained contact with a second He 177 and probably destroyed it, about 80 miles north of Anzio. They then made contact on a third He 177 and pursued it for nearly 100 miles through evasive action. Several bursts were fired at this target before it disappeared. In each combat our Beaufighter experienced heavy return fire and it was later discovered that several shells had hit our aircraft. There is naturally much elation over these victories.

But there was also some less happy news during the month. 'Capt. Brake and F/O Gander had to bail out when their aircraft [Beaufighter ND178] was set afire by an enemy plane. We have few details, but the rescue launch is searching the area near Ponza Island [off the west coast of Italy, mid-way between Rome and Naples].' The bodies of the two crew men were never recovered.

Despite 'thick haze from the deck to 5,000 feet' over base and between San Volturno and Naples, the crew of Beau ND260, comprising 1/Lt W Groom and his RO F/O Roth flew a fruitful mission on 15–16 April. Forty-five minutes after taking off for a patrol at 2215 hrs they were vectored on to a suspected bogey at 9,000ft and flying west. After chasing it out to sea and then back over land for some time they lost sight of what they thought was a Ju 87. Resuming their routine patrol, they were vectored on to another contact shortly after midnight. This one was flying over land at around 8,000ft, and travelling so slowly that Groom had to drop the Beau's wheels to avoid overshooting the target. Closing to 300ft, they identified a Ju 88 'from long, tubular fuselage, bathtub on starboard [side]'. The bomber was flying at 20 degrees above at twelve o'clock, when evidently suspicious of being spotted, it peeled off hard to starboard. Racking the Beau round to stay with it, Groom fired a brief burst of cannon. This made strikes on the starboard engine, whereupon the German burst into flames and went straight down into the sea. There was no return fire and no one was seen to bail out. Scratch one Ju 88, 30 miles north-west of Anzio.

Operations – May 1944

At the end of April, the Mediterranean Allied Air Force issued the air plan for a new offensive, code-named *Diadem*. Drafted by the TAF commander, the USAAF's Maj. Gen. John Cannon, its object was 'to make it impossible for the enemy to maintain his position in the face of a combined Allied offensive'. During the first eleven days of May, attacks on Axis targets consisting of supply dumps, road and rail bridges, motor transport and harbours were intensified. But the Allies were meeting some stiff opposition from Luftwaffe fighters and bombers and, for example, in the early hours of 13 May Ju 88s from bases in northern Italy and southern France carried out a fierce attack on Alesan airfield in Corsica by the light of white flares, and using *Duppel* (the German equivalent of Allied Chaff/Window*)*, practically wiped out the US 340th BG and its B-25 Mitchells.

In the early hours of the following day the 416th scored a hard-earned success against the marauding bombers. At 0355 Capt. Harris Cargill and his RO, F/O Freddie Kight, were scrambled in a Beaufighter in response to enemy aircraft reported in the Naples area. Immediately after take-off the Beau encountered large quantities of Window as it was vectored to a position 10 miles south-east of Castel Volturno (about 22 miles/35km north-west of Naples), at 10,000ft. But no contacts were made. Then, at 0401 hrs, the Beau obtained an AI contact at 3½ miles range and two o'clock high. The contact was identified as hostile as it took violent evasive action and dropped Window, making it difficult for the Beau to close to an effective attacking position.

Doggedly pursuing his quarry for fifteen minutes, Cargill managed to close to a range of 400ft, at which point the bandit was identified as a Ju 88. Reducing the range to 300ft in a steep turn to the south-east, he fired three bursts of four to five seconds each through the line of flight of the '88. Large pieces of the nose section and the canopy were seen to break off and a trail of white smoke appeared from the starboard side of the enemy aircraft. Whether this came from the engine or the wing root was difficult to determine due to the desperate evasive action being taken. Unfortunately contact was then lost when the quarry dived steeply, almost on its back, towards the town of Castel Volturno and was lost in the radar ground returns. No crash flash was observed. In assessing the combat it was found that one cannon had jammed after firing ten rounds. Another cannon had failed after sixty rounds due to faulty feed belt tension. Finally, one machine gun jammed after ten rounds, apparently due to excess rounds in the ammo box.

Operations – June 1944

This was apparently a quiet month for the squadron, with little if any combat recorded and certainly no victories scored. The diary simply states: 'From 14 June to 8 July three aircraft nightly operated from the Anzio beachhead.'

Not yet in service with the 416th NFS, Mosquito NF.XXX is shown here on test and evaluation, alongside a P-61 and a P-38, at Hammer Field, California, on 23 September 1944. (Dana Bell)

NF.XXX, with P-38, P-61 and P-59 pictured at Hammer Field, California, in September 1944. (Dana Bell)

Operations – July 1944

With its main base still at Pomigliano, the squadron was, by July, beginning to fly the occasional detached operation from Tarquinia, some 43 miles/64km north of Rome. On 22 July Col Kratz of the Night Fighter Training Group in California 'met the aircrew and discussed the new aircraft which we may receive'. This is a reference to Mosquitoes. The following day, after landing at Tarquinia, prior to mounting the now routine patrol, Lt Robinson accidentally ran into a culvert, buckling the undercarriage … 'and we have one Beaufighter less. The shortages of planes is now becoming acute.'

By now the 416th was part of the 62nd Fighter Wing, 12th Air Force, and on 24 July the 12th's boss, General Morris, and the 62nd's Col Israel presided over a formal parade and ceremony for the squadron. During this, Maj. Blake and Lt Moody were awarded the Distinguished Flying Cross 'for the extraordinary achievement in probably destroying one He 177, damaging a second He 177 and engaging a third, despite damage to their own aircraft by the enemy'.

The comparatively mild tone of the 416th diary entries at this point perhaps belies the hard slog that the Allied ground and air forces were undergoing in their drive up Italy. In mid-July American medium bombers attacked the important rail bridges at Casalmaggiore and Piacenza and the road bridge at Taglio and damaged several others. At the same time energetic preparations were being made for the invasion of the south of France, which would be named Operation Dragoon, and which would soon involve the 416th. To direct this, Headquarters, Mediterranean Tactical Air Force was transferred from Italy to Corsica, although the 416th, together with other air assets, would continue to be based in Italy until required elsewhere. Accordingly, the squadron diary recorded, on 27 July, that a detachment of four officers and twenty enlisted men would move from Pomigliano to Tarquinia – where they would operate under the 6505th Fighter Control Area (Provisional). Two Beaufighters would be based at Tarquinia and the detachment would, for admin purposes, be attached to the 345th FS, 350th FG. The entry went on: 'We have had a plague of tire trouble and it is becoming increasingly difficult to get replacements. There was one patrol from Tarquinia and one scramble. Lt Bateman and F/O Smith obtained several contacts but were unable to get up enough speed to intercept the bogey.'

THE MOSQUITO IN THE USAAF

Operations – August 1944

The first assault of Operation Dragoon got under way in the early hours of 15 August and four Beaufighters covered the huge convoy that, some days earlier, left Naples for the beaches of southern France. Winston Churchill had arrived in Naples on 11 August to see for himself progress for Dragoon and on the 14th he flew in the Dakota of Gen. Henry Maitland Wilson (Supreme Allied Commander Mediterranean) to Corsica to view events at first hand. Four Beaus escorted the Prime Minister and then landed at Borgo, in Corsica, to form a detachment to cover the landings. Another detachment was mounted at Alghero in Sardinia from where convoy patrols were flown. From Pomigliano a crew was scrambled to intercept a high-flying enemy reconnaissance intruder, but the Beau was unable to gain sufficient altitude. The diary ruefully records that on 24 August Lts Harris and Bateman 'flew to Brindisi (in south-east Italy) to pick up a replacement Beaufighter for the squadron. The aircrews are beginning to hope devoutly that the supply will soon be exhausted, so that we may get Mosquitoes.' A more upbeat entry occurs on the 28th. 'Several P-61s belonging to the 427th Night Fighter Squadron, fresh from the States, have arrived on our dispersal at Pomigliano. They are the cynosure [Dictionary: centre of attention and admiration] of all our air and ground crews.'

Operations – September 1944

In the early hours of 1 September, the squadron broke camp at Pomigliano and began the move to Rosignano, on the north-west coast of Italy. There, eight officers, twenty-four EMs and four Beaus were attached to the 427th NFS to patrol the Naples area until the 427th, with its new Black Widows, became operational and could take over the commitment. The remainder of the 416th's aircraft arrived the following day in formation, led by Col Banks, buzzing the airfield to announce their presence. Lt Johnson ground looped on landing and damaged a wing. The taxi strip and roads on the airfield were muddy and treacherous.

On 7 September Lt Frank Robinson was awarded the Soldier's Medal for heroism. The citation read:

> On 10 July 1944, when engine failure forced Lt Robinson to land his aircraft in the water off the coast of Italy, he made his way to

his dinghy, but his comrade was thrown into the water and was unable to inflate his life preserver. Although nearly exhausted in his efforts to reach the dinghy, Lt Robinson immediately left his place of safety and made his way through the rough sea and returned the stricken comrade safely to the dinghy.

After the ceremony Col Banks and a group of squadron execs drove to Pisa to gauge its suitability for night flying. The plan was to move there permanently once the runway had been repaired.

James Urso's outstanding work earlier in the year was given wide recognition by the Allies when he was awarded a British DFC and received a warm letter of congratulation from Air Vice-Marshal Sir Hugh Lloyd, Air Officer Commanding (AOC) Mediterranean Allied Coastal Air Forces. The AOC praised Lt Urso:

> for consistently good work with the 416th NFS and particularly in respect of your fine performances on the 8th of February when you got an Me 210 and on the 14th of May, when you destroyed a Ju 88. It gives me all the more pleasure that this fine decoration should have again been won by an American pilot in one of our US Beaufighter squadrons, and the award will do much to cement the very strong friendship which exists between yourselves and your British colleagues in the Coastal Air Forces. Our own Beaufighter squadrons have the greatest admiration for your performance and this award is extremely popular.

In making his first flight in a Beaufighter since his return to active duty, Urso gave a dazzling display of airmanship after the award ceremony.

The night of 26–27 September was, according to the war diary, an exciting one:

> The Squadron made its first offensive sweep of the Po Valley. Col Banks came down from Wing to fly the first mission with Lt Wirkus as his navigator. Four other crews all contributed to the excellent results in which six MT vehicles were destroyed and fourteen damaged, a factory and power plant damaged, and seven other targets were attacked. On this mission the 416th was joined by seven Beaus from its sister 414th NFS.

Operations – October 1944

Operations from Rosignano came to an end on the night of 30 September–1 October with a maximum effort in the Po Valley. Eleven Beaufighters were airborne on either night intruder missions or general patrols in the area. Seven MT vehicles were destroyed and eighteen damaged, one electric train was probably destroyed, an iron ore smelter was strafed and set on fire, and four bridges strafed. A 62nd Fighter Wing Operation Order issued on 28 September had already stated 'The 416th NFS will cease operations at Rosignano on 1 October and commence operations at 1201 hours at Pisa Airdrome. The Squadron will remain operational through the move.'

The move to Pisa was accomplished without incident and the operations from the new base got off the ground on the night of 3–4 October with another maximum effort. Four intruders scoured the Po Valley, two patrols got airborne, and five Beaus were scrambled. Although crews were vectored on to six 'bogies', no sightings or contacts were made. On the intruder missions Lts Robinson and Schultz destroyed an MT vehicle and probably destroyed two more. The aircraft was hit by flak, part of the nose was shot off, and the fuselage was holed. Lt Beaudette and F/O Hunter attacked four road vehicles, while the Underwood/Partain crew damaged two. The ubiquitous Urso/Wirkus crew achieved the biggest bag of all, destroying ten vehicles, probably destroying another and damaging yet one more. They also destroyed a locomotive and five railway cars. The night's work prompted a commendatory message from the 62nd FW's Gen. Israel: 'Please extend my heartiest congratulations to your officers and men for the fine work on the night of 3/4 October. Your unit is making a fine contribution to the defeat of the enemy.' One aircraft flew an air-sea rescue mission, though the outcome was not recorded.

Operations – November 1944

Despite the fact that the 416th had now been operating from bases in Italy since September 1943, support was still being provided from locations in North Africa, and on 17 November six men from the Radio Section left for a course of instruction at the Radar Conversion School in Algiers. But this November was important for another reason – Mosquitoes – and as the war diary reports:

On the 19th Lts Bonneau and Skrinar flew several crews to Algiers in the B-25 to pick up our new Mosquito aircraft. On the 29th Capt. Iribe returned from Africa in our first Mosquito and gave the base a display of buzzing which was astonishing for its virtuosity. Headquarters was less impressed! Later in the day three more of our Mosquitoes arrived. Everyone is enthusiastic about our new aircraft.

Several officers from XXII Tactical Air Command (which now controlled the 416th NFS) visited to inspect the squadron and view the Mosquitoes, which were the NF.XXX version, equipped with the new AI Mk X radar, the UK version of the American SCR-720 set.

Beaufighter KV944, flown by 2/Lt Joe Graham with F/O Roop as his RO, was lost on 17–18 while on an intruder mission in the Bergamo-Brascia area. Where they were finally laid to rest did not become clear until after the war.

On the last day of November three crews flew intruder patrols with the 414th NFS from the latter squadron's base at Pontedera. The 416th could look back on its work in November with satisfaction. Its score included 129 MT vehicles destroyed, 177 damaged; three locomotives destroyed and seven damaged; three railway cars destroyed plus seventeen damaged; and finally three miscellaneous targets destroyed together with twenty damaged. In addition, a Mosquito training programme had been set up at Foggia.

Operations – December 1944

With the focus on introducing and training on the Mosquito itself and its Mk X AI equipment, there was a lull in operations during the first half of December. On the 9th, for example: 'A quiet day. The ground crews toil mightily to get our Mosquito aircraft serviceable and in another day or two our pilots should be able to get transition time.'

The following day the air crews attended a lecture by the de Havilland and Rolls-Royce representatives, and several crews got in some transition hours. On the 11th, squadron pilots ferried in six Mosquitoes from Maison Blanche. 'They had been so well briefed that not a pilot buzzed the field!' All crews practised dusk landings in the new fighters and then two practice interceptions and patrols flown on the night of 17–18 December marked the first operational missions flown by Mosquitoes.

Operations – January 1945

Another period of comparative inactivity followed in early January, for the squadron was scheduled to move up into France. Somewhat fragmented in execution, the transfer began with a detachment of thirteen officers and twenty-seven EMs placed on temporary duty with the 425th NFS at Etain in north-eastern France. Equipped with P-61s, the 425th had flown out to France from England in August 1944 and had arrived at Etain the following November. The 416th's move began on 4 January, with Mosquitoes flown by Capt. Iribe, and Lts Coles and Bateman departing at noon, and ground personnel following a little later in four C-47s. At that point no one knew for certain where the squadron as a whole was bound. As a result the C-47s became widely dispersed, with two going to Lyons, one stopping off at Marseilles, and the fourth being grounded at Dijon because of the weather. By the 5th, three C-47s had made it to Etain, where the Luftwaffe had been very active. 'Here we learned the reason for our coming. The 425th needed additional air support and our five Mosquitoes would help relieve the strain on them. Our detachment is part of the XIX Tactical Air Command, 9th AF.' On the 10th the fourth C-47 with its complement of ground personnel stragglers arrived at Etain but three Mosquitoes were weathered in at Paris.

On 13 January the war diary reported:

> Good news today. At 1300 hours the first Mosquito ('764) landed at Etain. Lts Robinson and Schultz flew it from Pisa, with a night stop at Marseilles. There are five Mosquitoes somewhere in France, some in Paris getting their VHF changed to match this field's frequency. At about 1600 hours Lt Englert came in with another Mosquito from Lyons. Lt Johnson remained behind at Lyons, where someone tested the durability of his Mosquito and kicked a hole in his stabilizer.

The Iribe/Simpson crew flew in from Paris on the 14th. 'Rumoured they had a lovely visit.' The first operational mission was scheduled for the night of 14–15 but things didn't go according to plan:

> The patrols were called off because of a lack of oxygen, hydraulic fluid and other spare parts. As yet we haven't received any spares or other necessary equipment to operate. Someone remarked that

160

operating Mosquitoes here is about the same as 'Jerry' trying to operate Ju 88s from England.

Lt C Smith teamed up with Lt Stewart to fly a mission in a P-61 and afterwards reported that the Black Widow 'is a good airplane'. Two Mosquitoes were readied to fly to Brussels with the hope of picking up some sorely needed spares but adverse weather in northern Europe scotched the plan.

The Bateman/Tuck crew finally made it to Etain from Paris on the 16th, leaving behind Lt Coles with a flat tyre. On this date the Iribe/Schultz crew flew the first operational mission from Etain in a Mosquito, a patrol from 2000 to 2400 hrs that proved uneventful. Not so uneventful were activities in the early hours of 27 January. At 0300 hrs, Capt. John Davies and 2/Lt Hubbard Larson took off from Pisa in MT475 for what should have been a three-hour night intruder mission to strafe road vehicles in the Po Valley. After Davies had radioed, at 0415 hrs, that he was returning to base nothing further was heard from the Mosquito. Further attempts to contact the mute fighter proved fruitless. Dawn patrols of Pisa-based P-47s, instructed to look out for the missing machine, similarly drew a blank. A German report stated that a Mosquito had come down in the Lonate-Pozzolo area, and Davies and Hubbard were reluctantly listed as killed in action.

Tragedy struck again, on the 29th, when 1/Lt Frank Janisch and 2/Lt Eugene Franklin went MIA in Mosquito MM761 while on an intruder sweep of the Padova-Ferrara area. The wreckage of the fighter was found near Florence with Franklin dead and Janisch wounded. The latter was picked up by farmers but sadly he died some four hours later.

NF.XXX MM746 of 416th Night Fighter Sqn in Italy in 1945. (Lippincott via Garry Pape)

NF.XXX, MV564 'G' of 416th Night Fighter Sqn in Italy in 1945. (Lippincott via Garry Pape)

Another view of NF.XXX, MV564. (Lippincott via Garry Pape)

162

Operations – February 1945

February saw the squadron's first victory since re-equipping with Mosquitoes. At 2154 hrs on the last day of the month Capt. Lawrence Englert and 2/Lt Earl Dickey in MM746 were scrambled from Pontedera in response to a hostile aircraft that was reported to have dropped flares over Naples. At 8,000ft and 180mph the Mosquito was vectored 090 degrees to Florence by the *Cooler* GCI. Dickey picked out multiple targets on the radar scope but they all faded rapidly and no permanent contacts could be made. The crew was then given a vector of 270 degrees to Montecatini. *Canine* GCI then took over and reported an enemy aircraft 20 miles south-east of Florence at 23,000ft and 260mph. Despite an unserviceable supercharger, Englert climbed to 17,000ft and orbited, awaiting further instructions. A new vector was then given and to gain speed the wing tanks were jettisoned.

At 2247 hrs, 4 miles north-west of Pavullo, Dickey obtained an AI contact, head on, at a range of 7 miles. The Mosquito was now at 22,500ft, the enemy aircraft a thousand feet higher, with contact being maintained in a turn to starboard. Then, when the range had been closed to 5 miles, the starboard Merlin engine cut out. Chase was maintained on one engine. Contact with the GCI controller was lost but Englert continued to stalk the 'bogey', even when it dived to 17,000ft. The range was gradually reduced to 1,500ft at which point a visual identification was obtained. The wide wingspan with pointed tips and square tail fin bore the distinctive features of a Ju 188. Englert closed to 400ft and fired a two-second burst. The tail of the Junkers shook violently as strikes were made and it began a shallow dive towards the ground. After several more bursts it caught fire and after a large explosion started to shed large pieces. The Mosquito flew through the debris and brown smoke, and the enemy bomber spun down and hit the ground. No return fire was noted and no one was seen to bail out.

This was a fine victory but the Mosquito had not come out of it unscathed. Shortly after being vectored for base, the starboard engine caught fire. The fire was extinguished and the engine quickly feathered, but then the starboard wheel came down and could not be raised. At the same time the flight instruments failed. Englert headed doggedly towards base but realised that they were steadily losing altitude and their route took them through an 8,000ft mountain pass. At 2321 hrs the GCI controller picked them up about 40 miles south of Parma and twenty-four minutes later they were overhead their Pontedera base. However, their trials were not over; the control tower advised 9–10/10 cloud between 800 and 1,000ft over the airfield. Englert

NF.XXX MM746 of 416th Night Fighter Sqn in Italy in 1945. (USAAF)

attempted to descend through the cloud but with no instruments and the duff engine windmilling the task was beyond even him. On the way home directional control had only been achieved with radar operator Dickey hauling on the right rudder pedal with his hand. The Mosquito was therefore climbed to 4,000ft and the crew 'shook hands, wished each other luck and hit the silk', both landing near the base and suffering only minor cuts and sprains.

Apart from the destruction of the Ju 188, operational activity in February was minimal, although it did result in a brief but, at first glance, enigmatic entry in the war diary:

On the night of 16/17 February there were three patrols and two scrambles, but no chases resulted. Our crews are beginning to report mysterious orange-red lights in the sky near La Spezia and also inland. These 'foo-fighters' have been pursued, but no one has been able to make contact. GCI [Ground Control Interception] and intelligence profess to be mystified by these ghostly apparitions. The hypothesis that the 'foo-fighters' are a post-cognac manifestation has been disproved. Even the teetotallers have observed the strange and mysterious 'foo-fighters' which have also been observed by night fighters in France and Belgium.

The term 'foo-fighters' originated from the popular comic character of the time, Smokey Stover, a zany firefighter who called fire 'foo' and drove around in his 'foo mobile'. The strange lights and their wacky nickname was developed into a story by war correspondent Robert Wilson for a February edition of *Newsweek*. Wilson had come across the details while sharing a cognac with the crews of the 415th NFS during a brief visit to the squadron at their French base of Ochey, on New Year's Eve. He subsequently wrote:

Lt Donald Meiers of Chicago was flying a Beaufighter on an intruder mission over Germany. He was braced to meet Nazi planes or anti-aircraft [fire]. Suddenly an eerie light split the darkness around his plane. Looking up from his instrument panel, the horrified lieutenant saw two red balls of fire cruising alongside his wing tips. Thinking he had run into a secret anti-aircraft weapon, Meiers tensed and waited for a German on the ground to push a button and blow him up. But the balls merely kept pace with him for a while and then disappeared.

That was more than a month ago, and one of the first times Allied fighters encountered what they now call 'foo-fighters'. In addition to the wing tip balls, pilots have reported two other types. One is a group of three smaller balls which fly in front of their planes, the other a group of about fifteen which appear some distance away and flicker on and off. Apparently controlled by radio, the 'foo-fighters' keep formation with the planes, even when they dive, climb, or take evasive action. 'But they don't explode or attack us', Meiers said last week. 'They just seem to follow us like will-o'-the-wisps.'... Possibly they are the results of a new anti-radar device which the Germans have developed. On the other hand, they may be the exhaust trails of a smaller model of the radio-controlled Messerschmitt 163, a rocket-propelled flying wing.

Day bombers have met the Me 163, which has an explosive charge in the nose and is apparently designed to crash into Allied planes. When one pilot closely inspected the 'foo-fighters' tagging him, however, he detected nothing but the spheres.

With dramatic media headlines on the progress of the war appearing daily, the story was soon forgotten.

Operations – March 1945

The bad weather that had stymied Mosquito '746's safe return to terra firma continued on into March, somewhat hampering operations. Ground fog resulted in at least one aborted patrol. On the 2nd of the month a dance was held at the officers' villa 'for those fortunate individuals who were off 'ops' for the night. 'In view of the way the signorinas eat, we sometimes wonder if we "liberators" are the main attraction on these occasions' – was the rueful assessment of the event!

The celebrated Capt. Englert was now awaiting orders to return home but on 3rd of the month it was reported that 'he generously gave some of his valuable time to check Lt Boatman out in the notorious Mosquito'. Boatman had joined the 416th two months previously and would go on to fly the P-61. Many years later, in 1977, he recalled his experiences as a pilot on the squadron and the comparative merits of the British and American night fighters.

> I did not fly the Beaufighter and am not qualified to compare it with the Mosquito and P-61, which I did fly. These two aircraft were quite dissimilar – not only in physical appearance but in flying characteristics as well. Most notably, the Mosquito was superior in speed and fuel time, while the P-61 was superior in stability and crew comfort. It was the consensus of Mosquito pilots that one could never cease for an instant giving full attention to flying the airplane, and particular concentration was required during take-off and landing. The pre-flight cockpit check normally had to be performed prior to starting the engines unless one was assured of immediate clearance for take-off after taxiing out to take-off position; otherwise any delay might result in having to abort the flight due to rising oil and/or coolant temperatures. (Rolls-Royce Merlin engines heated up exceedingly fast during ground running.) Representations in the Pilots' Notes notwithstanding, the Mosquito did not perform well on one engine and, depending on the particular aircraft, it could prove difficult to hold an altitude, let alone climb on single engine operation.

166

The P-61, on the other hand, made far fewer demands on the pilot's proficiency and concentration due to its incredible stability, superb flying characteristics, and well-appointed and comfortable cockpit. Few, if any, aircraft could match the P-61 in single-engine performance. To lose one engine during operation of a P-61 would hardly constitute an emergency. If the foregoing comments appear to favour the P-61, I believe most pilots who have flown both aircraft would much prefer the Mosquito in combat primarily due to its superior speed and liberal fuel time. To fly a P-61 was safe and easy while to fly a Mosquito was to court danger and experience a severe test of one's flying capabilities. Mosquito pilots felt enormous respect for the aircraft.

Seven patrols of the front line were launched on the night of 4 March. Unfortunately, the crew consisting of F/O Quenton Bruton and his RO, F/O Boone, in NT247 crashed on take-off after they ground looped and their landing gear collapsed. Neither was injured but 'the Mosquito is a sad sight lying on its belly at the end of the runway'. The following night four patrols took to the skies, these proving uneventful apart from one chase. Lt Beaudette got a contact on an unidentified aircraft, but lost it when it dived into the radar ground scatter up near the Brenner Pass. There was another reminder of the Mosquito's reputation for requiring care on take-off when Lt Herbert King and F/O Prince also crashed at the end of the runway on take-off. Although their Mosquito, NT244, burned very quickly, they got out with only burns to their face and hands. They were taken to the in-theatre 105th Station Hospital for treatment.

A rapid ceremony took place in the Mosquito dispersal area on 6 March when Gen. Israel from HQ 62nd FW presented DFCs to Capts Englert and Urso, and to Lt Simpson. The ceremony was rapid because 'Brazilian fighters were taking to the air for their numerous day missions.' This is an interesting reference to the rarely mentioned presence of the Brazilian Air Force's First Fighter Group that, with its P-47 Thunderbolts, had arrived in Italy in October 1944 and had been attached to the US 350th FG, itself part of the 62nd FW.

'A rather dull night for operations – only three uneventful patrols' is recorded for 7 March, but this was spiced up by events on the social front:

Last night in a farewell spree for Lt Busic before he left for home, he and Capt. Englert accidentally fell into the moat at the base of the Leaning Tower of Pisa. So he took off with muddy shoes and a high water mark on his pink trousers. Lts King and Boatman made the liquor run to Naples to purchase some of that fine Neopolitan 'bath-tub' gin for the bar.

Pisa airfield was apparently plagued at this time by regular visits from enemy reconnaissance aircraft, as testified by events for the 8 March. '*Recce Joe #2* appeared last night, and Lts Kangas and Herron gave him a hot chase southward, getting very close at times, but he was thoroughly aware they were after him and took violent evasive action. Lt Robinson and F/O Boublik chased him when he came back north, following him to a point north of the Po River. There was much Window, and he again took evasive action, at which contact was lost. There were two other patrols during the night.' Towards the end of March the squadron moved to nearby Pontedera, itself in the province of Pisa.

Operations from the new base got off to an unfortunate start with the loss of Mosquito NT249 on the 29th. Pilot Lt Eldon Blake and navigator 2/Lt Max Galowich were killed in an incident in which the aircraft was written off, although the exact circumstances are not recorded.

The location is probably Pontedera, Italy, where the 416th Night Fighter Sqn's NF.XXX MT482 is parked amid the debris of war. (Author's collection)

Operations – April 1945

Intruder missions to enemy airfields, front-line and bridgehead patrols, and armed reconnaissance now formed the squadron's main roles. On the night of 21–22, four MT vehicles were destroyed with one damaged in the Po Valley. During a daylight armed recce on the 22nd two Mosquitoes destroyed one locomotive and three freight cars, one steam crane, five road vehicles, plus one ferry. One locomotive, thirteen freight cars and one MT vehicle were also claimed as damaged. Later that night, a singleton Mosquito notched up four MT vehicles destroyed and one damaged in the Po Valley.

Thus far the 416th had got off comparatively lightly in terms of losses, but the squadron now began to experience these from enemy anti-aircraft fire. On 22 April, 2/Lt Wesley Kangas, pilot and his RO, 2/Lt Jack Herron took off from Pontedera in MT482 at 1100 hrs for an armed reconnaissance of the Po Valley covering the Parma, Piacenza and Mantua area. They were due to land back at base at around 1300 hrs. When they failed to return, HQ 62nd FW was informed. The sector controllers tried in vain to contact the overdue Mosquito and the crew were posted as missing. On the same day Maj. James Urso led a hazardous daytime attack on a Po River crossing in support of the 5th Army. During a strafing run his Mosquito was hit by intense and accurate AA fire, which knocked out an engine. Urso ordered his RO, 1/Lt Talmidge Simpson, to bail out. Blinded and burned by flames and hampered by his harness, Simpson was experiencing great difficulty in exiting the crippled fighter and so, with complete disregard for his own safety, Urso stayed to help force his crewman out of the escape hatch. The Mosquito was now too low for Urso to bail out himself so he crash-landed the burning aircraft, sustaining life-changing injuries to his left foot. On the ground at San Benedetto he was treated by a German doctor, but then abandoned by the Germans in the course of their hasty retreat. Simpson, on the other hand, made a safe parachute descent and was also picked up by the Germans.

Operations – May 1945

After the welcome information that Lt Simpson was safe and well in Florence after his bail out, the man himself appeared back on the squadron on 7th having been a PoW for a short time. Somewhat conflicting information about impending re-equipment with the P-61 now crops up in the war diary. On the morning of the 7th, Lts Ellis and King set off for Naples to pick up two of the new fighters, but apparently returned empty handed. The diary remarks, rightly or wrongly: 'It seems all new Black Widows will be sent elsewhere now, none used for training purposes in this theater.' Perhaps this is explained by the momentous news received that afternoon that the war in Europe was over. Would the P-61s be needed after all? The following day, the 8th, was 'VE Day and Hangover Day. A holiday, but very quiet.'

Although there was victory in the West, the war in the Pacific still raged and on 9 April a movie at the officers' villa was 'preceded by our first Recognition Film of Japanese aircraft – boos and hisses!' Activities reported that day include: 'An afternoon training flight on P-61s.' That the 416th now actually had some of the Northrop fighters on charge seems to be confirmed by the diary entry for 16 May: 'We have only four P-61s now, all orders for new ones having been cancelled. Lt Ellis had a single [flight] in a P-61, made a good landing. Not as interesting as a single engine in a Mosquito.' The Black Widow seems to have edged quietly into service with the squadron without fanfare or fuss.

Operations – June 1945

'The Mosquitoes will be taken away and replaced by P-61s. We will fly no more Mosquitoes for training purposes,' announces the diary report for 1 June; it seems that the 416th's brief time with the Mosquito was over. The British night fighters would soon be ferried away for return to the RAF. The exemplary work of Maj. Carl Morrison, who had taken over as CO of the squadron in September 1944, was recognised on 4 June by the award of a well-deserved DFC. The citation read:

> On 22 April 1945, Maj. Morrison led his squadron in its first daylight low-level strafing mission in the Po Valley, Italy. Skilfully manoeuvring through intense and accurate anti-aircraft fire which destroyed three aircraft, he caused the dispersal of several convoys, and the destruction of a great number of motor transports, trains and ferries. On more than 60 combat missions his outstanding proficiency and steadfast devotion to duty have reflected great credit upon himself and the Armed Forces of the United States.

With the war now over, the accent for the time being was on relaxing socially and on taking stock of what had been achieved. As far as the future was concerned, the war diary speculated, on 12 June: 'We have suspected for some time that we'd be in the Army of Occupation. It now seems that we'll be on our way to either South Germany or Austria before the end of July.' It would be a little longer than that. In the meantime there was still the occasional Mosquito echo, and on the 15th: 'Three British officers [were] here investigating the loss of Mosquito and ferry pilot. It seems the Mosquito landed in Southern France, took off again and crashed soon afterwards. We know this story all too well. The Mosquito may have everything else – but could hardly be called a safe airplane.' The Mosquito in question was MT479, which, while being ferried back to RAF charge on 7 June by Fg Off Brian Armitage and Sgt Sidney Baker, crash-landed in Italy, killing the pilot and injuring the navigator.

News was received from HQ 12th AF that Lt Joe Graham and his RO, F/O Richard Roop, missing from a night intruder sweep in their Beaufighter on 17–18 November 1944, were buried in a cemetery at Mirandola, in north central Italy.

Of the 416th's Pontedera base, the war diary reports, 'The area is rapidly becoming a shambles, with tents being torn down, and much packing and carpenter work in evidence.' Many new faces were appearing on the squadron to replace those long-serving members either being redeployed or sent home. 'If this keeps on, we will have an entirely new squadron with possibly no one left of the old regulars but the CO,' opined the war diary.

With the Second World War at an end, the squadron became part of the US army of occupation, moving to Horsching, Austria, in August 1945. A year later there was a final move to Schweinfurt, Germany, where it inactivated on 9 November 1946.

Oral Interview with Talmidge Simpson

In January 2008 historian Norman Malayney interviewed Talmidge Simpson, a navigator with the 416th NFS, then frail and in his mid-80s. The following is a transcript of their conversation.

Norman Malayney (NM): When did you join the 416th?

Talmidge Simpson (TS): On 11 April 1943, a couple of months after it was formed in Florida.

NM: Do you know why they formed the 416th?

TS: I think they already knew the commitment, or requirement, for combat aircraft in the Mediterranean, so they decided to form another squadron.

NM: What type of aircraft did you train on initially?

TS: That was the Douglas A-20/P-70 in Florida.

NM: Why do you think the USAAF was supplied with British Beaufighters?

NM: Well, the Beaufighter seemed to be a ready-made night fighter. But the main reason was that the ole Beaufighter had four 20mm cannon, whereas the P-70 was poorly armed. And one of those limeys across there had cranked that thing up to fire 720 rounds a minute.

NM: So you preferred the Beaufighter to the P-70?

TS: The Beaufighter had a top speed of around 330mph and was a lot tougher plane than the P-70 too. It could tear down more trees than a caterpillar tractor if it crash-landed in a forest. And, of course, the Mosquito, compared with what we were trying to come up with, we didn't have anything comparable.

NM: So, in the Beaufighter, the radar operator sat in the back and gave the pilot directions on to the target, right or left?

TS: No, no – it was port or starboard. If you said right or left to them limeys they'd cut yer up real quick!

NM: How many missions did you fly?

TS: Every time you came back from a mission you recorded it. But I caught my pilot not writing them down. I said: 'What are you doing?' He said: 'Simpson, the minute you and I get forty missions they gonna send us back to the States. Then we'll head right for the Pacific – and we don't wanna go there.'

NM: When you got to England, I believe you went to a British base?

TS: Yes, the pilots went to Cranbrook [Cranfield] I think. And we [radar operators] went to Acklington, north of Newcastle, where we trained in aircraft flown by RAF pilots.

172

NM: So the RAF trained you on the equipment and you linked up with the pilots later on to form crews?

TS: Yes, the pilots tended to pick radar operators who they knew performed well. And I should mention that in the radar operator's position we had a fixed Thompson sub machine gun. Someone asked what this for and was told that if your pilot loses his way you shoot him with it! [The weapon was a 0.303 machine gun]. During our training in England we flew with a lot of Canadians, Australians and New Zealanders.

NM: How did you get to North Africa?

TS: Another radar operator temporarily took my place alongside my pilot and I went by sea to North Africa [in August 1943]. We all congregated in Cairo and then they put us on a little ole narrow-gauge railway and sent us to Algiers to fly front-line support. The place was a heckuva mess but the British took good care of us.

NM: When did you move up to Italy?

TS: After operating from Bone in Algeria and Bizerte, Tunisia, we started flying from Lecce, Italy, in September, and then moved to Grottaglie.

NM: Early air operations over Italy presented quite a confused picture, with Allied and German aircraft mixed up and the added hazard of anti-aircraft fire. What were your impressions?

TS: Yes, for example it was difficult to tell a Mosquito from a Ju 88. And it was difficult to catch a Ju 88 in a Beaufighter.

NM: How were you directed to your targets?

TS: We were vectored on to an area where there had been air activity by a GCI controller. Then the radar operator might pick up a target on his screen, direct the pilot to a contact enabling him to obtain a 'visual'.

NM: The records suggest you were attacked by friendly P-39s [Airacobras].

TS: I didn't experience that personally, but I believe it did happen. The trouble was [friendly] pilots didn't switch on their IFF. One time we were vectored on to a contact which was rated as hostile. It didn't have its IFF on but I said it looked like an A-20. Then it flipped up, switched its landing lights on and we saw it was friendly.

NM: Your missions were flown over both land and sea. Did you attack anything on the ground?

TS: I remember one time we came across a convoy of nineteen enemy road vehicles. We shot them up but didn't have enough ammunition to get 'em all.

NM: When you converted from Beaufighters to Mosquitoes did you receive any training on the Mk X AI radar?

TS: Yes, if I remember we sent teams of instructors to, I think, Naples for courses who then came back and passed on the training. We also gained fresh operators who were familiar with the equipment.

NM: Did you find it better to fly in the Mosquito than the Beaufighter in that you sat alongside the pilot?

TS: Yeah, but there wasn't a helluva lot more that you could do. I felt better – a bit like sitting next to someone in an automobile. Oh, I should mention that one of our pilots was Maj. Davies who had a fine reputation, and was involved in training the Doolittle raid aircrew.

NM: Who was 'Recce Joe'?

TS: That was a [German] reconnaissance type plane – a Ju 88 that came over and photographed things like the Bay of Naples. Sometimes at night using flash photography.

NM: You were flying with Maj. James Urso when you were shot down on 22 April 1945. Can you describe what happened.

TS: We were hit by ground fire over a place called San Benedetto, near Bologna. I jumped out of the Mosquito when we were on the north side of the [river] Po, but when I hit the ground I was on the south side. Urso didn't have time to bail out and crash-landed the Mosquito, which blew his left leg off. He survived the war and became a Denver County Court judge for thirty years. He was a good pilot. One night I happened to fly with our squadron CO, Col Banks, and he got talking about pilots. I said, Colonel, I fly with the best pilot in the 416th and the Colonel said: 'That's right, you mean me?' And I said: 'No, I mean my regular pilot, Paul Rives!'

Known 416th NFS Beaufighters

V8678
V8693
V8746
V8769 – Crashed UK 21.6.43
V8809
V8816 – Crashed 1.8.43
V8828
KV903
KV904 – Crashed UK 4.8.43
KV905 – Crash-landed UK 15.7.43
KV909
KV912
KV914
ND260 *(Ref: Combat Report)*
ND274 *(Ref: Combat Report)*

Chapter 4

492nd Bombardment Group

Special Duties Operations Take Off

USAAF Special Duties operations from the UK, or Carpetbagger missions as they came to be known, have their genesis in a letter from the HQ Detachment, Office of Strategic Services, European Theatre of Operations US Army (ETOUSA) to the Commanding General, ETOUSA, dated 12 October 1943, and titled 'Supply of Resistance Groups'. It set out in clear terms what was to be achieved:

OBJECT

1. To deliver supplies to Resistance Groups, prior to the initiation of military operations on the Continent for the purpose of building up stocks of equipment necessary for organised resistance in guerrilla warfare.
2. To transport the personnel of *Jedburgh* teams and deliver supplies to Resistance Groups in conjunction with military operations on the Continent.

The letter goes on to cover several other major headings of the coming operations such as 'Authority' (the chain of command for tasking), 'Potentialities of Resistance Groups' (strength, organisation and activities), and 'Equipment and Supplies Required'. Under the heading 'Proposals' the Special Operations (SO) Branch of OSS is tasked with undertaking the delivery of supplies to supplies to resistance groups in a plan co-ordinated with the UK's SOE. The need for a storage, packing and departure centre is discussed along with the operation of suitable aircraft, the number of squadrons likely to be needed (three), and the requirement for reception parties. Finally, the letter stresses: 'An early decision on the advisability of initiating such a program is essential if even a limited number of operations are to be undertaken before the first of the year as past experience has shown that considerable time is consumed in training crews for the type of operations contemplated.'

Spurred on by the letter, events moved quickly; experienced crews from the 4th and 22nd Anti-Submarine (AS) Sqns of the USAAF's short-lived and soon to be disbanded 479th AS Gp were earmarked to form the nucleus of the US Special Duties force. The crews were briefed on their forthcoming duties at a meeting held on 24 October at Bovingdon, a USAAF base home to several miscellaneous units and conveniently close to 8th AF HQ at nearby Bushey Heath. The meeting included representatives from the 22nd AS Sqn – Lt Col Clifford Heflin (who would command the nascent Special Duties group), Maj. Robert Fish (who would take over from him as Group CO), Capt. Oliver Akers and Lt Robert Sullivan; Cols Kirk and Williamson from Eighth Bomber Command; Col Oliver from HQ 8th AF; Col Haskell and Maj. Brooks from OSS; and Gp Capt. Edward Fielden, the current Station Commander of RAF Tempsford, home to the RAF's two SD squadrons, Nos 138 and 161. Fielden had previously been the first commander of 161 Sqn, from February to October 1942.

RAF SD operations, begun as far back as August 1940, were now in full swing. The US crews were therefore detached to Tempsford to gain experience with their RAF counterparts. The night-time sorties from the Bedfordshire base soon began to take their toll. On 3 November Capt. James Estes climbed aboard Halifax DT726 to act as co-pilot to Plt Off Henry Hodges and his 138 Sqn crew. They took off at 1920 hrs and headed for a drop zone at Livron-sur-Drôme in south-eastern France. But just before midnight the aircraft crashed into high ground in the Central Massiff, killing everyone on board. 1/Lt Burton Gross was lost in another Halifax, EB129 of 161 Sqn, which, with Australian Plt Off Murray Line at the controls, took off at 1950 hrs on an OSS mission to France. Lines apparently lost control of the bomber in cloud at 3,000ft after engine failure and crashed at around 0200 hrs, 45km west of Chartres.

The detachment was planned to last until the end of the year and while this was going on the first two USAAF squadrons tagged for the SD role were formed at Alconbury in November with B-24D Liberators, the 36th BS on the 6th and the 406th BS on the 11th. (The addition of Mosquitoes to the Special Operations fleet would follow on later in the war.) Initially administrative support was provided by the resident 482nd BG, a specialist radar-equipped pathfinder outfit flying both B-17s and B-24s. For this reason, the first loss of a 36th BS Carpetbagger B-24, 42-40474 on 27 December while on a navigation training mission, is recorded as a 482nd aircraft. The Lib, flown by Capt. Robert Williams, crashed near Moretonhampstead, Devonshire, killing all eight crew.

In early January 1944 Col Heflin received orders to assemble a detachment of personnel for approximately thirty days of detached duty at Tempsford. This was to consist of nineteen officers and thirty-four EMs from the 406th BS, plus eight officers and nineteen EMs from the 36th BS. The first operational SD missions were to be flown from the RAF base, where, in the short term, more comprehensive support was available. These duly took place, the 36th BS flying six missions, and the 406th nine.

Then, in mid-February, the two SD squadrons took their leave of the 482nd BG, were reassigned to 8th AF Composite Command, and moved to Watton in Norfolk, then home to a so-called 'Provisional' group, the 802nd Reconnaissance Group (which in August 1944 would be activated as the 25th Bomb Gp, another USAAF Mosquito unit.) For political and operational reasons Watton was not found ideal. The airfield was, by this time, very busy with the work of the USAAF's 3rd Strategic Air Depot, which had been constructed on the south side of the base to repair combat damaged B-24s of the 2nd Air Divn. The two squadrons were therefore shunted off to Harrington, Northamptonshire, at the back end of March.

At the same time as this station move, the 36th and 406th Squadrons were used to form the 801st BG (Provisional), the first SD group. Shortly afterwards, on 11 May, the 788th and 850th Bomb Sqns were added to complete the 801st's establishment. Then, in another administrative twist, the four squadrons were redesignated the 856th, 858th, 859th and 857th Bomb Sqns respectively on 13 August. The designation '801st BG (P)' was merely an interim one as the 'Provisional' qualification suggested and on 5 August the 801st was finally allotted number plate of the 492nd BG, a short-lived conventional bombardment group that had flown its first mission on 11 May 1943 from North Pickenham as part of the 2nd AD and then ceased operations in August that year.

A contemporary document for general consumption entitled *Characteristics of Carpetbagger Flying* describes the modus operandi of the work:

The purpose of the Carpetbagger Project is to fly 'Special Operations' to deliver supplies to resistance groups in enemy-occupied countries; to deliver personnel to the field and occasionally to bring personnel back from the field. Combat with the enemy is avoided as it only endangers the success of the

B-24 *Beverly Joy* of 801st Bomb Gp at Harrington. (Eberly Family Special Collections, Penn State University Libraries)

mission. Enemy anti-aircraft installations and detector posts are skirted as widely as possible in order not to reveal the presence or destination of the Carpetbagger aircraft.

To avoid action with the enemy, flights are ordinarily made at night and at low-level. When it is necessary for an aircraft to cross enemy-held areas equipped with anti-aircraft defences, a route is chosen which will expose the aircraft to the fire of light guns only. Thus, the altitude attained seldom exceeds 7,000 feet. As soon as a dangerous area is passed, the airplane drops down to 2,000 feet or lower.

The majority of Carpetbagger flights are made during the moon period, or those nights when the moon is out, making the ground visible to the navigator and bombardier. In order that accurate drops may be made, pilots endeavour to get down to within four hundred to six hundred feet of the ground, and to reduce their flying speed to 130 miles per hour or less. The low speed reduces the chances of damage to the parachutes when they open.

Non-moon period flights at night are made with the use of special navigation equipment – *Rebecca*, S-phone and radio altimeter.

179

B-24D of 858th Bomb Sqn with Rebecca radar at Harrington. (Author's collection)

By means of this equipment the percentage of accuracy can be even greater than with ordinary visual pilotage. But reception parties must have the ground counterparts of S-phone and *Rebecca* equipment, and be able to use them expertly – something which is very difficult in territory occupied by the enemy. Thus, even in dark periods, aircraft can fly low altitudes with only slight increase in risk. However, dark period operations are possible without S-phone or *Rebecca* provided the reception signals consist of bonfires and provided there can be reference to prominent landmarks which can be distinguished in the dark, such as rivers and lakes.

The Operational Cycle

Another contemporary document entitled *The Operational Cycle* gives a vivid description of the *Carpetbagger* process over a thirty-six hour period, and includes individual personnel involved at the time. The following is an edited version.

Targets Received and Plotted
This process begins at 1700 hours, at which time the Conference Room at Air Operations Headquarters, OSS in London gives S-2 [Intelligence], Captain Sullivan at Harrington, the list of approved targets for the following night, over the scrambler telephone. The targets are designated by names and numbers (e.g., 'Wheelwright 11', 'Mixer 7'), which refer to targets kept on file and described in detail on Air Transport Forms #6. During the evening, S-2 plots those targets on a large operational map covering a wall of the Deputy Group Commander, Lieutenant Colonel Fish. The map is on a scale of 1 to 500,000, or about ten miles to the inch. It shows topographical features, such as elevations, rivers and forests. Any areas where 'Special Operations' flights are prohibited are clearly indicated on the map.

When a target is plotted, it is indicated by a tab pinned to the map. The comparative priorities of the missions is shown by pieces of colored paper attached to the pins. British, or 'Special Operations Executive', targets proposed for the same night are also plotted with distinctive tabs.

Night's Targets Laid On
At about 0900 hours the following morning, the Station Weather Officer advises Colonel Heflin, or his Deputy, of weather conditions anticipated in the target areas, and at that time it is decided where it will be practicable to send *Carpetbagger* aircraft. Then the Commanding Officer, or his Deputy, select the list of targets for the night, considering the priority of requests for material in the field, the reception record of the particular location, the possibilities of enemy opposition, the distribution of desired missions and the availability of aircraft and crews. The list of selected missions is then telephoned to the London Conference Room by Captain Sullivan and if London has no practical changes to suggest, the list is confirmed for that night's operations.

Targets Assigned to Squadrons
At about 1100 hours, the Squadron Commanders, Majors St Clair, Boone, McManus and Dickerson, are called in and meet in front of the map with the tabs pinpointing the targets for the night. Together, the squadron leaders select targets for their crews, balancing the difficult with the comparatively easy, the distant with the near, so that each squadron will have about the same workload. Any disagreement arising is decided by the toss of a coin; or, Colonel Heflin may be called upon to make the decision.

Navigators Receive Targets

At around 1200 hours, the navigators of the crews receive their targets from the Squadron Navigator, who has received his list from Maj. Tresemer, Group Navigator, who has been advised of the targets by S-2.

In the meantime, S-2 officers have been gathering briefing data, and preparing maps and special instructions. At about 1500 hours, each crew navigator submits a flight plan to his Squadron Navigator, who brings all his squadron flight plans to the Group Navigator. The flight plans and courses are checked by the Group and Squadron Navigators, who make any necessary changes. A take-off time schedule is made up by the Group Navigator, who is an assistant S-3 [Operational Planning]. The take-off time schedule is posted and distributed to Squadron S-3s.

S-2 Briefs Crews

Also at about 1500 hours S-2 officers begin meeting with officer members of each crew. Maps are checked for location of the target (latitude, longitude and terrain features). The S-2 officers use large-scale maps to ensure accuracy. Each crew is briefed separately by an S-2 officer and has the opportunity to study the S-2 map and compare it to their own. Their maps are called 'target maps' and are on a scale of 1 to 250,000, or about five miles to the inch.

Final Briefing

At 1630 hours, a final briefing session is held for all crew members. A weather officer displays the weather map and gives a detailed description of conditions for each target area, stressing expectations en route and at home base for the return flight. Weather predictions cover direction and wind speeds, cloud and icing conditions, the likelihood of rain, sleet or snow. Then, Capt. Sullivan gives any special information which may affect the crew. Next, Lt Col Fish gives general flying and dropping instructions, and finally Maj. Tresemer gives instructions on the route to be followed while over England, and the point and altitude for crossing the English coast. He ends by giving a time check on which all crew watches are synchronised.

During the afternoon, enlisted crew members are briefed as necessary. The crew navigator briefs them on the course, the type of reception signal, the code recognition letters for the target, and terrain features approaching and around the target. The radio operators are handed a 'flimsy' just before take-off. This details all signal information including the code letters, the ground challenge and reply letter, and the colors of the day for flare signals over England, the navigational radio beacons, direction-finder stations in England, and other navigational information including the night's bomber code used in communication between bombers and home stations. If necessary, the Group Communications Officer, Capt. Silkenbaken, briefs radio operators on special information.

Crew navigators plot their targets on their mission maps, checking for flak concentrations, and select check points on the route. When the aircraft carries special packages or personnel to be dropped, Dispatchers are briefed by the Group Armament Officer, Capt. Cunningham, who is the Chief Dispatcher for the Group.

Preparation for Take-Off
During the day, aircraft scheduled for operations are given a half-hour test flight. Crews report to their squadron operations about two hours before take-off and are issued with emergency kit and survival rations. Up-to-date weather reports are received and any necessary adjustments made to the flight plan. About three hours before the first scheduled take-off all flight plans are notified to [the UK's] Air Defence of Great Britain [ADGB – and interim title for RAF Fighter Command] at Stanmore. The information passed includes the squadron and individual aircraft identification letters, times of crossing the English and enemy coasts, and planned landing times.

Loading of Aircraft
As soon as it is ready, the target list goes to the OSS Liaison Officer at Harrington, Capt. Vaughn, so that he can draw up a list of required containers and packages for which he arranges delivery to the airdrome. The containers are consigned to the Group Ordnance Officer, Lt Watkins, whose men deliver the containers, first attaching the parachutes, to the aircraft where Armament Section men are on hand to load the containers into the aircraft. Packages are similarly delivered to the Group Armament Officer for loading onto the aircraft. Finally, the OSS Liaison Officer and his staff check each aircraft for its correct load.

Leaflets, or *Nickles*, received from a warehouse at Cheddington, are delivered to despatching aircraft in bundles of 4,000 by the Armament Section. For security reasons, no leaflets are dropped near *Carpetbagger* targets. Personnel to be dropped are received at Harrington by the Armament Officer. They are then escorted, dressed and briefed by a representative from Special Operations, London, before being loaded onto aircraft.

Take-Off

After take-off aircraft make their way individually to their selected targets. Departures are notified to ADGB (Air Defence of Great Britain).

Interrogation of Crews

On return from missions, crews are debriefed by S-2 officers in the Intelligence Library. Free and frank exchange of information is encouraged. Crews, often jaded after difficult and hazardous missions, are handled with tact and flexibility. Sometimes there is comic relief. On return from one particular mission, Lt Merrill's 36th BS crew described how a French girl-agent they were due to drop over the Continent was so slow in getting into the heavy gear she was supposed to wear that she was not allowed to exit as the reception lights went out before she was ready. She sulked on the way home until nature put her under pressure. She was directed to the 'relief' tube in the rear of the aircraft. The despatcher gallantly turned his back on her while the girl struggled with her men's zipped-up flying suit in an effort to use the tube which, of course, had been designed for the male anatomy. Finally, the girl burst into laughter and when the despatcher turned round, demonstrated in quick-fire French and with appropriate gestures that her personal 'operation' had not been entirely successful and that she was considerably dampened below the waist – but not in spirit. On another occasion, Lt Rabbitt's radio operator (406th BS) swore blind that as the aircraft crossed over a target he heard a woman on the ground S-phone yelling in a cockney accent 'For Christ's sake, come back 'ere! Turn round and come back!'

End of the Mission

After debriefing, crews are given a two-ounce tot of whisky – a medicinal ration designed to soothe frazzled nerves. This is followed by a good breakfast which includes fresh eggs, and then bed. Anyone finding difficulty in getting to sleep is invited to ask the Medical Officer for a sedative. The operational cycle is over – until the next mission.

This became the pattern of the 492nd's Carpetbagger operations throughout 1944 using the B-24. But in November of that year a new thread of secret agent air operations by the OSS/USAAF partnership was begun in great secrecy – the so-called Joan Eleanor (JE) missions. These involved an aircraft flying over the Continent to make contact with Allied agents on the ground. The aircraft the USAAF used for these missions was the Mosquito, selected for its outstanding performance. To the normal crew of pilot and navigator was added a third member, a radio operator, located in the belly of the aircraft, whose task was to make contact with the ground-based agent and record intelligence information on specially installed radio transmitter/receiver equipment. Because the Mosquito was the aircraft of choice for the role, initial operations were mounted by the USAAF's only Mosquito unit at the time, the 25th BG at Watton. However, this had the effect of dividing OSS-driven air operations between Harrington and Watton. The work is first mentioned in intriguingly hushed tones in the records for November 1944 of the 25th BG, whose 654th BG Mosquitoes flew the first missions. The lack of detail is understandable given the classified nature of the project. It is not surprising that the OSS would wish to centralise its air effort on one base and responsibility for the missions would soon pass to the 492nd BG and its 856th BS at Harrington. This, paradoxically, would split the USAAF's Mosquito operations and support between Harrington and Watton – which would go on to cause difficulties, as we shall see.

The shift of responsibility for this particular aspect of Carpetbagger work and how it was to be managed was agreed at a conference held at 8th Air Force HQ on 10 October 1944. This was attended by representatives from the 25th BG, the 492nd BG and OSS, and the principal points agreed were as follows:

1. The Mosquito project would be known by the code word of Joan.
2. Although OSS could submit tasks directly on either the 25th or the 492nd Bomb Groups, 8th AF HQ would be the final approving authority for any mission. This would eliminate the necessity for submitting pinpoint requests to the UK Air Ministry, and would mean that all operations would be approved and executed within the sphere of the 8th Air Force.
3. All matters concerning modifications to the Mosquitoes would be handled directly between OSS and Col Leon Gray, CO of the 25th Bomb Group.
4. The operating areas for Joan Mosquitoes attempting to contact agents on the ground must be free from flak to enable the aircraft to orbit without the need to take evasive action. However, approach routes could be over flak areas provided these were not too concentrated.
5. Frequency of visits to the same 'target' area was not crucial provided the diameter of the operating area remained at between 60 and 100 miles. On the other hand, missions to the same spot should be spaced out as far as possible. While night Joan missions were the

norm, escorted daylight Mosquito missions could be considered, but only in emergency situations.

6. Finally, a review of the 'flak situation' map revealed an extremely limited number of approach routes to operating areas.

For the sake of continuity, and because the 25th BG's records contain virtually nothing about even the initial JE Mosquito missions, the work is described in its entirety here under the heading of the 492nd BG for the sake of continuity. Luckily, the fortunes of the Joan Eleanor project were recorded in a contemporary document called *The Joan Eleanor Log*, which, in the form of a diary, trace in reasonable detail, what went on.

Before looking at the actual missions it is useful gain an overall impression of the JE operations. Lt Marvin Edwards was a Mosquito navigator with the 856th BS and in 2006 he recalled his missions for the benefit of the OSS Society.

a. An exception [to the 8th AF daylight bombing campaign] was the operation carried out by the 492nd Bombardment Group. The 492nd was the air arm of the Office of Strategic Services (OSS). That was the unit I was assigned to as a navigator in Harrington, Northamptonshire in 1944. The activities at Harrington were classified 'Top Secret'. All aircraft were painted black, and all flights over Europe took place at night.

b. Most of the planes at Harrington were B-24 Liberators. Other aircraft were the Douglas A-26, the C-47 and the Mosquito. The B-24 was used for bombing raids and to drop supplies as well as agents to aid the Resistance. The clandestine missions to occupied Europe were all carried out under the name 'Carpetbagger'.

c. Allied agents in Germany were contacted from flying [airborne] Mosquitoes through a newly developed undetectable radio transmitter. In addition to serving as a navigator on B-24 flights, I served in the same capacity on highly successful Mosquito flights. The Mosquito was selected because of its high speed and ability to fly at the desired altitude of 40,000ft [sic]. The revolutionary transmitter/receiver equipment named Joan Eleanor was readily adaptable to the Mosquito.

d. These Mosquito missions involved a crew of pilot, navigator and special operator who spoke to the agent on the ground. A compartment was designed to hold this operator in the belly of the aircraft. The Mosquitoes had Merlin 72 engines. Heat in the cockpit stayed at room temperature. The planes were not pressurised, so oxygen masks had to be used.

e. We all noted that the engines of the American aircraft seemed to roar, while the Merlin seemed to purr. We were also impressed with the automatic supercharger that was activated at about 20,000ft. As we climbed to an altitude of 28,000 to 40,000ft the thrust was so strong that it seemed that we were taking off again.

f. Once we reached 40,000ft we felt secure – the German flak could not reach us. The only planes that presented any threat were jet fighters that the Germans developed near war's end, but their number was very limited. Since our plywood plane was at such a high altitude, the German radar would have difficulty spotting us. The plane was stripped of all excess weight and we had no armament of any kind. Even our Identification Friend or Foe (IFF) was removed.

g. These Mossie missions were code-named 'Red Stocking' [sic - *Redstocking*]. Part of the navigator's responsibility was to give directional corrections to the pilot once we reached our rendezvous area. We remained in an orbit not exceeding a maximum in width of 60 miles. Beyond that, the Joan Eleanor radio transmission and receiver equipment would not work. A prearranged meeting time was agreed upon, including coded BBC broadcasts beamed towards Germany.

h. The Joan Eleanor equipment was battery-operated. The transmission and receiving equipment carried on the Mosquito weighed about 40lb. It could pick up a voice on the ground in the 60-mile radius of the cone at 40,000ft. The transmitter and receiver were called Eleanor. The OSS agent on the ground carried the Joan section. It only weighed about 2lb and measured only 6.5 × 2.25 × 1.5in. While the transmitter used by the agent on the ground spread to about a 60-mile circle at 40,000ft, the cone narrowed to just a couple of feet at ground level. Therefore, the chance of the conversation being picked up by German direction finders was almost nil. The conversation that took place was recorded by the Mossie special operator on a wire spool. The spool was rushed to OSS HQ for analysis, and immediately given to the Allied High Command for use in planning future operations and strategy against Germany.

The Joan Eleanor Log

The origins and development of the JE radio equipment itself are covered in the section dealing with the 25th BG. For the day-to-day details of the missions flown we turn to the *Joan Eleanor Log*. It is interesting to note that at no point in the *Log* are the missions referred to as *Redstocking* flights. The term crops up only in the records of the 25th BG, first appearing in the January 1945 report.

Operations – 1944

RCA engineer DeWitt Goddard brought his Joan Eleanor equipment to Watton around 1 October 1944 for installation in Mosquito NS676, which had been allocated for OSS use. All the engineering work was carried out under the supervision of the 654th BS, but the facilities of the Communications shop were also utilised. On or around 22 October the first test flight took place, with '676 flown by Lt Geary, Lt Mishko as navigator and Lt Cdr Simpson as JE operator. Goddard operated the ground set with Capt. Sawyer observing. From a JE communications point of view the test was relatively successful but for some reason the aircraft seemed sluggish in the air. In a bid to find the cause, Geary made further test flights over the final days of October with the 654th's engineering officer, Capt. Jessie Abbot, on board but the answer proved elusive.

More test flights followed in November, during which 'many of the bugs were ironed out of the JE equipment'. First, it was decided to use a two-element antenna instead of a plain dipole. Next, a resistor was installed in the audio plate voltage lead to eliminate the howl in the SSTC-502 radio transmitter/receiver on low batteries.

Training was started on an agent code-named 'Bobbie' (located in Holland) and for this several missions were flown over London, together with a night mission on 9 November. 'Bobbie' was 'dropped in around Nov 11th' but bad weather apparently prevented the launch of a 'live' mission to make contact with him until 15 November. In the event, contact was not established and the sortie was deemed unsuccessful. To compound matters, the Mosquito's elevator controls jammed and pilot Doroski had considerable trouble controlling the aircraft.

The following day the Doroski/Mishko crew were again airborne in NS676 for what proved to be another 'no contact' event. On the return leg the Mosquito was diverted to Tangmere, where, on landing, the starboard oleo strut was cracked. This resulted in a week's sojourn at the airfield while repairs were made.

With NS676 unserviceable, another Mosquito, NS707, was hurriedly prepared for inclusion in the programme, in time for Doroski and Mishko to make an operational trip on 22 November. This time contact was made and it was established that 'Bobbie' was safe and well. The flight was not without incident and the pilot's seat became loose, making the aircraft something of a handful to fly. Mission number 4, in the now repaired NS676, headed off on 27 November, crewed by Walker and Mishko. Contact was successful and, apart from a diversion to Bradwell Bay on return, no problems were encountered.

On 25 November a trip was laid on to the Signals Corps at Burtonwood (Base Air Depot 1) to collect a large quantity of wire, cable and other equipment for installation in OSS aircraft. Plans were made to improve the communications engineering in Mosquitoes NS676 and '707. DeWitt Goddard left England for the US on 30 November and the following day the Walker/Conyer crew flew a successful mission to 'Bobbie' in NS676.

Work continued on the JE installation in NS707 over the first ten days in December and the Mosquito was painted black. For the time being no further work was planned on '676 – it was to be left as it was but would remain operational until modifications to '707 were completed. A special antenna was installed on '707 for LORAN, which, together with GEE, was fitted to the Mosquito.

JE missions 6 and 7, both to 'Bobbie', were flown on 10 and 12 December, both successful. Then, on the 15th, mission #8 was mounted. This consisted of Magee and Conyers in NS676 at high level to make contact with 'Bobbie', together with Walker and Mishko, on the deck in a night-photo ship to drop containers to 'Bobbie'. Contact with 'Bobbie' on the ground was established, but the two aircraft were, for some reason, unable to talk to each other on VHF. No drop was accomplished and the two containers were brought back to base.

The same mission was attempted again on the 16th but, despite trialling different radio antenna, VHF contact between the two-mission aircraft was still elusive. Although the high-level aircraft could communicate with 'Bobbie', the low-level 'drop' aircraft could not see the agent's identification lights.

A brand new A-26C (43-22500) was collected from Bovingdon on 18 December to join the JE programme. The Invader had been delivered initially to St Mawgan, was completely unmodified and still had ferry tanks installed. The *JE Log* reports that on 21 December OSS in London sought clearance for JE operation in the Munich area. However, the response from the 25th BG (still responsible for JE ops at this stage) was that radio contact with agents on the ground was viable but that equipment drops were not, due to the proximity of 'mountainous terrain'.

Two Dutch agents were given JE training in 'Area 'O' (details not specified) on 24 December, which included a flight over the area. Unfortunately, OSS's Maj. Hans Tofte decided that the pair 'were unfit to be sent out'. By no means everyone was suitable for the work! On the last day of the year, NS707 was flown on a training mission over London in preparation for agent 'Jack'. The tasking was abandoned when the radio cut out during contact.

1945

Operations – January 1945

The first news coming out of the JE programme at the turn of the year concerns the newly acquired A-26, which would soon be required to pair with the Mosquitoes on the *Redstocking* missions. The Invader was experiencing problems with its hydraulic system – apparently a fairly common problem (though a temporary one) throughout the fleet. The advice of the engineering staff at Bovingdon was sought and they recommended replacing the Bendix regulator and selector valve with British Vickers-manufactured components.

On 5 January mission #11 was flown in NS707, resulting in successful contact, but mission #12, flown the following night to 'Bobbie', proved a bit more problematic. With the A-26 in the low-level role and NS707 flying JE higher up in the hands of Robert Magee, the Mosquito aborted 60 miles from the target due to a blown radio valve. The Invader fared no better, failing to see any agent identification lights and suffering a broken radio antenna. Not surprisingly, no contact was made with the agent on the ground. Worse was to follow, and on return to base the Invader's undercarriage would not lower, necessitating a belly landing, fortunately without injury to the crew.

The Walker/Conyers crew flew mission #13 in NS707 on 10 January. Although contact was poor, two new agent pinpoints were obtained. Magee took the Mosquito up again on 15 January in a training mission for new crewman, Capt. Victor Layton, who, as a JE operator, would become the third member of the Mosquito crew. Contact was initially 'fair' but then Layton lost the ground for thirty minutes. For their part, ground could hear the aircraft all the time. Good contact was eventually re-established but on return to base, the weather closed in and the Mosquito was diverted to Manston.

RG157 'Q' of 492nd Bomb Gp at Harrington in early 1945. (Marvin Edwards)

In an effort to overcome problems with troublesome radio transmitter/ receiver aerials, the JE team drew on the expertise of the UK's Telecommunications Research Establishment (TRE) at Malvern, Engineering Officer Capt. Sawyer visiting the organisation on the 2nd. There would be a productive liaison between the JE team and TRE over the coming weeks. Much effort was also devoted to obtaining the ideally configured Invader to work alongside the Mosquitoes. On the 17th, A-26B 41-39329 was delivered to Warton and exchanged for A-26C 43-22524. After inspection back at Watton it was decided to try to exchange the newly acquired aircraft for one with a clamshell canopy. Warton was again contacted but the BAD reported that none was available with this modification. Despite ongoing engine problems with '524 the plan to swap it was abandoned as too difficult and work began on installing an absolute altimeter and the associated antennas in the bomber.

When the Walker/Mishko flew mission #14 in NS707 on the 22nd of the month contact with 'Bobbie' was good but the agent's batteries ran out after ten minutes.

Bad weather at Watton caught the headlines of the *JE Log* on 28 January. 'Heavy snow and slippery runways. Mosquito ran off the runway into snow piled on side and broke in half.' This was NS594 with the unfortunate Capt. Robert James at the controls. And on that date the Walker/Mishko crew flew JE mission #15 over the Stuttgart area in NS707. Around this time Mosquito NS725 (which had been delivered to Watton back in November 1944) enters the picture and is reported as awaiting the installation of a VHF interphone prior to starting work as a JE workhorse.

Operations – February 1945

February saw work finally start on installing VHF comms equipment in '725 and the Mosquito was given a coat of black paint. JE mission #16, the second mission to 'Jack', was flown on the 1st of the month by the Walker/Mishko/Layton crew in NS707. The starboard undercarriage of the Mosquito would not retract and so, somewhat surprisingly, the tasking was flown with it down, resulting in an approach to the target that was twenty minutes late. On the return trip the engines cut out for a brief instant. No agent contact was achieved.

The night of the 3rd and the following day proved eventful for the clandestine flying programme. The *JE Log* reports that a Harrington-based aircraft (presumably a B-24) made a run to 'Bobbie' but saw no lights in the target area. On the way out the aircraft was hit by anti-aircraft fire. That night the Walker/Mishko/Layton crew was tasked to fly a mission to 'Bobbie' in NS707 but, as inclement weather was forecast at their planned take-off time, they elected to fly to Dijon and mount the mission from the French airfield. However, things did not go as planned. At 0430 hrs on the 4th, Flying Control (at Watton) called the JE team on the 654th BS to report

Mosquito aircrew pictured at Harrington in February 1945. Back row: pilots Samuel Webb, Ralph Smith and James Kuntz. Front: navs Edward Kolawski and Marvin Edwards. (M Edwards)

that Walker had landed at Manston at 2.15 am with engine trouble. Arriving overhead Dijon, he had elected to return to Manston because of a lack of good night landing facilities in France. NS707's crew were duly ferried back to Watton in an A-26, leaving the stricken Mosquito at the Kent airfield.

With NS707 unserviceable, more Mosquitoes were needed to maintain the JE flight programme. Enter NS725 and '740. Of these, '740 had already been installed with LORAN and GEE and on 5 February was declared ready to fly a mission the following day, barring unforeseen problems. NS725 would be ready a day later. Both ships would need to be installed with a trailing wire antenna, which would not delay matters. 'NS740 checked in flight and looks a good ship.'

Attention turned briefly to the A-26 and a planning meeting decided that the Invader would be crewed by a pilot, two navigators behind the pilot operating LORAN and GEE, and a third navigator in the nose 'doing just pilotage and observing'. Arrangements were made for the A-26 to visit the Air Ministry Airborne Forces Experimental Establishment (AFEE) at RAF Beaulieu in Hampshire, where it could be modified for the agent dropping role.

JE mission #18 (#4 to 'Jack') took off half an hour after midnight on 7 February but experienced GEE problems and had to use dead reckoning to fly to the target. The crew were unsure of the position of the target and, failing to make contact with the agent, returned to Watton at 0450 hrs.

The following day, the 8th, NS740 was taken up on a 'test hop', climbing to 25,000ft, where it remained for about an hour. All systems worked satisfactorily except for the intercom on the navigator's position, which was noisy. During a subsequent short test flight the problem was traced to poor earthing of the microphone jack. Mission #19 (#15 to 'Bobbie') was planned for a 2230 hrs take-off that night. The weather proved 'fair', contact was established and the Mosquito touched down back at Watton at 0230 the next morning after an uneventful mission apart from an oil leak in the cockpit heater.

A mistake by OSS staff in the date broadcast for a contact with 'Jack' resulted in the cancellation of a mission to the agent planned for 9 February. (The task was rescheduled for three days later.) On the evening of the 9th, Walker and Mishko took off for a mission over Munich to test LORAN, but were diverted to Exeter early the following morning. Later on the 10th Roy Ellis-Brown collected Steve Simpson from Bovingdon in Mosquito NS581 after the latter's visit to OSS in London.

Mission #20 ('Bobbie' #16) was planned for 13 February, during which NS740 would attempt to make agent contact from 20,000ft, but the

Mosquito developed a coolant leak at take-off time and so 'gear switched to NS707'. During the night of 13–14 February the Walker/Mishko/Layton crew in NS725 flew JE mission #21 (#5 to 'Troy'). Contact was established in two bursts of twenty-five and fifteen minutes respectively in the hour before midnight but reception was poor most of the time.

At this point in the JE programme the operations and planning staff at Watton agreed to a drop north-west of Berlin and one north of the Ruhr, and to JE flights over those locations provided they were short and not more than once every five days. 'Want nothing east of Berlin due to Russians.' The night of 17–18 February saw JE #22 ('Bobbie' #17) with good contact made at midnight. 'Bobbie' was apparently equipped with new batteries. The mission was flown by a crew comprising Leon Gray, Robert Morrow and Steve Simpson in NS740. Their GEE equipment failed just before the target was reached and they had to rely on their SSTR-6 radio equipment for guidance to the agent. Later on the 18th a band of key personnel from JE/25th BG comprising Steve Simpson, Roy Ellis-Brown, John Walch (Navigation), Finis McClanahan (Intelligence), William Mishko and Robert Walker set off for the RAF's HQ 100 Group at nearby Bylaugh Hall in Norfolk to pick some brains in preparation for the Berlin missions. Of the visit the *JE Log* reports: 'Too little to eat for lunch but much good info and co-operation.' Times were hard and food rationing ruled!

During the month new code names for agents secreted on the Continent slid into the picture: 'Chisel', 'Hammer' and 'Mallet'. Bad weather prevented a planned photo mission for 'Chisel' on the 18th, but 325th Photo Wg staff said they had some photos of the area in question. Finis McClanahan set off to track down the pictures.

A training flight over London on 19 February for new JE personnel Richard Dolph and Karl Phyllis resulted in a close shave. Robert Magee lifted NS74 off the Watton runway at 1330 hrs with Victor Layton in the operator's seat. Good contact was achieved throughout the mission but the Mosquito narrowly missed colliding with a B-24 while flying through cloud.

The sixth mission to 'Troy' was mounted on the 24th by the Walker/Mishko/Layton crew in NS740. With take-off at 2320 hrs, the target was reached forty minutes later. The Mosquito circled around the target at a radius of 15 miles for thirty-seven minutes but was unable to make contact with the agent. This was despite all comms equipment proving serviceable during the pre-take-off checks.

Meanwhile, on the morning of the 24th, Walker, Mishko, Simpson, Fogarty and Baker set off in the A-26 ('524) for the AFEE at Beaulieu,

An unidentified PR.XVI running up engines at Harrington. (USAAF)

Hampshire, where the Invader would undergo tests for its agent dropping role. Modification work started as soon as they arrived, with 16in being sawn off from the rear of the bomb bay platform to enable jumpers' chutes to clear the main spar. For the actual tests, two dummies and one package were dropped. The package made a clean departure but the chutes snagged the turret, one also breaking off the IFF antenna. The next test, also involving two dummies and a package and initiated by bomb release, was more successful. Finally, two live jumps proved equally encouraging and the Invader returned to Watton that evening. Robert Walker took her up for a test flight the next day, when all systems were found to be operating satisfactorily.

On 26 February Lt Kingdon Knapp with Lt John Jackson as his navigator flew a *Skywave* long-range navigational mission over the Continent in a Mosquito. Jackson describes the tasking:

> We went in over the Ruhr at 26,000 feet. Using 128 feet of aerial we picked out signals difficult to read due to extra noise. However, fixes were obtained with a little difficulty. Between Nurnberg and Munich we let down to 3,000 feet indicated altitude. Near

Lts Samuel Webb (pilot) and Edward Kolawski (navigator) in front of their 492nd Bomb Gp Mosquito at Harrington. (USAAF)

Munich, as a test, I took a good fix with 3 feet of aerial out at an altitude of 3,000 feet. After about 10 minutes at this altitude we climbed to around 10,000 feet (this was just south of Stuttgart). Reception was still very good, and fixes were obtained nearly as far as the Charleroi area, where the rate 5 signal had a tendency to fade. At this point I wound in the aerial – to test short-aerial reception again – and could not let it out. While using LORAN I obtained an average of about one fix each 8 minutes and continued normal navigation, but the average while we were at low altitude was about a fix each six minutes. To take and plot a LORAN fix under ideal conditions requires from 3 to 4 minutes.

Mission #7 to 'Troy' was flown by the Knapp/Mishko in NS740 on the 25th. Victor Layton, the operator on the task, describes a frustrating night's work: 'Arrived over the target area on schedule at 2400 hrs. It had been arranged previously with the navigator that we would fly as close to the target as possible. During the 35 minutes while contact was attempted we were never more than 12 miles from the target. No contact, and landing at 0210.'

Training missions over Watton were flown on the final days of February and navigator Mishko commented: 'Flight [of 27th/28th] was at altitudes of 1,000 – 2,000 feet. Pilotage from the nose of the ship was excellent and we had little difficulty picking up our check points etc. Exhaust stacks [of the Mosquito] showed considerable light and pilot thought dampers should be put on if at all possible. Trip was very beneficial.' This was a two-hour mission flown in darkness just before midnight.

A graphic description of the last mission of the month is contained in a letter written by William Sawyer, the JE operator involved, to his OSS boss, Col William Jackson, a couple of days after the event. With Kingdon Knapp and John Jackson crewing NS725, the task was 'Bobbie 19' and Sawyer had this to say:

1. On the night of February 28th I talked to Bobbie on a contact scheduled for 2400 GMT. We flew at 25,000 feet and the contact started at exactly 2400 GMT. The contact lasted 25 minutes. The first and last parts were good but some difficulty was had keeping contact with him for about 10 minutes of the center portion of the 25 minutes.
2. Bobbie was definitely giving his prearranged 'trouble signal' all through the contact. There was no doubt about this after the first five minutes. No indication was made from the plane that trouble was sensed except to swear on one occasion. It was definitely felt that he should not be asked to spell his name, as (1) there was no mistaking his voice – it was Bobbie, and (2) his 'trouble signal' was very clear and outstanding.
3. I feel that Bobbie was operating under duress and was being told what to say, because (1) he seemed unwilling to say he was in trouble except by his undercover signal, (2) the coordinates for his pinpoint at which he wanted a drop were up in the North Sea, (3) he seemed to have excellent facilities for reading his messages containing intelligence which indicates he had a good light, (4) his intelligence seemed, in my opinion, a lot of valueless information, and (5) he seemed to have to be prompted on the date for the package delivery, as he hesitated considerably before replying to this question. He is usually sure of his dates and has them figured out ahead of time. As for his telling of the arrest of his friends and the possible capture of one of the JE sets, that may have been a move by the Germans into believing he had a code for his coordinates and may have botched them up in that way. All of these points are assumptions and seem logical to me, having talked to

Bobbie some seven different times and having had first-hand contact with the present situation.

4. After the first five minutes of contact time, the pilot, Lt Knapp, was asked to keep his eyes peeled for enemy aircraft as trouble was suspicioned. No enemy aircraft were seen. Lt Knapp left the area immediately after the contact was finished and headed north.

5. My opinion is that the Saturday package delivery should definitely not be attempted but that the BBC messages should continue for another week, with the mission being alerted and called off alternately. In about one week a JE contact flight should be made and further action should depend on the results of that contact.

6. I will fly another contact any time after next Thursday, March 8th, pending approval by the 25th Bomber [he means 'Bomb'] Group.

Operations – March 1945

Mosquito NS707 was brought into use for training missions in the opening days of March. When Lt Calhoun Ancrum flew his first trip as a trainee operator on the afternoon of the 5th, with the Knapp crew, bad weather closed Watton and they were diverted to Deopham Green, a B-17 base 10 miles to the east. The Mosquito was left there with an unserviceable fuel pump. Training completed, Ancrum was ready for his first operation, the first mission to agent 'Anzio', on 7 March aboard NS725. In the event, this proved to be something of an anticlimax. Despite circling the target area for thirty-eight minutes at a radius of between 12 and 16 miles no response could be raised. To compound the disappointing results, 27ft of trailing antenna could not be reeled in.

A training mission on the afternoon of the 9th, with Lt Oliver Emmel at the controls of NS707, featured a bit more drama, and the *JE Log* reports: 'Good contact. Hit tree on way to base and had to make emergency landing with one engine. Ran off end of runway. Antenna was broken off.' That night Kingdon Knapp, with Lt John Jackson in the navigator's seat, took NS725 up on the thirtieth JE mission (#9 to 'Troy'). Before take-off all systems had tested serviceable. Despite this, operator Calhoun Ancrum was unable to establish a satisfactory contact with the agent, even after the Mosquito had circled for twenty minutes and then flown directly over the target. Accurate flak was encountered just west of Ludwigshafen, which 'caused ship to jump about, but no damage'. This particular mission had been flown at 25,000ft.

RG157 'Q' of 492nd Bomb Gp at Harrington. (Marvin Edwards)

Never averse to picking other organisations' brains for ideas and equipment, the JE team decided to enlist the help of the RCAF. Thus, on 12 March the Knapp/Jackson/Ancrum crew climbed aboard one of the A-26s and set off for RAF Middleton St George in County Durham. The base was at that point home to two experienced Canadian Lancaster squadrons, Nos 419 and 428. The Canadians provided a quantity of flares and briefed on their use. This was in preparation for a planned A-26 mission on 13 March.

Tuesday, 13 March 1945 proved to be a milestone in the ongoing JE effort, for on that day Steve Simpson attended a meeting at HQ 8th Air Force Bomber Command, 'Pinetree' (High Wycombe). There he was informed by Col Arthur Pierce, Director of Plans, that JE operations would be moving to Harrington forthwith, where they would be under the auspices of the 492nd BG. (A 'bomber man', Pierce had until August 1944 been CO of the 466th BG, a B-24 outfit based at Attlebridge, Norfolk). Neither OSS nor 8th AF records indicate the reasons for the move at such a late stage of the war. The factors involved in reaching this decision would have been interesting; primarily, the logic in centralising all clandestine air operations at Harrington versus the desirability of concentrating all USAAF Mosquito missions at Watton (which by now had been operating the type for over a year).

The move got under way with commendable promptness, Steve Simpson visiting Harrington on the 14th, but unfortunately the move did not go smoothly. The *JE Log* states tersely that on 14 March: 'Simpson [goes] to Harrington and finds that they are not ready to receive us, but orders stand.' The physical move to Harrington started on the 15th and the *Log* goes on to describe events. 'Two trucks from London sent down and loaded at Watton. Trucks arrive at Harrington at 1800 hrs. Much confusion, as no one knows location of new [JE] shop. CO contacted thru S-2 [Intelligence] and finally Capt. Gibson from S-4 [Supply] arrives at 2015 to show us new quarters. Trucks unloaded and sent back to London. Mosquitoes 707 and 725 flown to Harrington by Knapp and Emmel – Knapp returns to Watton. Training of new Mossy crews started.' The following day Mosquito NS740 arrived at Harrington together with the relevant crew chiefs. Steve Simpson, Calhoun Ancrum, and other JE personnel, including George Fogarty (a JE operator), also arrived and were quartered in a Nissen hut. A JE support centre was established in another Nissen hut on the technical site.

An OSS report dated 26 March 1945 is scathing about the confusion and initial lack of support afforded the newly arrived JE team at Harrington, due, it said, to a mixture of poor communication, inexperience and misunderstandings. Steve Simpson's personal input to the report mentions 'complete chaos as far as engineering was concerned'. The report states that, in order to restore some sort of order to all this confusion: 'It was agreed with all concerned that the two Mosquitoes (NS584 and '686) were to be used exclusively for training of Harrington personnel, while Mosquitoes NS707, '725 and '740 were to be held, flown and operated only by Watton men for operational work.' A degree of friction between Simpson and Col Hudson Upham, the 492nd's CO, surrounding the policy for JE ops in general and the operation of Mosquito specifically is also suggested – although that is just the OSS perspective.

But the show had to go on and the same OSS report describes subsequent events. 'The first mission was flown from the Harrington station on the night of 18 March. Navigating officer, Lt Jackson, had considerable amount of difficulty in getting his weather information and there was little or no S-2 [intelligence] information as required on this type of Mosquito mission. There was no VHF, no communication flimsies, no colors of the day, and no emergency information given. Furthermore, our mechanics had to go all over the field to locate oxygen and gasoline trucks. There was no alert crew.'

The mission was JE #33 and #3 to 'Hammer'. Flying in NS725, the Knapp/Jackson/Ancrum crew were unable to make a contact due to jamming of the TR-6 equipment (the on-board transmitter/receiver), which was recorded on wire.

It was no consolation at all that JE A-26 operations were suffering the same organisational problems, as illustrated by events for an Invader mission on 18 March:

> Throughout the day orders were given and cancelled several times to fly the 'Chisel' mission in the A-26 ('524). It was brought to everyone's attention that the A-26 needed a 100-hour check, the radio altimeter needed calibrating, the LORAN and GEE needed checking, that Lt Emel had insufficient [pilot] hours in the A-26 and had not flown it more than twice at night. Maj. Tresemer [a navigator] had been in the A-26 only once before and had been completely bewildered by ground pilotage at such speed, and none of the crew … had ever flown together before and were unfamiliar with the ship as a whole.

Despite these obstacles plus a forecast of marginal weather over the Continent ('Ship had to pass thru terrific front going and coming. Mission should not have been flown.') the mission was launched at around 2200 hours. 'The ship did not return' and the crew consisting of Oliver Emel, John Walch (navigator), Edward Tresemer, and SSgt Frederick Brunner (gunner) were listed as MIA. The A-26 had crashed just north of its destination of Münster in Germany.

OSS reported similar shortcomings in airfield support before the launch of the tasking flown on 19 March, mission #4 to 'Hammer'. 'This has been constant trouble with every Mosquito mission flown. We now have more high-altitude depth penetration information since Cmdr Simpson sent Maj. Bozarth to Watton to bring back what was available there.' On the outward leg the right dome light in the JE compartment of NS725 burned out and again on the way home. Over the Continent the LORAN was jammed and so the Knapp/Jackson/Ancrum crew flew the five-and-a-half-hour mission by DR.

Technical problems bedevilled Mosquitoes NS725 and '740 during the course of attempts to fly the 'Chisel' mission #36 of 22/23 March. After '740 aborted the mission the Knapp/Jackson/Ancrum crew took off in '725 and later reported: 'Gas leak covered floor of JE compartment. Door was jettisoned. Took off with normal load and only 1400 lbs of oxygen pressure. Reached target too late (0134) after coming in low through friendly and enemy flak.'

The pace of Mosquito missions continued unabated but the *JE Log* strikes a familiarly negative note: '23–24 March – JE mission #37, 'Anzio' 32. Mosquito 707. Knapp/Jackson/Ancrum. 2105 to 0205. No contact. TR-6 jammed after 20 minutes. No VHF. Ship could receive tower but tower could not receive ship.' On that day navigator William Mishko's temporary duty at Harrington came to an end and Hugh Bozarth flew him back to Watton in NS686. The *JE Log* opined: 'He was a great help.' Maj. Albert Schaeffer (the 492nd's Deputy Ops Officer) flew a *Skywave* mission to the Continent in NS707 and in the absence of a report it was assumed that this was successful.

At this point, the *JE Log* records how the problems of servicing the JE aircraft at Harrington were overcome. 'Understand Capt. Fulton, the 856th BS engineering officer, will now maintain and co-ordinate the Mosquito and A-26 jobs. Up to now the six mechanics we brought [from Watton] have not known who to take orders from or what to do. Fulton is a good man and can handle the job.' It was suggested to Col Upham that Pinetree either provide jacks, hydraulic kit and Mosquito ground handling equipment, or that Mosquito NS740 was flown to Watton in order to have its various faults with brakes, hydraulic leak, left landing light motor and flap return cut-off rectified.

The problems with Mosquito pilot and navigator training that also dogged the JE programme at this juncture were not, it seemed, so easily solved. Kingdon Knapp and John Jackson were sent to 856th Sqn Ops on 25 March to instruct pilots and navigators respectively. There – 'Knapp is told pilots have gone to Watton and he doesn't know where the navigators are. They don't seem to want any help.' Jackson was equally luckless, and '… still unable to get navigators to instruct. Spent the afternoon at the [492nd] Group Navigation Section but navigators could not be located.' On a more optimistic note, Steve Simpson arranged for Hugh Bozarth to provide Albert Schaeffer with a local JE-role Mosquito training flight. Schaeffer immediately began acting as a steadying hand, co-ordinating the training of new pilots, Lts Webb, Kuntz, Smith and La Due. In essence they were sent to Watton for a seven-day course. Navigators, on the other hand, were still proving elusive. Lt Col Charles Bowman, the OSS Air Operations Officer, spent the afternoon of the 25th at Harrington and according to the *Log*, 'He saw plenty.'

The Knapp/Jackson/Ancrum crew took up NS740 for 'Chisel' #3 on the 26th but was unable to achieve the scheduled 0100 hours contact. On the way out a friendly fighter appeared off their wing tip, but it was called off by the ground controller.

Mission #5 to 'Hammer' proved more eventful than usual and the ubiquitous Kingdon Knapp recorded what happened after he took off in NS740 on the night of 27–28 March with his usual crew:

Was briefed to land in France as weather was bad in all of England. Take off was at 0005 hours. After contact was made [with the agent on the ground] Lt Ancrum told me he had important information, so I decided to land in England and hasten delivery of the wire [on which the agent's message had been recorded]. At the French coast I contacted Woodbridge and received a favourable weather report. Soon after, Coltishall called me and told me to land there. I proceeded there and as I was about to enter the circuit they told me to go to Woodbridge. By the time I got to Woodbridge the ceiling was 200 feet and visibility 800 yards. While trying to land we flew through gun batteries that were firing at V-1s. With great risk and excellent help from the navigator [Jackson] on the GEE, I was finally able to make a landing at 0630. At 0645 Lt Ancrum talked to OSS in London requesting transportation and was told it would not be available. We contacted Cdr Simpson at 0800 who arranged through London for a car. The car left London at 0950 and arrived at Woodbridge at 1350. It is thought that since the crew brought the wire back to England at great risk to themselves and the plane in order to get this information through quickly, the delay in securing transportation was criminal. This lack of co-operation does not encourage the crew to accept abnormal hazards beyond the line of duty. Flying time in Mosquito 740 was six hours and 25 minutes. [We had] 20 gals of gas on landing.

A delay in getting the Mosquito refuelled at Woodbridge held up take-off but Knapp and Co. finally arrived back at Woodbridge at 1800 hours.

Among the *JE Log* entries for 30 March is quiet satisfaction that, at last, the programme's three front-line Mosquitoes (NS707, '725 and '740) were all serviceable. Having achieved this, the Harrington engineers felt they could dispense with the three Mosquito crew chiefs detached from Watton. However, Col Gray, CO of the 25th BG at Watton, agreed that the crew chiefs could remain at Harrington alongside the 654th BS aircrew who flew the JE Mosquitoes at Harrington. Two 100 gallon drop tanks were procured for the Mosquitoes. The energetic figure of Albert Schaeffer again crops up in events. An enthusiastic pilot, he was busily experimenting with Mosquito climbing speeds and other performance figures. Kingdon Knapp, with rather more Mosquito experience under his belt, suggested that 'operational ships should not be used for this purpose as damage may occur to the engines which could prove disastrous on a mission'. In Knapp's view Schaeffer was a good pilot but needed more experience before flying [JE] missions.

The indomitable Schaeffer finally took the controls for his inaugural JE Mosquito mission on 31 March, with first-time navigator 2/Lt Edward Kolacki and Steve Simpson in the JE operator's seat. This was 'Tyl' mission #21 using NS707. The inexperience of the crew soon began to show, as Simpson reported later:

> New navigator in 707 and had expected trouble on holding course. Were a little late, being 30 miles from Point One at 2400. Had to continually correct navigator. Pilot climbed at speed as low as 160 and finally cautioned him when things got shaky. Contacted 'Bobbie' at 0003 GMT and stayed in area until 0040. He never did tune us in except first time. We orbited to right and left and passed over target twice, always getting a good signal. Began to hear what may have been radar and a strong signal on our frequency that was suspicious – so we left. Air filter blew a hole in bottom of plane.

With the tide of war turning against the Axis, greater use could be made of landing grounds on the Continent. Such was the case when, on 30 March, Kingdon Knapp took off in NS740 on 'Anzio 4' (the forty-first JE mission). Arriving over the target at midnight, no contact could be achieved with the agent on the ground, even after orbiting for twenty-five minutes. To make matters worse, the starboard engine started to run roughly and so Knapp made for ALG B-87 (at Rosières-en-Santerre in Picardy) where the Mosquito was found to have an unserviceable generator, resulting in a failure of the electrical system. This left the crew without either radio or intercom. On the ground, an engine was also found to have an oil leak from the camshaft cover.

Operations – April 1945

A new addition to Harrington's small Mosquito fleet arrived at 1100 hours on 1 April in the form of RG157. At the same time, TA614 was unserviceable due to brake and engine trouble. An apparent lack of Mosquito ground crew at this point did nothing to alleviate the situation. NS740 with its Knapp, Jackson, Ancrum crew returned from B-87 to report the details of their emergency landing in France. The spate of equipment failures led Steve Simpson to comment: 'These troubles indicate poor maintenance. Capt. Fulton [Engineering] thinks his men can now handle Mosquitoes OK and wants to return the Watton men. They can't learn in a week and mechanical difficulties [during the] last 3 missions have caused near disaster. Reason for oil leak on "Anzio 4" was that bolts were only finger tight on the cam case cover.' Finally, on the first day of the month, the *JE Log* reports tersely: 'Mosquito TA614 arrived at 1400. Needs a check over. Brake pressure bad.'

The somewhat less than satisfactory situation with Mosquito serviceability as a whole leads the *JE Log* to report, on 2 April: 'Fogarty [JE operator] inspects new Mosquitoes with Capt. Cain and Sgt Carrie of Sub-Depot [at Watton]. They make out a list of modifications and work is to start same afternoon.' On the same day a training flight was arranged for a new Mosquito crew comprising Maj. Schaeffer (pilot) and Lt Corson (navigator). That afternoon, NS725 was air tested in preparation for the coming night's work. During the flight all systems were checked but smoke poured into the cockpit and the VHF was unserviceable. The VHF generator was replaced, enabling the Knapp/Jackson/Ancrum crew to take off at 2345 hours with what should have been a fully serviceable aircraft for 'Hammer 6'. However, one hour from the target the LORAN and GEE went out. Ancrum was unable to make contact with the agent and so Knapp turned the Mosquito for home with the cloud ceiling at 200ft. In the circuit he failed to get green lights after selecting landing gear down and so radioed the tower, asking for a visual check as he made his approach. Receiving no response from the controller, Knapp buzzed the airfield to try to attract attention, but without success. Pressing ahead with the landing, he instructed navigator Jackson to maintain hydraulic pressure with the hand pump until the undercarriage locks were on. Back on the ground it was found that the indicator lights had simply shorted out and the landing gear was functioning normally.

A somewhat startling incident appears in the *JE Log* entry for 3 April, which possibly highlights the pressure being put on JE aircrew:

More adventures of the Rover Boys and the wooden birds [JE crews and Mosquitoes respectively!]. Maj. Schaeffer schedules training flight to Dijon at the request of [OSS] London office. Fogarty is to ride in back end of Mosquito '740 with Kolacki as navigator, Webb as pilot. Fogarty got in, oxygen pressure checked zero, interphone wouldn't work, so he hit emergency light to get organised. Pilot started taxiing without any check, so when he stopped at the end of the runway, Fogarty jettisoned door and jumped. Pilot was on command set and navigator had table over emergency light. We replaced door, adjusted oxygen, checked interphone, and tried again. Pilot took off and couldn't get the wheels up, but bomb doors opened. Pilot came in and made a ball-busting landing. Decides to go up with crew chief to check the undercarriage. Fogarty returns to the [engineering] shop. Lt Webb, the pilot, has just finished a course of instruction at Watton.

'Lt Col [Robert] Boone ground loops Mosquito '686 about 2000 hours. Looks like a complete loss.' So states a *JE Log* entry for 3 April. This is incorrect, for '686 soldiered on until 1948. The aircraft involved was in fact NS584 and the incident is officially described as a 'Take Off Accident'. In the midst of all this brouhaha, OSS's Col Bowman scheduled another mission for JE operator George Fogarty with Webb as pilot, but Fogarty was having none of it. 'Life is still sweet,' observed the *JE Log*.

The somewhat confused state of operations at this point prompted Steve Simpson and George Fogarty to meet with Col Upham, the 492nd's CO, to discuss the training of JE operators in Mosquitoes flown by pilots who were not properly checked out on the aircraft, the return of mechanics to Watton and Warton, and who should be responsible for the management of Mosquito conversion training. Upham agreed that Simpson's team would supervise JE conversion training, that only the Knapp/Jackson crew would fly JE missions until at least two more pilots had been trained, that Mosquito NS686 would return to Watton, and that all mechanics would return to their parent units.

The *JE Log* takes on a more optimistic note with the arrival, around 4 April, of two fresh Mosquitoes, RG157 and TA614. At the same time the *Log* reports the arrival of a party of RAF 'instructors', led by a Sqn Ldr

Hailstone, with Sgt Bean as his deputy. Whether the USAAF had officially requested help from the RAF to ease the operational and maintenance problems with the Mosquitoes is not clear. In any event, the Brits received a warm reception.

Flight planning went ahead for another mission, 'Anzio 5', on the night of 5–6 April, with NS740 earmarked for the task. But when operator George Fogarty reminded Kingdon Knapp of the hard landing experienced by the

RG157 'Q' of the 856th Bomb Sqn, 492nd Bomb Gp at Harrington in 1945. (Marvin Edwards)

492nd Group Mosquitoes at Harrington in 1945. Nearest the camera is TA614 'R'. (Marvin Edwards)

Mosquito earlier in the month, the pilot insisted on a landing gear retraction test. This revealed a bad leak on the down lock hydraulic system. Knapp was, instead, allocated NS725. Despite flying over the target at three levels, including one at 2,000ft to let 'Anzio' hear the engines, no contact could be established.

The hard-pressed Kingdon Knapp, who had recently been so vocal against the use of the dedicated JE-dedicated Mosquitoes for training new pilots, was now slated to fly the first 'Luxe' and 'Pickaxe' missions in NS725 on the night of 8–9 April. Preparations for this did not go well. On checking the Mosquito, Knapp found that the artificial horizon was unserviceable – 'with 20,000 feet of cloud to fly through'. This prompted a visit to the parked Mosquito by 492nd BG execs, Lt Cols Robert Fish and Rodmans St Claire, where, according to the *JE Log*, 'Knapp insists that somebody give him a written order to fly.'

Preparations for the mission continued but the task now became a little more complicated with a request from OSS London for a contact with 'Hammer' to be added to the itinerary. The plan now was to stage at ALG Y-2 (Lunneville, France) on the way out to the targets and to stage at ALG B-78 (Eindhoven, Holland) on the way back. Allocated NS740 for the job, Knapp took the Mosquito up for an air test after lunch on the 8th, only to

Joan Eleanor crew. L-R: William Mishko (nav), Kindon Knapp (pilot) and William Sawyer (OSS Joan Eleanor operator) in front of NS725 at Harrington. (N Malayney via W Sawyer)

find that the landing gear wouldn't raise or lower and the VHF was not functioning properly. The problems were eventually rectified in time for a 1910 take-off with Jackson and Ancrum crewing. After completing the first part of the mission, Knapp touched down at Lunneville at 2055 hours, more or less as planned. After a meal for the crew and fuel for the aircraft they were off again to complete the remainder of the mission – which resulted in contacts with all three agents. Turning the Mosquito for home, Knapp was informed by the ground controller that the weather had closed Eindhoven (where the only radio channel working was 'Air Sea Rescue') and that he should instead head for ALG B-58 (Melsbroek – Brussels). Touchdown at the Belgian airfield was at 0600, where the aircraft was again refuelled. After breakfast Knapp went to the air traffic control tower for departure clearance but was informed that the weather in England was bad. Of Harrington, Watton, Northolt and Manston only the latter airfield was open. Knapp reported: 'The Control officer drove us out to the plane and stood by as we started. I followed his taxi instructions which were given as we drove out as I had no radio. I ran up the engines, received a green light to taxi to the runway and another to take off. Landed at Manston at 0815 [on 9 April].'

The Knapp crew had a well-deserved if brief respite when the Schaeffer/Corson/Fogarty crew was detailed for 'Faro 1' (the forty-fifth JE mission), planned for 9–10 April. They later reported: 'Hit target right on time, circled for 35 minutes, no contact. Everything perfect, except probe popped out of antenna at target and had to be held in by hand. Diverted to Tangmere on return because of uncertain weather, where we were very well treated.' Tangmere was at this point an RAF fighter airfield in the county of Sussex on the south coast of England.

The indefatigable Knapp crew was back in harness for 'Faro 2' and Luxe 2' on 10–11 April. 'Faro' was contacted but operator Fogarty had no luck at 'Luxe'.

Training of potential JE operators continued apace and a Liberator was used for an introduction to the art because its roomy interior could accommodate more than one student. Andre Pecquet was one such individual and had his baptismal B-24 mission on 11 April. 'Contact was held 100 per cent for about 50 minutes with assorted students. It was their first time and they did very well. Pecquet is now ready for training in the Mosquito.' The Anglo-Frenchman already had a distinguished career as an OSS radio operator and in June 1944 was part of special operations unit led by British Army Maj. Desmond Longe that, under the code name

'Mission Eucalyptus', parachuted into a field in south-eastern France to train guerrillas in the receipt and use of parachute-delivered weapons.

Albert Schaeffer's crew now began to shoulder more of the JE tasking and were rostered for the first 'Buzzsaw' mission, planned for 11–12 April. The report of the mission, flown in NS707, was as follows: 'Took off at 2350 (had to return to replace defective TR-6) [the vital transmitter receiver]. Target Leipzig. Reached target at 0100 GMT. At 0030 noticed gasoline dripping into aft end of fuselage, forming a puddle half an inch deep. Pulled up antenna and goosed for home. Landed Harrington 0255 with no further untoward incidents. TR-6 seemed to lack sensitivity.' Not surprisingly agent contact was not achieved.

A review of Mosquito serviceability on 13 April showed that NS707 had a cracked landing gear, '725 was out for inspection, while '740 was flyable but had a magneto drop of 150 on each engine. This situation enabled the Knapp crew to take off in '740 for a 'Luxe' and 'Pickaxe' mission over the night of 13–14 April, when contact was made with both agents.

The Schaeffer/Corson/Fogarty crew stepped up to the plate again for the 'Buzzsaw 2' and 'Faro 3' mission of 14–15 April. For this multi-target mission NS740 staged through Brussels, but diverted into Woodbridge on the way home due to a lowering cloud ceiling. Operator Fogarty complained that an oil trap leaked all over him during flight. Andre Pecquet had his first familiarisation ride as a JE operator in the back of a Mosquito with Kingdon Knapp at the controls. During the flight: 'All the lights in the rear went out.'

Two-target missions were now becoming the norm, but the mission 'Mallet 1'/'Hammer 7', flown on 15–16 April in NS725, was aborted when all electrical equipment failed on the approach to the first target. The Mosquito landed back at Manston after four hours in the air.

After the Schaeffer crew assembled on 16 April for 'Faro 4'/'Buzzsaw 3' the mission turned troublesome. Staging at Brussels, their departure was delayed because: 'They didn't get the gas truck out.' Because of the forty-minute delay Schaeffer decided to miss out 'Buzzsaw 3', enabling the Mosquito to arrive over 'Faro' on time. Here they were again stymied when, after ten minutes over the target, the oxygen failed. They stooged around for twenty minutes more before dropping to 10,000ft and heading for home.

Brussels was again used as a staging post for 'Hammer 8'/'Mallet 2', programmed for 18–19 April and requiring thirty minutes over each target. Despite the timely arrival of Schaeffer and Co. over both targets, no contacts were achieved. 'No enemy action, no nothin',' reported Fogarty.

'New Mosquito still suffering from generator trouble,' reports the *JE Log* entry for 20 April. This presumably refers to RG157. Of the other Mosquitoes, NS740 was on a fifty-hour check, while Knapp was flying NS725 on a JE mission, and pilot John Webb crewed with new navigator Marvin Edwards and operator Andre Pecquet to fly a *Skywave* mission in NS707.

Mission 'Hammer 9'/Mallet 3' got as far as Brussels before aborting. Taking off from Harrington on 20 April in NS725, the Schaeffer crew were planning to use the B-58 ALG as a forward operating base. Again, the Gremlins stepped in and on the way out the Mosquito developed engine problems. Schaeffer contacted Harrington to hold NS707 as a standby aircraft, and described what happened next: 'Attempted to fly back, but engine got worse, so landed [he doesn't say exactly where – possibly Brussels?] and cabled for 707 to be sent over.' NS707 was ferried over by a crew consisting of Lt James Kuntz (pilot) and Lt Edward Kolawski (nav) and Schaeffer continues: 'Right engine aneroid out, and after two unsuccessful attempts at take-off, flight was abandoned. Crew came in from Harrington and got both ships flyable (?) by 23 April. Returning to Harrington, hydraulic system failed on '707 and brakes failed on '725.'

Mosquito RG157 flew its inaugural JE mission on the night of 23–24 April. This was 'Farmer 2'/'Chauffeur 2', with Knapp at the controls, John Jackson in the nav's seat and Andre Pecquet as radio operator. 'New aircraft 157 used for first time. Some trouble experienced, but should be all right soon. Gas in rear compartment.' Of the two targets, only 'Chauffeur' resulted in a contact.

A defective TR-6 radio, resulting in a forty-five-minute delay in take-off, prevented success with 'Hammer 10'/'Mallet 4' on 23–24. The Schaeffer crew were in NS707 and reported: 'Arrived target about 25 minutes late for "Hammer", but tried calling. No luck.'

NS725 *The Greek* of 492nd Bomb Gp at Harrington. (Harrington Museum)

Left: Lts Edward Kolawski (nav) and James Kuntz (pilot) in front of the 492nd Bomb Gp's *Patty* – possibly TA614. (Dana Bell)

Below: RG157 'Q' of the 856th Bomb Sqn, 492nd Bomb Gp at Harrington in 1945. (Ben Shaver)

No missions were scheduled for 24 April, but work continued on Mosquito RG157 'to correct deficiencies' and on TA614 to prepare it for a test flight on the morning of the 25th. Came the 25th and disaster struck. Lts James Kuntz (pilot), Richard Green (navigator) and Sean Nater (JE radio operator) were rostered to fly a *Skywave* mission. The *JE Log* tersely reports: '[NS]707 goes on *Skywave* with Kuntz, Green and Nater. Engine went afire and crew jumped. Kuntz and Nater all right. Green (navigator) not heard from. Green was killed ...' In the subsequent British Accident Investigation Report pilot James Kuntz described exactly what happened:

The engines had been run up by the groundcrew about 2 hours prior to my entering the aircraft. I warmed the engines up and taxied to the take-off point. Just after leaving the ground I noticed that the port engine boost gauge was reading 14 lbs/sq inch, against the 12 lbs/sq inch from the starboard engine. Everything else was normal. The engines behaved normally until four and a half hours after take-off, when we were returning from our mission. We were flying at 5000 feet ... Instruments were reading normal. My first indication of trouble was fluctuating and backfiring of the port engine, accompanied by fairly heavy volumes of smoke and fluctuation of the port boost gauge. As soon as the trouble occurred, I pulled the throttle back and when I tried pushing it forward the backfiring accompanied by explosions began again, and the throttle lever vibrated in sympathy with the bangs. I pulled the throttle back and feathered. Before the feathering operation was complete I noticed the engine was on fire. Immediately the propeller stopped, smoke started to come into the cockpit and caused us considerable discomfort. I then ordered my crew to bale out. Lt Nater baled out at 2500 feet and Lt Green at approximately 2200 feet. Concerning baling out, Lt Green opened the inside door and jettisoned the outer door. He then tried to go out feet first, but had difficulty in getting through the door and returned to his seat. At that time he noticed he had not his leg straps fastened [on his chest-type parachute]. He asked me if it would be all right to bale out with his leg straps unfastened, and I told him that he would have to have at least one leg strap fastened. I saw him working with one leg strap, he seemed a little excited but said nothing to me and then left the aircraft feet first. Lt Nater had already gone by this time.

213

The jettisoning of the door hatch made only a little difference to the density of the smoke in the cockpit. During this time I had got the aircraft trimmed for single-engined flying … Before leaving the aircraft I went over to the navigator's seat when the aircraft went into a dive to port. I levelled the aircraft and went out feet first, at which time the aircraft would be travelling at about 180 mph. I had no difficulty in getting out. I did not turn the port fuel cock off nor operate the fire extinguisher. I only noticed the fire in the early stages, when it was not intense and consisted merely of smoke and sparks. As I was descending by parachute I had my back to the aircraft, but in spite of this and the bright moonlight I was conscious of the aircraft going away from me by the glow around me. During the trouble we called 'Blue Fire', Manston, and got a vector of 110 degrees. I had intended to land at Manston if the fire went out.

Kuntz and Nater landed safely but Green was killed. The latter's body was recovered several days later, separate from his parachute, which was found with the harness attached but the leg straps undone. In the investigator's opinion the loss of the Mosquito was caused by the pilot's failure to turn off the fuel and press the fire extinguisher button. 'Had he done this it is thought that the fire would have been put out as it did not appear to be one of the bad types.' Of Kuntz, the report noted: 'He was not experienced in Mosquitoes.' Thus was lost one of the precious JE Mosquitoes, though not, it should be said, on an actual JE mission.

After the briefest of interludes a 'Farmer' and 'Chauffeur' mission was flown on 27–28 April by the Knapp/Jackson/Pecquet crew in NS740. This was described as: 'Rough trip due to weather. Ventilation vent jammed. Antenna lock did not lock. Compelled during contact to hold antenna up by hand.'

The rectification work performed on RG157 rendered it serviceable for the 'Pickaxe 6'/'Luxe 7' mission slated for 28–29 April. The crew line-up was Schaeffer/Corson/Ancrum. The tasking was bedevilled by problems from start to finish, as the *JE Log* notes: 'GEE went out shortly after take-off from forward staging airfield. Fluxgate compass could not be turned off at Dijon. No key for gas caps in engine nacelles. No emergency oxygen bottles in plane. No relief can for JE operator. Leak from gas[oline] overflow pipe in JE operator's compartment. Gas was coming from under metal disc at hole junction and from pipe itself. Radar sweep interference. Orbits [over target] could have been improved.' Despite this litany of snags, contacts were made over both targets.

A new crew, comprising Lt John Webb (pilot), 2/Lt Edward Kolawski (nav) and Lt Sean Nater (JE operator) was assembled to mount the 'Sultane'/'Boyard' mission of 29–30 April. Flying RG157, they staged at the now well-used airfield of Dijon, and then attempted to make contact from 30,000ft. Unfortunately, all intercom and radio comms failed over the last target. Insufficient time between the targets had been allowed for, and Webb had to buzz the target field, which itself was difficult to pinpoint because of a blanket of snow, four times to get the identification lights turned on.

In a final throw of the dice, yet another fresh crew was tasked with a 'Chauffeur' mission on 1–2 May. On this occasion navigator Marvin Edwards flew his first and only JE mission, crewing with pilot Kuntz and JE operator Andre Pecquet. Again, the Gremlins made their presence felt with a vengeance, and shortly after the 1805 hours take-off the VHF, interphone and GEE on RG157 failed. The Mosquito returned to base at 1845 hrs and equipment was transferred to NS740. The crew took off for a second time in the replacement Mosquito, only to find that the pilot and JE operator were unable to hear the navigator. The hapless crew returned to Harrington yet again, where the interphone on '740 was repaired. After a third departure the starboard engine registered unacceptably low revolutions, and the mission was aborted and the job abandoned. This was the final mission of the JE programme, and perhaps a somewhat anticlimactic note on which to finish. But such is war.

492nd Bomb Gp Mosquito named *The Greek.* (Dana Bell)

Review of Joan Eleanor Mosquito Operations

With the fog of war cleared and the dust of combat settled it is interesting to assess the short but intensive burst of Joan Eleanor operations. The total number of missions flown varies, depending on which source of reference is consulted, but eighty-six is a fairly safe figure to centre on. (Of these, three were flown by A-26 Invaders, with a crew of four drawn from the usual JE manpower pool. On the third and final A-26 mission, the aircraft was MIA). Analysing the success of the Mosquito missions, the results are as follows:

Contacts   – 38 (46 per cent)
No Contacts – 39 (47 per cent)
Aborts   – 5 (6 per cent)
Cancelled   – 1 (1 per cent)

The apparently high rate of unsuccessful contacts should be seen in its true perspective. Almost half were due to the fact that there was no response from the agent on the ground. Mechanical failures of the aircraft accounted for around 7 per cent of failures, while unserviceability of JE equipment caused 1 per cent. The difficulties facing agents in reaching the agreed target location at the right time and then operating the JE equipment in the required secrecy helps explain the high incidence of lack of response from the ground.

But in retrospect the most disruptive factor to the mounting of JE Mosquito ops was the move of the programme from Watton to Harrington in March 1945. There was an initial lack of preparedness at the latter base and a misunderstanding of the day-to-day management of missions between Col Hudson Upham, the 492nd BG's CO at Harrington, and Lt Cdr Steve Simpson, the JE executive. The OSS's Lt Col Bowman described Upham as 'a very fine officer, recently arrived from the United States with no experience of our type of activity and unwilling to make definite decisions'. A contemporary OSS report on the conduct of JE air operations states: 'From the beginning it seemed to be Colonel Upham's understanding that Cmdr Simpson was merely there [at Harrington] for a short time in an advisory capacity. The Colonel intended putting radio personnel in the JE shop to learn the job, and that all intelligence including the handling of the [airborne JE equipment recording] wire, the dispatch of the missions, the selection of routes based on the signal[led] plans, was to be done by [the 492nd] Group S-2. This was not Cmdr Simpson's understanding.' At the end of March 1945 an exasperated Simpson memo'd Lt Col Bowman: 'Please Colonel – who am I and what am I at Harrington?'

And there was confusion about who should maintain the JE Mosquitoes – engineers from Watton or Harrington. The engineering staff at Harrington were unfamiliar with the Mosquito and this probably led to comparatively poor serviceability. Finally, there was vigorous discussion about the use of individual airframes for training and those for actual operations, along with where to train aircrew. It seems that every aspect of the operation courted controversy. However, a more productive partnership was eventually forged between Albert Schaeffer, the 492nd BG's training officer, and Steve Simpson.

Shining through all this organisational discord and indecision was the performance of the aircrew, who doggedly flew the almost nightly missions in all weathers. It is invidious to single out individual personalities but certain names catch the eye in the JE narrative. In the early days, from November 1944 to February 1945, Robert Walker shouldered the lion's share of the piloting work, with a couple of regular navigators. Thereafter, throughout March and April, the crew comprising pilot Kingdon Knapp and navigator John Jackson slogged away night after night over the Continent, almost to the point of exhaustion. Behind them in the Mosquito on numerous occasions, and equally deserving of the spotlight because of his dedication, was JE operator Calhoun Ancrum, vital to the missions because of his linguistic talents.

RAF Mosquitoes were never operated by a crew of more than two – pilot and nav – and so the role of Calhoun Ancrum and his fellow 'third man' JE operators, incarcerated in the belly of the aircraft, was an unusual and uncomfortable one. It is worth a brief look at a typical day's work. Working closely with OSS HQ, the first task of the rostered operator was to study the agent, or team, to be contacted that night, and acquaint himself with the JE signal plan and the special alphabet used, which varied according to the language and origin of the team. These signal plans and alphabets had to be memorised, as did the contact locations, recognition and danger signals. A call was then made to OSS Communications in London to obtain the necessary intelligence questions and operational messages. This information might need to be translated into French or German. Once the Mosquito crew had completed their flight plan the operator was given details of the route to be taken, which he had to memorise so that if he had to bail out at any point, he would know roughly where he was.

The next event was an 'operational meal', which avoided gaseous foods, such as eggs, for the crews flying at high altitudes. Following the meal was a briefing by the Base G-2 (Army Intelligence) officer that covered Allied ground activity in the planned area of the mission. Arriving at the aircraft earmarked for the task, all personal kit was checked, together with the on-board JE communications equipment. Immediately after take-off all equipment was given another check, with the TR-6 and recording equipment being turned on for five minutes every half hour to prevent it freezing up. On return from missions, which sometimes lasted five or six hours, the JE recording reel would receive priority handling if it contained any particularly 'hot' items of intelligence. Finally, there was a short debrief with the G-2 officer.

Disposal of the Mosquitoes

All the Mosquitoes used for JE operations began their working lives with the 25th BG at Watton before filtering over to Harrington. As already mentioned, NS707 was lost over the UK in April 1945 after an engine fire. The other Mosquitoes that flew operationally, NS676, NS725, RG157 and NS740, all ended up with the scrap man in 1947, although '740 enjoyed a short instructional post-war life as 6232M. The post-war OSS analysis of air operations ruefully reports: 'On the last day of the war, when it was too late to use them, three brand new Mosquitoes were assigned to the J/E operation.' In all probability these were NS686, '709 and TA614. They did not last long in USAAF ownership, all returning to RAF control in June 1945. Of interest, TA614 became G-AOCN on the civil register before becoming 4X-FDL-92 with the Israeli AF.

PR.XVI G-AOCN, ex-TA614 of 492nd Bomb Gp. (Brian Harris collection)

Chapter 5

The F-8 Saga

An important but less well-known element of the USAAF Mosquito story is the part played by the Canadian-built aircraft, known in US service as F-8s. The F-8 saga is interesting in that it began long before the Hatfield-produced PR.XVIs entered service with the 25th BG at Watton in 1944. Back in 1928 the de Havilland Aircraft Co. in Britain had decided to establish a branch in Canada, de Havilland Aircraft of Canada Ltd (DHC). The new plant soon moved to a permanent airfield at Downsview near Toronto in Ontario and began assembling civilian Moths. In 1937 production of Tiger Moths began and the possibility of meeting military requirements was examined. The outbreak of hostilities gave this added stimulus and Downsview's production capabilities, staff, engineering facilities and airfield size were increased to cope with more modern types. Following the type's highly successful first flight on 25 November 1940, and subsequent large-scale orders, the Mosquito might naturally be a candidate. British factories were being bombed and dispersal of production made sense.

The possibility of producing the Mosquito in Canada and the USA was thus formally examined early in the Second World War. With Canadian industry reorganised to support the British war effort, the country's energetic Minister of Munitions and Supply, Clarence 'C D' Howe made a near-fatal sea journey to England in December 1940 (his ship, SS *Western Prince* was torpedoed and sunk and his aide, Gordon Scott, did not survive the incident) 'to discuss matters with the customers'. Early in 1941 he watched displays by the Mosquito and Lancaster, and would have been impressed by both. In April 1941, the American ambassador to the UK, John Winant, together with Maj. Gen. Henry 'Hap' Arnold and Maj. Elwood 'Pete' Quesada of the US Army, travelled to England for three weeks to evaluate UK aircraft production needs and analyse British air operations. Their programme included a display of the Mosquito at Hatfield on 20 April. (Lettice Curtis, the legendary Air Transport Auxiliary pilot, was based there at the time and says: 'We were all hustled off the airfield.') When Arnold returned to the USA he took details of the aircraft back with him.

The Americans, however, were not comfortable with the idea of building a British aircraft, even less a wooden one, though they would be content to operate the Mosquito when it 'better filled roles being flown by US types.' Discussions with the Canadians, on the other hand, proved more fruitful, and in August 1941 a contract for Mosquitoes was placed with DHC.

In September 1941 the de Havilland Company in the UK sent W D Hunter, the senior Hatfield designer, and Harry Povey, its chief production engineer, to Downsview to advise and assist with getting the new contract under way. Povey had played a leading role in galvanising the woodworking industry to support the manufacture of Mosquitoes in the UK. He now displayed the same zeal at Downsview, working tirelessly alongside Philip Garratt, head of DHC, and Hunter to ensure that the first Canadian Mosquito was rolled out within a year of contract signing. Their hard work was rewarded when KB300, a B.VII, was completed and ready for its first flight on 23 September 1942. The original plan was for Geoffrey de Havilland Jr to fly out to Canada to be at the controls, but his departure had been delayed by bad weather and he did not reach Downsview until the 27th. With the race on for production, delay was not an option and the privilege went instead to DHC's chief test pilot, Ralph Spradbrow. The flight went well, and was all the more remarkable for up to that point Spradbrow had flown nothing larger than an Anson. For wartime security reasons there was a news blackout and few Canadians were aware of the momentous event. Ralph Bell, the Canadian Director of Aircraft Production, was there to witness the successful flight and immediately sent a message to Hatfield acknowledging the efforts of Garratt, Hunter and Povey, which had made this milestone possible.

Geoffrey de Havilland Jr was, however, on hand for the prototype's second fight on 2 October and was pleased with the Mosquito's performance. By then press and public had been made aware of the Mosquito's existence and the Downsview workforce turned out in strength to watch the display, which included a number of runs over Toronto. Later in the month and into November, de Havilland Jr gave a series of displays in Canada (including Ottawa) and America (including Wright Field, Ohio). In December Gen. 'Hap' Arnold arranged for a temporary no fly zone of the airspace over Washington DC for de Havilland to give a stunning display over the city in KB300.

De Havilland Jr returned to England by air in early January 1943 but before he did so he gave a display over Toronto in aid of a War Bonds sales drive. Of this he later wrote: 'This was a truly amusing show to do, and one gained a fine impression of speed going well below the tall skyscrapers with 400 mph indicated.'

Back in the second week of September 1942, Hatfield-produced Mosquito B.IV DK287 was loaded aboard the SS *Oregon* at Liverpool for shipment to Canada and Downsview to be used as a pattern. With it went Francis 'Pepe' Burrell, the Mosquito prototype flight shed engineer at Hatfield. This initiative got off to an unfortunate start when '287 was damaged while being unloaded at Halifax docks. However, Burrell accompanied de Havilland Jr on some of the test pilot's early flights in KB300. Little is known about DK287 while in North America except that it met an untimely end, crashing near Wright Field, Ohio, on 14 September 1943. The USAAF pilot, Lt Osmond Ritland, bailed out and survived.

With de Havilland Jr safely back at Hatfield and Ralph Spradbrow taken ill while on a visit to the UK, de Havilland's chief production test pilot at Hatfield, Pat Fillingham, was sent out to Downsview to help with test flying the Canadian machines. Leaving England in early February 1943, he took with him Flt Lt Gerald Wooll, an ex-1 PRU pilot who had made a forced landing in neutral Switzerland on 24 August 1942 following engine failure in Mosquito DK310. After a brief internment he was repatriated in exchange for two Luftwaffe pilots. With a severe shortage of experienced Mosquito pilots in Canada, the British pair made a valuable input to the flying programme at Downsview, which was not without incident. During

Mosquito B.IV DK287 was sent to Downsview, Canada, in 1942 as a pattern for Canadian production. (Author's collection)

a test flight on 26 April an engine caught fire and Wooll and his observer, T J 'Tim' Stone, were forced to bail out over the eastern side of Toronto.

During 1942–45 Downsview produced a total of 1,033 Mosquitoes, in eight different marks. These were: B.VII, B.XX, FB.21, T.22, B.25, FB.26, T.27 and T.29. Of this total, some forty-one airframes were allocated USAAF serial numbers, comprising seven Mk VIIs and thirty-four Mk XXs. In addition, they were allocated British serial numbers, all in the 'KB' series. Both the B.VII and the B.XX were based on the British B.IV, though the latter was fitted with Canadian and US instruments and equipment. Both versions were fitted with Packard-built Merlin engines. Some B.XXs found their way to RAF units in the UK: Nos 128,139, 162, 608, 627 Sqns and 1655 Mosquito Training Unit/16 OTU. (See Appendix B for details) It is the Mosquitoes that ended up in US hands that form the focus of this chapter.

The first Mosquitoes destined for the USAAF, Mk VIIs, began to roll out of Downsview in mid-1943, all following a fairly standard pattern of acceptance through handling and modification centres in the USA. Appendix B gives the individual aircraft movements.

Of the initial batch of Mk VIIs, two airframes had interesting careers. The first of these, KB315, has become something of a celebrity primarily because of its nickname *The 'Spook'*, but also because a little is known of what it achieved. From Downsview it went, in June, to Colorado Springs

Canadian-built Mosquito (possibly 43-34938, KB140) at Downsview. (BAE Systems)

photo recon training base, followed by brief spells at Peterson and Bolling Fields, before being prepared for overseas service. Then, in October, it was ferried to Prestwick, Scotland, by a crew consisting of Maj. James Setchell (pilot) and Capt. Jerome Alexander (navigator). According to Setchell's son, the route was Goose Bay, Bluie West One (Greenland), Meeks Field (Iceland) and Prestwick. Once in the UK, Setchell took *The 'Spook'* down to St Mawgan in Cornwall, from where he ferried it to North Africa. Arriving at La Marsa, Tunisia, he probably joined up with the resident 5th Photo Gp

B.XX KB131 (F-8, 43-34933) at the Bell Modification Center, Buffalo, New York. (Bell Aerospace Textron, Buffalo NY)

Fresh off the Canadian production line at Downsview, this Mosquito is already in USAAF markings as an F-8. (BAE SYSTEMS)

Maj. James Setchell with
KB315 *The 'Spook'*.
(Author's collection)

B.VII KB315 (F-8 43-34926) *The 'Spook'* before being ferried to North Africa by
the Setchell and Alexander crew. (NARA)

before moving on to San Severo, Italy, in December. According to the
American Air Museum, *The 'Spook'* flew through intense flak on both
15 and 16 January 1944 yet returned with valuable photo reconnaissance
information, earning Setchell the DFC. Some sources say that the Mosquito
was lost in a crash landing on 19 August 1944, though this is difficult to
verify. (Setchell had spent very brief periods as CO of the 5th Photo Gp in
January 1943, and the 3rd Photo Gp in November 1943).

B.VII 43-34926 (KB315) later named *The 'Spook'* at Wright Field, USA. (USAAF)

Maj. James Setchell with KB315 *The 'Spook'* at Prestwick, Scotland, en route to La Marsa, Tunisia, between 6 and 15 October 1943. (J Setchell)

B.VII KB317 (43-34928), the first USAAF F-8 Mosquito, was delivered to Wright Field, Ohio, on 1 June 1943. (Dana Bell)

B.XX 43-34933 (KB131) at an airfield in the USA. (DHC collection)

B.VII 43-34926 (KB315) *The 'Spook'* at an airfield in the MTO. (Joe Halliday via Dana Bell)

Another Mk VII with a distinctive nickname was *Faintin' Floozie III*, and by process of elimination this was probably KB312. After standard processing into USAAF service via Colorado Springs, Peterson and Wright Patterson, Lt Col Karl Polifka flew her to North Africa along the South Atlantic ferry route in November. A highly regarded pilot, Polifka would be decorated for his reconnaissance work in the MTO and would later take over command of the North African Photo Reconnaissance Wing from Elliott Roosevelt on the latter's return to England.

A third Mk VII set off for North Africa in late 1943, but didn't make it. On 27 November Maj. Harry Eidson took off in KB326/43-34929, from Miami, Florida, with the South Atlantic Ferry Route in his flight plan. Calling at Natal, Brazil, to refuel he then made for his next staging post, Wideawake Field on Ascension Island, which he reached without incident. But less than an hour out of Wideawake his troubles began when an engine temperature went into the red. With a long overwater leg ahead of him, prudence ruled and he decided to return to Ascension. But with loss of power and gear and flaps down the Mosquito became difficult to control and his arrival turned into a crash landing. Eidson walked away from the write-off but would need to make alternative arrangements to reach combat in the Mediterranean.

Deliveries of Mk XX Mosquitoes began in May 1944, KB130 and '131 going to Eglin Field, Florida, the proving ground for aircraft armament

Canadian-built B.XX KB149 (43-34943) at Downsview, Canada, in 1944. (Bae Systems)

Mosquito B.XXs at Downsville, Canada. Visible in the line on the left is KB158 (43-34952). (de Havilland Aircraft Museum)

In July and August 1944, B.XXs KB139, '180 and '182 transited through Grenier, New Hampshire, USA. (USAAF)

B.VII 43-34926 (KB315) *The 'Spook'* possibly at La Marsa, Algeria, in 1944. (Dana Bell)

B.XX 43-34946 (KB152) after a landing accident at Robins Field, USA, on 21 April 1944. (T Theonig collection)

B.XX KB171 (43-34930) after a take-off accident at Fort Dix, New Jersey, on 11 March 1944, when piloted by Maj. Frederick Borosdi. (NARA)

(and the primary training location for Jimmy Doolittle's B-25 raid on the Japanese mainland in April 1942). Thereafter, throughout 1944, practically all the Mk XXs went initially to the aircraft modification centre at Niagara Falls for the installation of American equipment. What seems to be common to all the Canadian-built Mosquitoes is that throughout 1944 they moved rapidly between major centres of specialist activity in the USA before allocation to specific duties.

Back in September 1943 bids by the USAAF for Mosquitoes had included the possible allocation of Canadian-built Mk XXs. Now, between May and July 1944, delivery of these to the UK took place. Sharp and Bowyer in *Mosquito* state that: '… 11 F-8s were now with No. 375 Servicing Squadron, USAAF, Watton. Early machines, all had been maintained at Rome/Romulus and Hunter Field, and they were all that came from 25 scheduled. Cracked side cowlings, damaged leading edges and control surfaces, oil leakages, all were apparent. They were passed to the RAF for renovation in exchange for PR.XVIs.' The individual Aircraft History Cards mention Rome/Romulus and give an idea of which airframes were involved.

B.XX KB131 (F-8, 43-34933) at the Bell Modification Center, Buffalo, New York, in 1944. (Bell Aerospace Textron, Buffalo, NY)

Col Newman and Capt. Gordon collecting B.XX (F-8) 43-34943 (KB149) for delivery to Romulus Field, Michigan, on 13 January 1944. (USAAF)

Another F-8 for which an interesting description of activity exists is KB186/43-34960. This airframe was assigned to the NACA Langley Memorial Laboratory at Langley Field, Virginia, from 24 August 1944 until 19 January 1945 for tests of lateral and directional stability and control characteristics. The air tests were flown by William 'Bill' Gray Jnr during October and November 1944 and on completion he wrote wrote a report for the AAF Air Technical Service Command. In his introduction, Gray stresses that his data has no bearing on the performance characteristics of the Mosquito, 'which were not measured in these tests, but which were considered to be exceptionally good.' He did, however, note one particular vice of the aircraft: 'The rudder control was inadequate during take-off and landing and was insufficient to fly the airplane with one engine inoperative and the other engine delivering power for level flight with the flaps and gear down.' That characteristic caught many a military pilot out.

In retrospect the F-8 programme gives the impression of being undistinguished, with individual aircraft on the whole performing low-profile, but probably quite useful, work at the various Army establishments

B.XX KB186 (F-8, 43-34960) at Langley Field, Virginia, for stability tests in 1945. (NACA)

around the Continental United States. They did at least provide American pilots with some initial experience of handling the feisty Mosquito from mid-1943 onwards before the USAAF got stuck into operations proper from early 1944 with PR.XVIs and later with NF.XXXs.

Chapter 6

Mosquitoes with the US Navy

A small number of Mosquitoes found their way to the US Navy during the Second World War for test and evaluation. Known details are set out below.

PZ467 With its nose-mounted, rapid-fire 57mm Molins gun, this Mk XVIII 'Tsetse' was shipped out to Patuxent River Naval Air Station (via Dorval, Quebec, Canada) arriving on 30 April 1945. Allotted the Bureau of Aeronautics Number 91106, it took part in a programme to evaluate the use of large-calibre, airframe-mounted weapons against surface vessels. A number of test sorties were flown against floating targets anchored in Chesapeake Bay, after which engineering officer Lt (jg) Walter Deschler, who flew as an observer, commented that during sustained bursts of fire the Mosquito hesitated in the air due to recoil. Later, registered NX66422 and named *The Silver Streak*, the Mosquito found its way into US civil ownership.

FB.XVIII 'Tsetse' PZ467, with 57mm Molins gun, marked as AT-2, ready for armament test and evaluation with the US Navy in 1945. (Alex Crawford)

FB.XVIII, ex-PZ467, in the USA in 1947 with pilot Jean Doar. (N Malayney via Alex Crawford)

FB.XVIII, ex-PZ467, pictured in the USA in 1947 when registered NX66422 and named *The Silver Streak*. (via Alex Crawford)

KB300 This B.VII was ferried to Naval Air Station Anacostia, Washington DC, in March 1943 for evaluation by the US Navy. Despite author enquiries to the National Naval Aviation Museum in Pensacola, and Naval History and Heritage Command, no details of the evaluation have surfaced.

B.VII KB300 at Anacostia, USA, in April 1943. (worldwarphotos)

KB115 Another Mosquito that appears to have been trialled by, or perhaps just demonstrated to, the US Navy was this Canadian-built B.XX. Photographs, with the caption 'Naval Air Experimental Station, Navy Yard, Philadelphia, March 1944', show it airborne over what appears to be the US countryside. The only other movements recorded for the aircraft are that it served with the UK's Royal Aircraft Establishment and was struck off charge on 1 November 1946.

Canadian-built B.XX KB115 airborne from the US Naval Experimental Station, Philadelphia, in March 1944 (Dana Bell)

Chapter 7

Postscript

Some Mosquitoes escaped the scrap man's axe at the completion of their wartime careers with the USAAF and either served on under a new owner or were preserved in part or in whole in museums. The details of one or two notable ones are set out below.

Leonard Cheshire's Mosquitoes

In 1946, after a distinguished wartime career as a bomber commander, Victoria Cross holder Group Captain Leonard Cheshire founded an organisation for ex-servicemen called Vade in Pacem (VIP, meaning Go in Peace). This set out to create a 'classless colony in which training, prosperity and fulfilment would result from united effort and mutual support'. To support and provide publicity for this initiative, Cheshire bought two ex-25th BG Mosquito PR.XVIs, NS811 and NS812, which were allocated the civilian registrations G-AIRU and G-AIRT. Cheshire acquired them through Marshalls of Cambridge, who advised him on 23 October 1946 that they were ready for collection from 44 MU at Edzell in Scotland. The newspaper the *Sunday Graphic* sponsored one of them, but unfortunately the insurance for the Mosquitoes came to a crippling £750, which he could ill afford and which probably explains why he kept them for such a short time. Both aircraft were very soon destined for the Israel Air Force. G-AIRU crashed at Ajaccio, Corsica, on 17 July 1948 on delivery, while G-AIRT was flown to Nice on 16 July en route to Israel but was written off on 13 January 1957.

The Loss and Dig of NS555

NS555 of the 802nd Recon Gp (Prov) took off on 8 June 1944 on a *Rooster* mission to photograph the D-Day beaches, crewed by pilot Capt. Walter Gernand and 8th Combat Camera Unit photographer Sgt Ebbet Lynch. Some time later, on the return flight it crashed near High Wycombe,

Buckinghamshire, killing both men, as described in the 25th Bomb Gp narrative. In 1972 The Chiltern Historical Aircraft Preservation Group carried out an investigation of the site and in 1980 group member A L Mason wrote to the author describing the dig:

> We recovered one of the Merlins from the site of the crash on a railway embankment on the Wycombe-Bourne End line, close to the A40 road. Gernand's graduation ring was found and traced to Baylor University, Waco, Texas, and after lengthy correspondence the pilot's mother was traced. She presented the ring to the University where it is now exhibited as part of a memorial to the pilot. I have documented the 'dig' and have photographs of the ring, but so far have no picture of the actual aircraft. The Merlin and other components, including parts of the camera, are stored at Booker Airfield, near High Wycombe, where we hope to set up a small museum in the near future.

The group presented the Merlin to the de Havilland Aircraft Heritage Centre – now the De Havilland Aircraft Museum – in April 1995, where it is now on display.

The Loss and Dig of NS582

This Mosquito was lost during a night *Joker* mission to Duisburg, Germany, on 25 October 1944. Pilot Lt George Brooks was killed but navigator Lt Richard Taylor survived. (Details in 25th Bomb Gp narrative). A crash investigation team led by Erwin Vanden Broecke visited the crash site at Vladslo in Belgium for a second time in 1998 with a metal detector and, with permission from the landowner, confirmed they were dealing with a Mosquito. The crash site was located near a polder stream in clay soil and a dig team assembled on 13 August and began work with a 'crane'. Fifteen minutes later pieces of scrap emerged, and after half an hour of digging an oxygen cylinder and a fragment of landing leg came to the surface. Efforts to locate one of the Merlin engines proved elusive, but a second landing gear was found together with large pieces of wood and the wing main spar. From the state of the components it was clear that aircraft and engines had disintegrated on impact, suggesting a high impact speed and 'small angle of approach'.

POSTSCRIPT

The final haul amounted to two oxygen cylinders, the support frame of the Merlin engine, together with a crankshaft and other engine fragments. A turbo supercharger, which was initially reluctant to leave the earth, was eventually retrieved, along with a landing gear motor, the two landing gears, four shock absorbers and two tyres, and a bomb hook. According to Erwin Broecke, '582's navigator Richard Taylor was traced and remembered the crash well. He also confirmed it was their thirteenth mission.

Ex-USAAF Mosquito PR.XVIs for the Royal Navy

In the immediate post-war years the RN took on charge some thirty-eight ex-air force Mosquito PR.XVIs, some ex-RAF but around fifteen of which had served exclusively with the USAAF's 25th Bomb Gp. Typically, these particular airframes were stored at 44 MU Edzell, Scotland, following the end of hostilities for a couple of years and then served in the Fleet Requirements role with the Navy's 771 Sqn at Ford in the UK, and 728 Sqn based at Hal Far, Malta. Duties included communications, training and exercises with the Fleet, over the years 1948–52.

At the end of hostilities PR.XVI NS753 was allocated to the Royal Navy and received the civilian registration G-AOCK, but during the war it was on the strength of the 653rd Bomb Sqn. (MAP)

A Mosquito for the National Museum of the USAF

Although not an-ex USAAF machine, the museum owns immaculately restored 'NS519', resplendent in authentic markings as 'P' of the 653rd Bomb Sqn, 25th Bomb Gp, Watton, 1944. This is actually RS709, which was built as a B.35 by Airspeed and then converted to a TT.35. It served first with 236 OCU, the maritime reconnaissance conversion unit, at Kinloss, Scotland, as a support aircraft. From there it moved on to 3/4 Civilian Anti-Aircraft Co-operation Unit at Exeter, Devon, a specialist target facilities outfit. After support to the military, '709 was sold on 11 July 1963 and put on the civilian register as G-ASKA, playing a star role in the films *633 Squadron* (1963) and *Mosquito Squadron* (1968). In 1966 it was part of the Skyfame Collection at Staverton, Gloucester. Allocated the US civilian registration N9797 in August 1969, it was then acquired by American collector Kermit Weeks in 1981. It later carried the registrations N98DH and G-MOSI. It has been on loan to the Experimental Aircraft Association Museum at Oshkosh, Wisconsin, since 1991.

No. 3 Civilian Anti-Aircraft Co-operation Unit's TT.35 at Exeter in 1963. It would eventually be displayed in the Wright Patterson Museum in USAAF markings. (Bill Fisher)

Mosquito TT.35 N9797 (ex-RS709, ex-G-ASKA) of Vintage Aircraft International at Booker, UK, on 10 July 1971. (John Bolt via Peter Davis)

TT.35 ex-RS709 with No. 3 Civilian Anti-Aircraft Co-operation Unit, posing as PR.XVI NS519 'P' of 653rd Bomb Sqn, 25th Bomb Gp at the Wright Patterson Museum. (USAF)

Acknowledgements

I would like to say special thanks to Dana Bell, whose enthusiasm and interest in the early days and recent most generous donation of his photograph collection is much appreciated; to Garry Pape for his kindness in providing 416th NFS data; and to Norman Malayney for forwarding the Daily Operations Reports for the 416th NFS from the US National Archives. In addition, the following people have provided invaluable assistance: Alex Bainbridge (Eberly Family Special Collections Library, Penn State University Libraries); Elizabeth C Borja (Reference Services Archivist at the National Air & Space Museum) for F-8 Aircraft History Cards; Martin Bowman; Hugh Bozarth; Bill Cannon; Wayne Comment; Alex Crawford; Marvin Edwards; Brick Eisel; Thomas Ensminger; Tom Fields; Peter Frost; Dick Gamma; Lynn O Gamma; Maria Hanna (Nat Archives, Washington DC); Robert Howle; Peter George; Gene Goodbread; William Grey; Hayden Hamilton; Jennings Heilig; Harry Holmes; Karl Kjarsgaard; Garry Lakin (de Havilland Aircraft Museum); Barbara Ann Lee (AFHRC, Maxwell AFB, Alabama); Vic Maslen; A Mason (Chiltern Historical Aircraft Preservation Gp); Frank McKee; Peter Moss (for IT assistance); Sylvia Naylor (National Archives, College Park, Maryland); Wiley Noble; Garry Pape; Budd Peaslee; Vivian Rogers-Price (Director – Roger A Freeman 8th AF Research Center, USA) Elliott Roosevelt; Peter Rustman; George Sesler; Joseph Stenglein; Roy Tebbutt at the Carpetbagger Aviation Museum, Harrington; Andrew Thomas; Gordon Thompson; Warren Thompson; John Tipton; Chuck Tolley; Russel Zorn.

Abbreviations & Glossary

AD	Air Division
AFS	Advanced Flying School
AHU	Aircraft Holding Unit (RN)
ALG	Advanced Landing Ground
Aphrodite	Remotely controlled B-17 drone, filled with explosives, planned to be dumped on a target
ASN	Aviation Safety Network
'Baby'	the explosive-filled drone in the *Aphrodite* missions
BAD	Base Air Depot (BAD 1 – Burtonwood; BAD 2 – Warton; BAD 3 – Langford Lodge)
'Blower'	Supercharger
Bluestocking	Weather recon mission over Europe to assist the operational planners in their selection of targets
CAACU	Civilian Anti-Aircraft Co-operation Unit
CAS	Chief of the Air Staff (UK)
Categories (aircraft operational state)	
'C'	Allocated to Instructional Airframe duties (for ground training)
'E'	Write-off
CCU	Combat Camera Unit
CFS	Central Flying School
DBR	Damaged Beyond Repair
Dilly	Night photography of enemy V-1 activity in France
EM	Enlisted Men
ERS	Emergency Rescue Squadron
ETO	European Theatre of Operations
FIDO	Fog Intensive Dispersal Operation
F/O	Flight Officer (USAAF rank)
Frantic	Shuttle missions to Poltava, Ukraine

FRU	Fleet Requirements Unit (RN)
FTR	Failed to Return From
FTU	Ferry Training Unit
Gee	Allied radio pulse system by which aircraft could fix their position by reference to three transmitting stations in England
GIA	Ground Instructional Airframe
Gp	Group
Graypea	Chaff dispensing mission flown by 653rd Bomb Sqn
H2X	US version of British H2S – airborne radio set that could paint a shadowy image of the ground below on a cathode ray tube for its operator in an aircraft above.
IP	Initial Point
Jedburgh	Teams of Allied agents, usually consisting of three individuals – a commander, an exec officer, and a radio operator – parachuted, usually by night, onto the Continent. (aka 'Jeds')
Joker	Night flash bomb photography
KIFA	Killed in Flying Accident
KIA	Killed in Action
LORAN	LOng RAnge Navigation – Long-range radio navigation aid
MAAF	Mediterranean Allied Air Force
MIA	Missing In Action
Mickey	H2X radar trials & ops
NACA	National Advisory Committee for Aeronautics
NARA	US National Archives & Records Administration
NMI	No Major Injuries
No-Ball	Attacks on V-1 launching sites
Oboe	Ground-controlled blind bombing radar system
OCU	Operational Conversion Unit
OSS	Office of Strategic Services. US intelligence agency formed during the Second World War.

PFC	Private First Class
RAF Del	RAF Delegation
RDU	Receipt & Despatch Unit (RN)
Rebecca/Eureka (Transponding radar)	A short-range radio navigation system used in the dropping of airborne forces and their supplies. It consisted of two parts: the Rebecca airborne transceiver and antenna system, and the Eureka ground-based transponder.
Redstocking	Mosquito mission in support of OSS tasks
Redtail	Monitoring of actual bombing ops by a 'Command Observer' from Wing HQ flying in a Mosquito
RNARY	Royal Naval Aircraft Repair Yard (RN)
RO	Radar Operator
ROS	Repaired On Site
Rooster	Experimental rear-looking radar
RIW	Repaired in Works
RTU	Returned to Unit
RV	Rendezvous
Seaweed	Photo reconnaissance of French sea ports
SHAEF	Supreme Headquarters Allied Expeditionary Force
Sharon	Long-distance B-17 weather missions to the Azores
Skywave	LORAN calibration flights to determine navigational effectiveness of aircraft equipment and ground emitting radar chains at various distances and locations
SOC	Struck Off Charge
SOP	Standard Operating Procedure
S-phone	A UHF duplex radio telephone system developed during the Second World War for use by SOE agents working behind enemy lines to communicate with friendly aircraft and co-ordinate landings and the dropping of agents and supplies.
VCAS	Vice-Chief of the Air Staff (UK)
WO	Warrant Officer
WRS	Weather Reconnaissance Sqn

Sources

Babington-Smith, Constance, *Evidence in Camera*, David & Charles, 1974.

Bagshaw, Deacon, Pollock & Thomas, *RAF Little Rissington: The CFS Yrs*, Pen & Sword, 2006.

Brookes, Andrew, *Air War Over Europe*, Ian Allan, 2000.

Christie, Carl, *Ocean Bridge*, Midland Publishing, 1995.

Curtis, Lettice, *The Forgotten Pilots*, G T Foulis, 1971.

Davis, Richard G, *Carl A Spaatz and the War in Europe*, Smithsonian Inst Press.

Delve, Ken, *The Military Airfields of Britain, East Anglia, Norfolk & Suffolk*, Crowood, 2005.

Downing, Taylor, *Spies in the Sky*, Little, Brown, 2011.

Fairbairn, Tony, *Action Stations Overseas*, Patrick Stephens, 1991. *RAF Gibraltar*, Tempus, 2002

Freeman, R, *The Mighty Eighth*, Arms & Armour, 1989.

Mighty Eighth War Diary, Jane's, 1981.

Mighty Eighth War Manual, Jane's, 1984.

Camouflage & Markings: British Aircraft in USAAF Service, 1942–45, Ducimus.

Goddard, George, *Overview: A Lifelong Adventure in Aerial Photography*, Doubleday, 1969.

Hansen, Chris, *Enfant Terrible: The Times & Schemes of General Elliott Roosevelt*, Able Baker Press, 2012.

Harrington, Janine, *RAF Foulsham 1942–54*, RAF 100 Gp Assn, 2012.

Holmes, Harry, *The World's Greatest Air Depot: The US 8th Air Force at Warton 1942–45*, Airlife, 1998.

Leaf, Edward, *Above All Unseen: The Royal Air Force's Photographic Reconnaissance Units 1939–45*, Patrick Stephens, 1997.

Malayney, Norman, *The 25th Bomb Group (Rcn) in World War II*, Schiffer Military History, 2011.

Maurer Maurer (Eds), *Air Force Combat Units of World War II*, Office of Air Force History. 1983.

– *World War II Combat Squadrons of the United States Air Force*, Smithmark, 1992.

McLean, Steven, *Squadron of the SAAF & their aircraft 1920–2005*, Self Pub, 2005.

Middlebrook, Martin & Chris Everitt, *The Bomber Command War Diaries*, Viking, 1985.

Morris, Richard, *Cheshire – The Biography of Leonard Cheshire VC OM*, Penguin, 2001.

Nesbit, Roy Conyers, *Eyes of the RAF: A History of Photo-Reconnaissance*. Sutton, 1998.

Olsen, Jack, *Aphrodite: Desperate Mission*, Putnam, 1970.

Pape, Garry R & Ronald C Harrison, *Queen of the Midnight Skies*, Schiffer Military History, 1992.

Parnell, Ben, *Carpetbaggers: America's Secret War in Europe*, Eakin Press, 1993.

Persico, Joseph, *Piercing the Reich*, Sphere, 1980.

Rawlings, John, *Coastal, Support & Special Sqns of the RAF & Their Aircraft*, Janes, 1982.

Rust, Kenn, *Twelfth Air Force Story*, Historical Aviation Album, 1975.

Saunders, Hilary St George, *Royal Air Force 1939–1945, Vol. III, The Fight is Won,* HMSO.

Scutts, Jerry, *Lockheed P-38 Lightning*, Crowood, 2006.

Sesler, George R, *Aerial Intelligence of the 8th Air Force*, Taylor Publishing, 1986.

Sharp, C Martin & Michael Bowyer, *Mosquito*, Faber, 1967.

Smith, David J, *Action Stations 7: Military Airfields of Scotland, the North East and N. Ireland*, PSL, 1983.

Smith, Starr, *Jimmy Stewart: Bomber Pilot*, Zenith Press, 2005.

Spooner, Tony, *Warburton's War*, William Kimber, 1987.

Sturtivant R + Mick Burrow & Lee Howard, *Fleet Air Arm Fixed-Wing Aircraft Since 1946*, Air Britain, 2004.

Documents

UK National Archives

AIR 27/1524 – ORB for 256 Sqn, RAF

AVIA 5/24/W2189 – Accident Investigation Report – *Loss of Mosquito NS707*

AVIA 5/24/W2129 – Accident Investigation Report – *Loss of Mosquito NS757*

SOURCES

Folder: *Mosquitoes for the USAAF*

RAF Museum
Individual Aircraft Movement Cards

Roger A Freeman Eighth Air Force Research Center
National Museum of the Mighty Eighth Air Force, Pooler, Georgia

US Air Force Historical Research Agency
Reel A0666 – 492nd BG/856th BS
Reels B0093, B0094, B0095 – 25th BG

National Archives, College Park, Maryland, USA
Document RG226, Entry 190, Folder 40 – *Joan Eleanor Log Book*

National Air & Space Museum
USAAF Aircraft History Cards, ACR-88, Roll 49

US National Archives, Washington
Daily Operations Reports for the 416th NFS

Miscellaneous
RAF Acklington War Diary
McFarland, Stephen L, *Conquering the Night.* [US] Air Force History and
     Museums Program study on the USAAF in the Second World War, 1997

Harrington Museum
Characteristics of Carpetbagger Flying
Carpetbagger Ops – The Operational Cycle
492nd Bomb Group Records

Washington National Records Center
Outline History, 416th Night Fighter Squadron
War Diary, 416th Night Fighter Squadron

Oral History
Talmidge Simpson (navigator with 416th NFS) interviewed by Norman
     Malayney on 12 January 2008

Websites

www.ww2.com/threads/dh98-mosquito-loss-records.51595 has details from
    ARCs 600squadronassociation.com
www.aahs-online.org_journals_files_583214
www.aeroflight.co.uk
www.airhistory.org.uk/dh_/DH98 production list
airforcehistoryindex.org
www.americanmuseum.com
www.aviationarcheology.com
www.aviation-safety.net
www.axis-and-allies-paintworks.com
casmuseum.org
www.cia.gov
earlyradiohistory.us
www.fieldsofhonor-database.com
www.harringtonmuseum.org.uk
http://militarybases.com/colorado/peterson
http://militaryradio.com
www.peterson.af.mil
www.usafunithistories.com
www.virtualmuseum.caw
forum.12oclockhigh.net (Vance Chipman)
www.stelzriede.com/warstory.htm

Appendix A

Serial Numbers of UK-Built USAAF Mosquitoes

Sect A: PR.XVI

Ser No	Remarks
MM308	Alconbury for H2X conversion 22.2.44; DBR in crash landing 12.5.44 (pilot 2/Lt Henry Stewart & nav H Gruis OK); SOC 22.8.44
MM310	To Langford Lodge 2.2.44; written off in belly landing at Warton 17.6.44 (pilot Charlie Himes OK)
MM311	To Alconbury 22.2.44 for H2X conversion; MIA 7.8.44 (crew both killed); some sources say 'Not Delivered'
MM337	Burtonwood 11.2.44; Nuthampstead Feb 44 – 8th Recon Gp (Sp) (P); landing accdt 3.3.44 (pilot Ed Maslow & instr pilot Oliver Emmel both OK); Cheddington Mar 44 – 802nd Recon Gp (Sp) (P); Watton 21.2.45; 10 MU 16.6.45; SOC 31.7.46
MM338	Burtonwood 11.2.44; Watton Apr (?) 44 – 653rd BS; 10 MU 16.6.45; to Armee de l'Air 20.10.47
MM340	Burtonwood 12.2.44; Nuthampstead Feb 44 – 8th Recon Gp (Sp) (P); ground looped at Warton 18.3.44 (pilot Charles Himes OK); Watton 21.2.45; 44 MU 10.8.45; SOC 29.1.47
MM342	Burtonwood 14.2.44; Cheddington Mar 44 – 802nd Recon Gp (Sp)(P); Watton – 653rd BS 'P'; minor accdt 20.1.45 (pilot Joseph Polovick OK); to RN Det 44 MU Edzell 25.3.47; AHU Stretton 27.3.47; Gosport/RNARY Fleetlands for repair 3.47; AHU Stretton 5.5.47; DH Leavesden 7.1.48; AHU Stretton 11.5.49; RNAS Yeovilton Holding Sect 15.3.51; RDU Culham 20.7.51; Airwork FRU Hurn 17.10.52; AHU Lossiemouth 6.10.53; scrapped 13.1.58
MM344	Burtonwood 12.2.44; Cheddington Mar 44 – 802nd Recon Gp (Sp)(P); take-off accdt at Cheddington 22.3.44 (pilot George Hand OK): Watton 30.9.44 – 653rd/654th BSs; 10 MU 16.6.45; SOC 25.7.46

Ser No	Remarks
MM345	Burtonwood 12.2.44; Cheddington Mar 44; Watton – 653rd BS 'Z' named *The Beast*; landing accdt 8.10.44 (pilot Robert Grimes OK); landing accdt 7.12.44 (pilot George Hand OK); ground looped 20.2.45 (pilot Warren Davis OK); ROS by 71 MU 27.2.45; 10 MU 16.6.45; SOC 25.7.46
MM346	Burtonwood 16.2.44; Cheddington Apr 44; Watton 12.4.44 – 802nd Recon Gp; ground looped on take-off 11.6.44 (pilot Robert Shoenhair OK); 653rd BS 'M' 9.8.44; 44 MU 21.2.46; to Gosport/RNARY Fleetlands 17.12.46; port engine failed on test flight – crashed 1 mile from end of runway at RNAS Stretton, Cheshire 9.12.48 – crew of Lt B Nash & AM D Hancocks unhurt
MM364	Burtonwood 7.3.44; Cheddington Mar 44; Watton Apr 44 – 802nd Recon Gp/654th BS 'C'; take-off accdt 29.8.44 (pilot Clayton Hackman OK); landing accdt 14.1.45 (pilot George Vanderleest OK); 27 MU date ?; to RN 22.8.45; AHU Stretton 1.49; 771 Sqn Ford 9.9.50; overshot runway 4.12.50 but repaired; at AHU Lossiemouth 7.53; sold to R A Short for scrap 25.11.53
MM368	Burtonwood 8.3.44; Cheddington Mar 44 – 802nd Recon Gp; Watton 802nd Recon Gp/ 653rd BS; Incidents: (1) While taxiing for t/o, 7.8.44, pilot 2/Lt Ford Porter selected landing gear retraction instead of flap lever. Damage to engines, main gear & bomb bay doors. (2) Take-off accdt 27.11.44 (pilot 2/Lt Simon Pilson); (3) Landing accdt 20.4.45 (pilot 2/Lt Lyall Barnhart): 57 MU 22.8.45; to RN & AHU Stretton 25.10.46; DH Leavesden 1.49; AHU Stretton 1.50; RNAS Yeovilton 1.51; RDU Culham 1.52; sold to R A Short for scrap 23.7.53
MM370	Burtonwood 11.3.44; Cheddington 4.4.44; Watton – 654th BS; Lost over target Le Havre 13.8.44 (pilot Sanner PoW, cameraman Kurjack KIA)
MM371	Burtonwood 11.3.44; Cheddington 4.4.44; Watton Apr 44 – 653rd BS 'Y'; landing accdt 18.12.44 (pilot 2/Lt Jerry Roberts OK)
MM384	Burtonwood 11.3.44; Watton Apr 44 – 802nd Recon Gp/654th BS; landing accdt 26.4.44 (pilot Richard Peterson OK); ground looped 18.9.44 by pilot Lt Claybourne Vinyard (nav Lt John O'Mara))
MM385	Burtonwood 11.3.44; Cheddington Mar 44 – 802nd Recon Gp; take-off accdt at Cheddington 24.3.44 (pilot Capt. Thomas Hughes OK); de Havilland, Hatfield, for repair 11.4.44; 10 MU 4.11.44; Watton 19.1.45 – 654th BS; 10 MU 16.6.45; 51 MU where sold for scrap to Lunzer & Co. 23.7.47

Ser No	Remarks
MM386	Burtonwood 4.5.44; Watton – 653rd BS; crashed Wendling, Suffolk 6.11.44 (crew both killed)
MM387	Burtonwood 18.3.44; Watton – 653rd BS; written off after landing accdt 13.4.45 (pilot John Larkin OK); SOC 7.5.45
MM388	Burtonwood 19.3.44; Watton 9.2.45 – 654th BS; crash landing at Hatfield 2.9.44 (Vance Chipman); landing accdt Alconbury 18.2.45 (Robert Howle); ground looped Chalgrove 18.6.45 (pilot John Hoover); 71 MU 27.2.45; SOC 19.10.45
MM391	Burtonwood 12.3.44; Watton 30.4.44 – 653rd BS; belly landing at Watton 9.9.44 (pilot John Noble); 10 MU 16.6.45; 51 MU 11.12.45; to French AF 3.7.46
MM393	Burtonwood 14.3.44; 10 MU 16.6.45; SOC 13.2.47
NS508	Burtonwood 4.4.44; Watton – 8th Light Weather Sqn/653rd BS 'G'/654th BS
NS509	Burtonwood 4.4.44; Watton – 653rd BS 'H'; shot down over Germany 21.1.45 (crew both KIA)
NS510	Date of delivery to USAAF not listed. Recorded involved in landing accident at North Pickenham on 25.7.44 while piloted by Jonah Good bread/Warren Barber of 8th WRS, 802nd Recon Gp
NS512	Burtonwood 5.4.44; Watton – 653rd BS; landing accdt 13.4.45 (John Larkin – CO 654th BS – NMI); SOC 5.5.45
NS513	Burtonwood 4.4.44; Watton – 653rd BS; written off in landing accdt at Watton 14.9.44 (Lt Ford Porter OK).
NS514	Burtonwood 5.4.44; Watton – 653rd BS 'L'; written off in take-off accdt at RAF Tangmere 22.10.44
NS515	Burtonwood 6.4.44; Watton – 653rd BS; crashed on take-off 22.11.44 (crew both killed)
NS516	Burtonwood 11.4.44; Watton – 653rd BS; landing accdt North Pickenham 11.4.45 (pilot Lt Edward Hodges); SOC 4.5.45
NS518	Burtonwood 12.4.44; Watton – 802nd RG; take-off accdt 3.6.44 (pilot Lt Harold James OK) – minimum damage
NS519	Burtonwood 12.4.44; Watton – 653rd BS; crashed after take-off 27.12.44 – Lt Morton Hunt – OK; SOC 15.1.45
NS533	Burtonwood 4.5.44; Watton – 653rd BS 'Q'; shot down by P-51 12.8.44 (pilot killed, nav evaded)
NS535	Burtonwood 12.5.44; Watton Jun 44 – 802nd BG, 8th Sp Sqn 'A'; landing accdt at North Pickenham 13.6.44 (pilot Lt Otto Kaellner OK)

Ser No	Remarks
NS537	Burtonwood 8.5.44; Watton – 8th Light Weather Sqn; FTR from weather recon mission over N Sea 7.7.44 (crew KIA)
NS538	Alconbury 4.7.44; 654th BS 'F'; exploded in mid-air 3 miles SE of RAF Newmarket, UK 8.9.44 (crew both KIFA)
NS551	Burtonwood 12.5.44; Watton – 802nd BG, 8th Sp Sqn/654th BS; 10 MU 16.6.45; to School of Photography; became 5952M on 13.6.46
NS552	To USAAF 31.5.44; 654th BS 'G'; landing accdt Warton 21.9.44 (pilot Peter Dustman) – minor damage; T/O accdt 23.3.45 (pilot Morton Hunt – substantial damage but crew OK); repaired by 71 MU at Watton; 10 MU 16.6.45; SOC 25.7.46
NS553	Burtonwood 15.5.44; Watton – 654th BS 'P'; landing accdt Snetterton Heath 26.5.44 (pilot Otto Kaellner OK); 10 MU 18.6.45; SOC 25.7.46
NS554	Burtonwood 13.5.44; Watton – 8th Sp Sqn/654th BS 'P'; 44 MU 22.6.45
NS555	Watton 19.5.44; 8th Sp Sqn 'A'; lost control in cloud on return from mission and crashed near High Wycombe, UK, 8.6.44 (crew killed)
NS556	Watton 7.6.44; 654th BS 'J'; landing accdt at RAF Foulsham after engine failure 21.3.45 (pilot Lt Richard Geary OK); SOC 27.2.45
NS557	Watton 7.6.44; 8th Sp Sqn; landing accdt Langford Lodge 6.8.44 (pilot 2/Lt James Matuska OK); SOC 28.8.44
NS558	Watton 14.6.44; 8th Sp Sqn; H2X prototype for USAAF; struck barrage balloon near Gravesend, UK and crashed killing crew 21.6.44
NS559	Watton 9.6.44; 8th S Sqn/654th BS; landing accdt Watton 1.2.45 (pilot Lt Alan Bateman, nav Lt H Mann OK); ROS by 71 MU 8.2.45; 10 MU 16.6.45; SOC 25.7.46
NS568	Watton 23.5.44 – 654th BS; crash landing 2 miles west of RAF North Pickenham, UK 6.11.44 (pilot killed, nav injured); SOC 30.12.44
NS569	Watton 15.6.44 – 654th BS; take-off accdt 4.4.45 – DBR (pilot John Murphy OK); SOC 18.4.45
NS570	Watton 14.6.44 – 653rd BS; shot down by night fighter over Germany 24.9.44 (crew both PoWs)
NS574	Watton 1.7.44; Benson 12.7.44 (probably to 540 Sqn, RAF); 27 MU 19.9.44; to French AF 12.7.46

Ser No	Remarks
NS577	Watton 5.7.44; Benson 12.7.44 (probably to 540 Sqn, RAF); 27 MU 17.8.44; to French AF 9.8.46
NS581	Watton 17.6.44 – 654th BS 'Q'; 10 MU 16.6.45; 22 MU 15.12.45; SOC 15.8.47
NS582	Watton 17.6.44 – 654th BS 'R'; Crashed in Belgium 25.10.44 (pilot KIA, nav RTU)
NS583	Watton 17.6.44 – 654th BS; crashed in Germany during *Joker* mission 8.2.45
NS584	Alconbury 19.7.44 – 654th BS 'D'; Harrington – 492nd BG; had bulbous nose housing H2X; DBR in T/O accdt 3.4.45 – DBR (pilot Lt Col Robert Boone CO of 856th BS OK)
NS585	Watton 29.6.44 – 8th Light Weather Sqn/653rd BS 'D'; 22 MU 24.10.45; to French AF 10.7.46
NS590	Watton 2.7.44 – 654th BS 'SB'; Incidents: (1) take-off accdt 27.8.44 (pilot Otto Kaellner) (2) landing accdt 7.12.44 (pilot Lt John Carter) (3) landing accdt 5.5.45 (pilot Lt Lyndon Lakeman OK); 10 MU 18.6.45; SOC 4.9.47
NS591	Watton 23.6.44 – 653rd BS 'S'; to French AF 17.7.46
NS592	Watton 29.6.44 – 653rd/654th BSs; to RN Det, 44 MU Edzell 26.11.46; Gosport on RNARY Fleetlands charge 1.12.46; AHU Stretton 15.2.47; DH Leavesden 31.7.47; AHU Stretton 19.3.48; 728 Sqn, Hal Far 28.5.48; SOC Hal Far, Malta 4.8.49
NS593	Watton 5.7.44 – 654th BS; failed to return from PR mission to Nijmegen-Eindhoven area 18.9.44 (crew both KIA)
NS594	Watton 29.6.44 – 653rd BS 'U'; ground looped 28.1.45 (Lts Robert James & Terence Hall OK); SOC 27.2.45
NS595	Watton 7.7.44 – 654th BS; ground looped during take-off – substantial damage 9.3.45 (pilot Robert Hastie OK); 10 MU 18.6.45; SOC 25.7.46
NS596	Watton 6.7.44 – 654th BS; ran out of fuel and crash-landed – DBR 27.11.44 (pilot Lt Wallace Rouse & nav Lt Allen Morrow OK); SOC 25.7.46
NS619	Watton 9.7.44 – 654th BS; damaged in landing accdt 22.3.45 (pilot Kenneth McGriffin OK); SOC 3.5.45
NS620	Watton 10.7.44 – 653rd BS
NS625	Alconbury 2.8.44 – 654th BS; lost on ops over Germany 19.8.44
NS626	Watton 19.7.44; to French AF 25.5.46

Ser No	Remarks
NS630	Watton 22.7.44 – 653rd BS; hit trees on landing in bad weather, killing crew 22.11.44
NS632	Watton 28.7.44; 653rd BS; to French AF 13.3.46
NS634	Watton 22.7.44; 653rd BS; to French AF 13.3.46
NS635	Watton 25.7.44. 653rd BS; named *Patches* – Capt. Robert Lee); shot down by B-24 gunners 4.4.45 – crew PoWs
NS636	Watton 28.7.44; 653rd BS; to French AF 26.4.46
NS638	Watton 31.8.44; crashed on training flight in UK 23.12.44 (crew killed)
NS650	Watton 25.8.44; 654th BS; sought sanctuary at Malmo-Bulltofta airfield, Sweden 3.4.45 (crew Podwodjski/Proulx); then to RAF Chalgrove; Mount Farm as 5710M 9.10.45
NS651	Watton 25.8.44; 654th BS 'F'; named *Woodpecker's Delight;* u/c collapsed in take-off accdt 5.3.45 (crew Evans/Spaight OK); 44 MU 22.6.45; SOC 1.11.46
NS676	Watton 3.10.44; 654th BS; 856th BS/492nd BG 18.3.45; had bulbous nose housing H2X; 10 MU 18.6.45; 57 MU 1.12.45; sold to Lunzer & Co. for scrap 7.8.47
NS677	Alconbury 18.8.44; Watton; 654th BS; shot down by flak over Germany 1.11.44 – crew PoWs
NS686	Alconbury 9.9.44; Watton – 654th BS; 856th BS/492nd BG 18.3.45; had bulbous nose housing H2X; 44 MU 22.6.45; as 6233M 20.1.47; to Enfield Rolling Mills for scrap 8.7.48
NS707	Alconbury 18.10.44; Watton – 654 BS; 856th BS/492nd BG 18.3.45; crashed Winchfield, UK killing crew 25.4.45
NS708	10 MU 5.10.44; Watton 29.11.44 – 653rd BS; written off in landing accdt at ALG B-120, Bremen 30.5.45 (pilot Lt Richard Kenny OK)
NS709	Alconbury 24.10.44 – 654th BS; 856th BS; bulbous nose housing H2X; 10 MU 18.6.45; SOC 25.7.46
NS710	10 MU 5.10.44; Watton 30.11.44 – 653rd BS 'L'; to French AF 25.7.46
NS711	10 MU 2.11.44; Watton 31.12.44 – 653rd BS; shot down over Germany by friendly fighter 25.3.45 (pilot Stubblefield killed, nav Richmond PoW)
NS712	10 MU 5.10.44; Watton 29.11.44 – 653rd BS 'O'; 10 MU 16.6.45; SOC 25.7.46

Ser No	Remarks
NS725	10 MU 6.10.44; Watton 2.11.44 – 654th BS 'L'; 492nd BG 15.3.45; 10 MU 16.6.45; SOC 4.9.47
NS730	10 MU 9.10.44; Watton 29.11.44 – 653rd BS; DBR in take-off accdt at Exeter, UK, 4.2.45 (pilot Wallace Rouse OK); SOC 21.2.45
NS739	10 MU 19.10.44; Watton 7.12.44 – 653rd BS 'F'; named *Pamelia* with Vargas *Flying Girl* on nose; 44 MU 10.8.45; 274 MU (probably Oulton); SOC 30.9.47
NS740	10 MU 18.10.44; Watton 2.12.44 – 653rd BS 'M'; 492nd BG 18.3.45; 44 MU 10.8.45; allocated ser no 6232M 20.1.47; sold to Enfield Rolling Mills for scrap 8.7.48
NS742	10 MU 19.10.44; Watton 7.12.44 – 653rd BS; to RN det 44 MU Edzell 1.4.47; AHU Stretton 14.5.47; DH Leavesden 1.49; AHU Stretton 7.49; 728 Sqn Hal Far (526/HF) 2.6.50; AHU Hal Far 30.4.51; Lee-on-Solent 25.1.52; RDU Culham 20.2.52; AHU Lossiemouth 23.10.52; became G-AOCJ on civil reg 18.5.55; to Israeli AF as 4X-FDG-91, 30.10.56
NS743	10 MU 19.10.44; Watton 7.12.44 – 654th BS 'Z'; 44 MU 22.6.45; to Fleetlands for spares for RN 7.11.47
NS744	10 MU 23.10.44; Watton 18.12.44 – 653rd BS 'M'; DBR in landing accdt at RAF Manston 9.4.45 (pilot John Carter & nav W Loden OK); SOC 17.5.45
NS745	10 MU 28.10.44; Watton 18.12.44 – 653rd BS 'S'/654th BS; 10 MU 16.6.45; SOC 4.9.47
NS748	10 MU 28.10.44; Watton 31.12.44 – 653rd BS 'A'; ground looped at Watton & destroyed 19.4.45 – (pilot Lt John Carter OK); SOC 14.5.45
NS752	10 MU 28.10.44; Watton 18.12.44 – 653rd BS; MIA from weather mission 25.3.45 (pilot 1/Lt Bernard Bucher PoW, nav 1/Lt Louis Pessirilo KIA)
NS753	10 MU 28.10.44; Watton 7.12.44 – 653rd BS; to RN det 44 MU Edzell 11.46; Gosport/RNARY Fleetlands 19.12.46; 771 Sqn Ford 4.11.48 – 11.49; RDU Culham 7.52; AHU Lossiemouth 23.4.53; on civil register as G-AOCK 25.5.55; burnt 10.60
NS754	10 MU 28.10.44; Watton 14.1.45 – 653rd BS; 10 MU 16.6.45; SOC 25.7.46
NS756	10 MU 2.11.44; Watton 16.12.44 – 653rd BS; 10 MU 16.6.45; to French AF 17.10.46

Ser No	Remarks
NS757	10 MU 2.11.44; Watton 31.12.44 – 653rd BS; crashed at RAF Shepherds Grove, UK 9.4.45 (pilot 1/Lt Robert James & nav 1/Lt Terence hall both KIFA); SOC 10.5.45
NS758	10 MU 4.11.44; Watton 19.1.45 – 653rd BS, named *Southern Belle*; to French AF 14.8.46
NS772	10 MU 2.11.44; Watton 19.2.45 – 653rd BS; RN det 44 MU Edzell 26.11.46; various RN second-line units; sold for scrap to R A Short 25.11.53
NS773	10 MU 4.11.44; Watton 17.1.45 – 653rd BS; RN det 44 MU Edzell 13.12.46; RDU Anthorn 16.12.46; RNARY Fleetlands 19.2.47; Gosport 8.47; DH Hatfield 6.48; SOC 1.2.49
NS774	10 MU 5.11.44; Watton 14.1.45 – 653rd BS 'M'; crash-landed at Watton 25.3.45, extensive damage but pilot Lt Warren Borges OK; 27 MU 1.8.45; 22 MU; sold to Lunzer for scrap 15.8.47
NS775	10 MU 5.11.44; Watton 17.1.45 – 654th BS 'F'; RN det 44 MU Edzell 12.46; Gosport/RNARY Fleetlands 16.12.46; various RN second-line units 9.48; sold for scrap to R A Short 18.11.53
NS782	10 MU 20.11.44; Watton 17.1.45 – 653rd BS; ground looped Watton 8.3.45, extensive damage (pilot Robert James OK); Cat 'E'/SOC 10.4.45.
NS783	10 MU 20.11.44; Watton 28.1.45 – 654th BS; 10 MU 11.6.45; to French AF 16.7.46
NS785	10 MU 15.11.45; Watton 19.1.45; to French AF 6.9.46; to Israeli AF 21.2.51
NS792	10 MU 23.11.44; Watton 22.3.45 – 654th BS; shot down by 'friendly' P-51s 9.3.45 – pilot killed, nav injured
NS793	10 MU 23.11.44; Watton 28.1 45 – 654th BS; 10 MU 18.6.45; 273 MU; sold for scrap to BKC Alloys 29.4.48
NS794	10 MU 25.11.44; Watton 19.3.45 – 654th BS; 10 MU 10.6.45; to French AF 22.9.46
NS796	10 MU 15.12.44; to USAAF 19.4.45; 44 MU 22.6.45; sold for scrap 16.7.47
NS802	10 MU 2.12.44; to USAAF 20.4.45; earmarked for British South American Airways but instead sold to Phoenix & Clifton Ironworks 8.7.47
NS804	10 MU 30.11.44; Watton 20.4.45; RN det 44 MU Edzell 1.4.47; various RN second-line units (Stretton/Yeovilton/Culham) 16.5.47; sold for scrap to R A Short 23.7.53

Ser No	Remarks
NS805	10 MU 4.12.44; to USAAF 20.4.45; 44 MU 22.4.45; to French AF 9.5.46
NS811	10 MU 8.12.44; to USAAF 19.4.45; 44 MU 22.6.45; sold to Gp Capt. Leonard Cheshire as G-AIRU 19.12.46; prepared for smuggling to Israeli AF 5.7.48; written off in crash at Ajaccio, Corsica 17.7.48
NS812	10 MU 16.12.44; to USAAF 20.4.45; 44 MU 22.6.45; sold to Gp Capt. Leonard Cheshire as G-AIRT 19.12.46; prepared for smuggling to Israeli AF 5.7.48; flown to Nice en route to Israel 16.7.48; written off 13.1.57
RF979	Watton 17.1.45 – 654th BS 'D'; 57 MU 6.12.45; 51 MU 30.1.47; SOC 25.7.48
RF983	Watton 14.1.45 – 654th BS 'O'; 10 MU 18.6.45; to French AF 16.7.46
RF985	Watton 17.1.45 – 654th BS; landing accdt Alconbury 19.2.45 (pilot Roger Gilbert & nav John Jackson both OK); RN det 44 MU Edzell 7.46; various RN second-line units 9.5.47; sold for scrap to J G Williamson 21.6.54;
RF986	Watton 11.1.45 – 654th BS 'W'; RN det 44 MU Edzell; Gosport/RNARY Fleetlands 26.11.46; various RN second-line units 1.49; 771 Sqn (593/LP) 31.5.50; sold for scrap to R A Short 25.11.53
RF988	Watton 17.1.45 – 654th BS 'J'; 10 MU 18.6.45; SOC 13.2.47
RF989	Benson 3.1.45; Watton 1.2.45; reportedly with 60 Sqn SAAF at Brindisi, southern Italy in May 1945; SOC 6.9.45
RF992	Watton 17.1.45 – 653rd BS 'R'; 10 MU 16.6.45; to French AF 4.7.46
RF996	Watton 17.1.45 – 654th BS 'Y'; abandoned over Germany after engine failure 20.3.45 – crew PoWs
RF999	Watton 14.1.45 – 'T'; RN det 44 MU Edzell 7.46; RNARY Fleetlands 16.12.46; various RN second-line units inc 728 Sqn Hal Far 1.49; sold for scrap to R A Short 25.11.53
RG113	Watton 14.1.45 – 654th 'S'; DBR in landing accdt at Watton 6.4.45 (pilot 1/Lt John Pruis & nav 1/Lt Claude Moore both OK); SOC 23.4.45
RG145	Benson 9.3.45; Watton 22.3.45 – 653rd BS; minor damage in landing accdt at Watton 17.4.45 (pilot Lt Warren Davis OK); 71 MU (probably repaired on site); sold for scrap 16.7.47

Ser No	Remarks
RG146	Benson 11.3.45; Watton 22.3.45 – 653rd BS 'J'; marked 'WX-J' on underside of wing; 44 MU 24.8.45; sold for scrap 11.2.46
RG148	Watton 23.3.45 – 654th BS; 10 MU 16.6.45; to French AF 10.5.46
RG154	Benson 11.3.45; Watton 22.3.45 – 654th BS; 44 MU 21.3.46; 27 MU 16.12.46; to French AF 18.8.47
RG155	Benson 9.3.45; Watton 22.3.45 – 654th BS; 10 MU 16.6.45; to French AF 11.9.46
RG156	Benson 14.3.45; Watton 22.3.45 – 654th BS; 44 MU 24.8.45; SOC 30.1.46
RG157	Benson 13.3.45; Watton 22.3.45; 856th BS 'Q'; 10 MU 18.6.45; 57 MU – sold for scrap to Lunzer 7.8.47
TA614	Watton 23.3.45; 492nd BG 'R' 1.4.45; to RN Det Edzell 7.46; 728 Sqn, Hal Far 22.9.49; AHU Hal Far 31.8.50; 728 Sqn 20.10.50; AHU Hal Far 28.2.52; Lee-on-Solent, UK 29.2.52; Brooklands Avn (Sywell) for overhaul; AHU Lossiemouth 25.11.52; R A Short 25.11.53; Regd G-AOCN 25.5.55; To Israeli AF as 4X-FDL-92

Sect B: NF.XXX

Ser No	Remarks
MM746	Damaged after attack on Ju 188; SOC 20.3.45
MM761	To 416th NFS in the Mediterranean – date unknown (dels of NF.XXXs to USAAF began in 11.44); missing 29.1.45
MM764	To 416th NFS NW Africa
MM765	To 416th NFS NW Africa; crashed on t/o 16.2.45 at Rouvres, France
MM769	To 416th NFS NW Africa; SOC 29.10.45
MT462	To 416th NFS 12.44; SOC 3.1.45
MT464	To 416th NFS 12.44; SOC 3.1.45
MT465	To 416th NFS 12.44; later to Belgian AF, with which crashed 15.6.49
MT475	To 416th NFS; missing 27.1.45
MT478	To 416th NFS 30.11.44; SOC 31.5.45

Ser No	Remarks
MT479	To 416th NFS 12.44; to RAF & 4 Ferry Unit; crash-landed 60 miles NW of Lyons 7.6.45 after engine failure during ferry flight from Italy to England; Fg Off Brian Armitage RAFVR (P) – KIA, Sgt Sidney Baker RAFVR (N) – Inj
MV564/G	To 416th NFS Pisa, Italy 29.11.44 (probably the first NF.XXX for USAAF); lost 22.4.45
MT482	To 416th NFS; MIA 22 Apr 45.
NT244	To 416th NFS; crashed on t/o Pisa, Italy 5.3.45
NT247	To 416th NFS; SOC 11.8.48
NT248	To 416th NFS; crash-landed San Benedetto 22.4.45
NT249	To 416th NFS Pisa, Italy; Missing 29.3.45

Sect C: T.III

Ser No	Remarks
LR516	10 MU Hullavington 30.12.43; Mount Fm 21.1.44; Nuthampstead Feb 44 – 50th FS/802nd Recon Gp (Prov); Written off at Nuthampstead in take-off accdt during training on 27.2.44 when flown by Maj. George Doherty (P) & 2/Lt Oliver Emmel (P2)
LR530	Precise date & location to USAAF uncertain; taxiing accdt Watton 24.3.45 (pilot Edward Hodges); landing accdt Watton 10.4.45 (pilot Andrew Horvath); allocated ser no 5910M 29.3.46
LR534	Precise date & location to USAAF uncertain; Landing accdt (ground looped) during training at Bury St Edmunds on 27.4.44 (crew Lts Carl S Satterlund & Dennis Scanlan); to RAF – 464 Sqn; 204 AFS; 231 OCU; FTU; sold for scrap 6.8.47
LR553	To USAAF but nothing more known
LR556	Photos from 25th BG pilot Robert Hastie clearly show camouflaged T.III in USAAF markings; then to RAF: 305 FTU; 51 OTU; 54 OTU; CFS; 'Lost ht on single engine overshoot nr Moreton-in-Marsh 4.7.49.' ASN confirms written off on 4.7.49 while flying from Little Rissington: 'The pilot intended to overshoot an asymmetric approach and make a further circuit but did not realize that he still had full flap selected and hence the ac would not maintain height, nor would it accelerate. A forced landing was made (nr M-in-M)'

Sect D: FB.IV

Details on the Aircraft Movement Cards suggest the following two airframes were earmarked, and might have seen limited, unofficial use by the USAAF.

DZ357. Bone, North Africa 1.2.43; 540/256 Sqns; missing from air test off Malta 28.12.43; Cat E 1.2.44.

DZ368. Taken on charge by USAAF 6.11.42; preparation for USAAF via Benson; 540 Sqn; crashed in forced landing 4 miles SW of Newbury, Berkshire 20.5.43 – Cat E.

Notes
ASN = Website aviation-safety.net
RAF Maintenance Units (MUs)

10 – Hullavington, Wiltshire
22 – Silloth, Cumbria
27 – Shawbury, Shropshire
44 – Edzell, Angus (Scotland)
51 – Lichfield, Staffordshire
57 – Wig Bay/West Freugh (Scotland)
71 – Slough, Berkshire (Repair & Salvage unit – esp Repair On Site)
273 – Polebrook, Northamptonshire

Details of accidents occasionally included as they indicate the whereabouts of individual aircraft and who flew them.

Appendix B

Serial Numbers of Canadian-Built USAAF (F-8) Mosquitoes

Ser No	Mk	USAAF Ser No	Remarks
KB306	B.VII	43-34931	Wright Fld 6.1.44; to RCAF; departed RCAF St Hubert on 25.6.45 on ferry flight to USAAF Houlton, Maine
KB312	B.VII	43-34924	Colorado Springs 6.43; Peterson Fld 8.7.43; Bolling Fld 18.7.43; Wright Patterson 28.7.43; poss to UK 4.11.44
KB313	B.VII	43-34925	Colorado Springs 6.43; Peterson Fld 5.6.43; Toronto 16.8.43; lost wing recovering from a dive after take-off from RCAF Amherst, NS 4.2.45 while operated by RAF Transport Cmd's 45 (Atlantic Ferry Gp. Flt Lt (?) John Bradley (P) & J McIntyre (Canadian civ N) both killed
KB315	B.VII	43-34926	Colorado Springs ?.6.43; Peterson Fld 8.7.43; Bolling Field 22.7.43; Patterson Fld 23.7.43; *The 'Spook'*. Ferried to La Marsa, Algeria, in Oct 43; crash landing 19.8.45; DBR; w/o
KB316	B.VII	43-34927	Peterson Fld, Colorado Springs 6.43; damaged in take-off accdt 1.7.43 – Lt Brian Moyers (P) OK; became instructional ac for USAAF
KB317	B.VII	43-34928	Early details missing from AHC; Langley Field 19.8.43; dep USA 19.2.44 'To be delivered by Material Cmd pilots'
KB326	B.VII	43-34929	Wright Field 3.9.43; Written off in landing accdt at Wideawake Fld, Ascension, on 27.11.43 when flown by Lt Harry Eidson – crew both OK

Ser No	Mk	USAAF Ser No	Remarks
KB130	B.XX	43-34932	Eglin Fld 3.1.44; Niagara Falls 11.5.44; Hunter Fld 7.6.44; Written off at Hunter Fld 16.6.44 after engine failure. Lt Joseph Taylor (P) OK
KB131	B.XX	43-34933	Eglin Fld (Air Proving Ground Command) 3.1.44; Niagara Falls (Bell Mod Centre); Hunter Fld 16.7.44; Rome, NY 17.7.44; Crashed on take-off after engine failure 2 miles SSE of USAAF Rome, NY 7.8.44. Lt William Cass (P) killed
KB132	B.XX	43-34934	Niagara Falls 3.1.44; Hunter Fld 5.4.44; Orlando 5.4.44; Bolling Fld (3rd AF Staging Area) 12.4.44; Hunter Field 3.5.44; Savannah 10.5.44; Hunter Fld 5.6.44; Romulus 6.6.44; Rome 7.6.44; Bangor, Maine 6.7.44; to RAF in UK 2.2.45; then 16 OTU; 50 MU. SOC 15.9.45
KB138	B.XX	43-34936	Niagara Falls 13.2.44; Hunter Fld 27.3.44; Wallatia 15.4.44; Hunter Fld 29.4.44; Atlanta Fld 4.5.44; Romulus Fld 11.5.44; Indianapolis 22.5.44; Romulus 1.7.44; To RAF 2.2.45; 13 MU 3.3.45; 44 MU 6.6.45; SOC 15.11.46
KB139	B.XX	43-34937	Niagara Falls 24.1.44; Nashville Airport 6.4.44; Orlando Fld 9.4.44; Savannah Fld then Hunter Fld 3.5.44; Romulus Fld 10.5.44; Rome 5.7.44; taxiing accdt at Grenier Fld, NH 9.8.44 – pilot Perry Collins OK; swung into snow bank at RCAF Greenwood, NS 19.1.45, Cat 'C'. Fg Off D McDonald RNZAF (P) OK
KB140	B.XX	43-34938	Niagara Falls 21.1.44; Pittsburgh 27.4.44; Hunter Fld 29.4.44; Rome (for 'Project 92721') ?.7.44; To RAF 2.2.45; 16 OTU; 71 MU 26.9.45; SOC 13.10.45
KB141	B.XX	43-34939	Niagara Falls 28.2.44; Hunter Fld ?.?.44; New Castle 27.4.44; Pittsburgh 28.4.44; Rome (via Atlanta & Romulus) ?.7.44; w/o at USAAF Rome, NY, during take-off accdt, 15.7.45. Lt Donald Kline (P) OK

Ser No	Mk	USAAF Ser No	Remarks
KB145	B.XX	43-34935	Niagara Falls 15.1.44; Orlando Fld 23.3.44; Middletown, Pa (Air Depot) 6.4.44; Orlando Fld 7.4.44; Final Destination Patterson Fld
KB146	B.XX	43-34940	Niagara Falls 29.2.44; Hunter Fld 10.5.44; Romulus 8.6.44; Rome, NY 18.6.44; Bangor, Maine 19.7.44 (Project 92721); to RAF 2.2.45; 608 Sqn 5.5.45; 162 Sqn 12.6.45; SOC 21.6.47
KB147	B.XX	43-34941	Niagara Falls 6.3.44; Hunter Fld 1.5.44; Knoxville 5.5.44; Romulus (awaiting pilot 8.5.44/mech trouble 9.5.44/awaiting pilot 10.5.44/grounded by Higher Authority 11.5.44); Final destination Rome, NY; poss to RCAF
KB148	B.XX	43-34942	Niagara Falls 9.3.44; Hunter Fld 2.5.44; Romulus 13.5.44; del to Canada by RAF crew 1.2.45; to RAF 2.2.45; 13 MU; 139 Sqn 22.2.45; swung off runway on landing at RAF Upwood 13.4.45; DBR. Fg Off Thomas Parsons (P) and Flt Lt Richard Burgess (N) OK; SOC 10.5.45
KB149	B.XX	43-34943	Take-off accdt due mechanical failure at USAAF Romulus, Mich 15.5.44. Lt Harry Peattie (P) OK; SOC 30.11.45
KB150	B.XX	43-34944	Niagara Falls 20.2.44; Hunter Fld 27.5.44; Rome, NY 22.1.45; SOC 30.11.45
KB151	B.XX	43-34945	Niagara Falls 20.2.44; Raleigh (mech trouble) 4.5.44; Hunter Fld 8.5.44; Romulus 7.6.44; Rome, NY (Project 92721) 7.9.44; SOC 30.11.45
KB152	B.XX	43-34946	Niagara Falls 15.2.44; Hunter Fld 8.4.44; Ground looped at USAAF Robins Fld, Elberta, GA 21.4.44. Lt Howard Thoenig (P) and Nav OK; 'Washout – Surveyed 26.4.44'; 'Final Destination – Project 92721'

Ser No	Mk	USAAF Ser No	Remarks
KB153	B.XX	43-34947	Operated by DH Canada. During test flight from Downsview, ground looped on landing and ploughed into chain link fence. Pilot OK; to RAF; 16 OTU; crashed 28.1.45 nr RAF Barford St John, Oxon, killing Flt Lt Jack Richardson RAAF (P) & Flt Lt Leonard Butcher RAF (N)
KB154	B.XX	43-34948	Niagara Falls 9.3.55; Hunter Fld (via Nashville) 6.6.44; Final Destination Rome, NY; SOC 30.11.45
KB155	B.XX	43-34949	Due to be del to Niagara Falls but this apparently 'Deleted' due to mech trouble. Arrived Orlando 4.4.44
KB156	B.XX	43-34950	Niagara Falls 13.2.44; Hunter Fld 28.4.44; mech trouble/apparently earmarked for UK; Rome, NY 18.6.44; Bangor, Maine, 9.7.44; to RAF 2.2.45; 139 Sqn; 162 Sqn 26.5.45; 163 Sqn 7.7.45; 9 MU 24.8.45; SOC 10.1.47
KB157	B.XX	43-34951	Niagara Falls 15.2.44; Hunter Fld 8.5.44; Romulus 6.6.44 (Project 92721); earmarked for UK; to RAF – probably 16 OTU. (There is confusion online between the ultimate fate of this airframe and KB153). Probably disposed of 28 Jan 45 (Mosquito Fates website)
KB158	B.XX	43-34952	Niagara Falls 16.2.44; Hunter Fld 27.4.44; Rome Jun/Jul 44; earmarked for UK (Project 92721); Bangor, Maine 7.44; to RAF 2.2.45; SOC 12.3.45
KB159	B.XX	43-34953	Niagara Falls 16.2.44; Hunter Fld 6.4.44; 'Project 90307'; ground looped 11.4.44 and w/o. Lt Charles Puzzo (P) OK
KB171	B.XX	43-34930	'Unveiled' by actor Pat O'Brien at Downsview, Ontario, on 19.4.43 for the 7th Victory Loan Campaign; Wright Fld 3.9.43; Class 20 13.3.44

Ser No	Mk	USAAF Ser No	Remarks
KB180	B.XX	43-34954	Niagara Falls 9.3.44; Hunter Fld 2.5.44; Romulus (earmarked for UK) 6.6.44; Bangor, Maine 17.7.44; Rome 26.7.44; Grenier 28.7.44; to RAF 2.2.45; 9 MU 13.9.45; 274 MU North Creake 5.2.46; SOC 31.7.47
KB181	B.XX	43-34955	Niagara Falls 27.2.44 (Project 92721); Hunter Fld 1.5.44; Romulus 6.5.44; earmarked for Rome, NY but non-avail of pilot, mech trouble & weather prevented this; Grenier 28.7.44; to RAF; damaged by RAF 24.8.44; SOC 21.6.47
KB182	B.XX	43-34956	Niagara Falls 19.3.44; Hunter Fld 2.5.44; Romulus 10.5.44; earmarked for Rome, NY, under Project 92721, 7.6.44; earmarked for UK via Bangor, Maine 16.7.44; illegible (Lour?) Fld 20.7.44; to RAF 2.2.45; 13 MU; 163 Sqn 8.2.45; RIW by DH 27.3.45; SOC 17.5.45
KB183	B.XX	43-34957	Niagara Falls 20.2.44; earmarked for Hunter Fld under Project 92721 but delayed by weather & mech trouble; Raleigh 4.5.44 (where again delayed by weather/mech trouble; Hunter Fld 7.5.44; earmarked for Romulus but more weather/mech trouble delay; Bangor, Maine 17(?).7.44; ground looped Goose Bay 21.7.44 – Lt William Munn (P) OK
KB184	B.XX	43-34958	Niagara Falls 28.2.44; Pittsburgh (weather diversion) 7.4.44; Hunter Fld (for Project 92721) 28.4.44; Atlanta 8.5.44; Romulus 10.5.44; 'Grounded by Higher Authority 11.5.44'; Rome, NY 7.7.44; Bangor, Maine 17.7.44; to RAF; RAF Sqns 162/139/162/163; SOC 28.11.46

Ser No	Mk	USAAF Ser No	Remarks
KB185	B.XX	43-34959	Niagara Falls 4.4 44; Hunter Fld 1.5.44; Romulus 8.5.44; Rome, NY 4.7.44; Bangor, Maine 7.7.44; to RAF 2.2.45; 163 Sqn; 139 Sqn 18.2.45; Missing 2/3.4.45 (out of RAF Upwood, Hunts); thought shot down by Oblt Kurt Welter of 10/NGJ11 flying an Me 262. Flt Lt Geoffrey Nicholls (P) & Flt Lt Jack Dawes (N) killed
KB186	B.XX	43-34960	Due at Niagara Falls 18.3.44 but delayed; Langley Fld 23.8.44 for stability and control studies; La Guardia ??; to RCAF (?); SOC 30.11.45
KB187	B.XX	43-34961	Niagara Falls 10.3.44; Hunter Fld 2.5.44; 'Class #26, 1.8.44; Final destination Project 92721; minor accdt at 36th St Airport, Miami, FL, on 15.6.44. Lt J Grogan (P) OK
KB188	B.XX	43-34962	Niagara Falls 21.3.44; Hunter Fld 1.5.44; Augusta 4.5.44; Pittsburgh (weather diversion) 5.5.44; Romulus 6.5.44 (mech trouble, awaiting pilot etc); Rome NY 12.7.44; earmarked for UK 16.7.44; Bangor, Maine 19.7.44; to UK; landing accdt at Watton, UK 30.7.44. Lt Joseph Brannock (P) & nav OK; to RAF 2.2.45; 16 OTU; 9 MU 27.8.45; SOC 31.12.46
KB189	B.XX	43-34963	Niagara Falls 19.3.44; Hunter Fld 3.5.44; Romulus 6.5.44; 'Grounded by Higher Authority' 11.5.44; earmarked for UK 6.6.44; Rome, NY (awaiting pilot/weather delay) 16.7.44; Bangor, Maine 17.7.44; to RAF 2.2.45; 608 Sqn; 162 Sqn 28.4.48; 163 Sqn 7.7.45; 9 MU 24.8.45; SOC 31.12.46
KB190	B.XX	43-34947	Niagara Falls 20.3.44; awaiting del to Romulus but apparently this did not go ahead. Instead, del to Canada by RAF crew for Canadian Car & Foundry

SERIAL NUMBERS OF CANADIAN-BUILT USAAF MOSQUITOES

Sources
USAF Aircraft History Cards (AHCs), ACR-88, Roll 49, National Air & Space Museum RAF Aircraft Record Cards, RAF Museum

Notes
Oxon = Oxfordshire, UK
AHC = Aircraft History Card

The Airfields:
- Atlanta Fld, Georgia – air freight terminal
- Niagara Falls, New York – aircraft modification centre
- Hunter Fld, Savannah – training base for medium bomber crews
- Eglin Field, Florida – proving ground for aircraft armament
- Bolling Fld, Washington DC – training & organisation base for personnel going overseas
- Grenier AAF base, New Hampshire – was, from 1 January 44, the HQ of the N Atlantic Divn of the USAAF's Air Transport Cmd, responsible for ferrying aircraft overseas.
- Raleigh AAB, North Carolina – AAF Air Technical Service Command airfield, known as Raleigh-Durham
- La Guardia Fld, New York City – air transport base
- Romulus Fld, Michigan – home of 3rd Ferrying Gp
- Colorado Springs Army Air Base – established in April 1942 at Colorado Municipal Airport). The base's mission at this point was reconnaissance training under the auspices of the Army Air Force Photo Recon Trg Unit (PROTU). From May to October 1942 the base prepared reconnaissance squadrons for deployment to overseas theatres.
- Patterson Fld – test and evaluation centre.

Operational Losses of USAAF Mosquitoes in the Second World War

Date	Ser No	Unit	Crew	Circumstances
8 Jun 44	NS555	8th Recon Sqn	Capt. Walter Gernand (P) – KIA Sgt Ebbet Lynch (8th CCU) – KIA	Loss of control in cloud. Crashed UK return from mission
21 Jun 44	NS558	8th Recon Sqn	Capt. Richard Clounch (P) – KIFA 1/Lt Connor O'Connor (N) – KIFA	Struck barrage balloon near Gravesend, UK
7 Jul 44	NS537	8th Light Weather Sqn	1/Lt John Mann (P) – KIA 2/Lt William Davis (N) – KIA	FTR from weather recon
7 Aug 44	MM311	8th Recon Sqn	1/Lt Walter Thompson (P) – KIA 2/Lt Carl Edgar (N) – KIA	MIA from *Mickey* mission over Germany. (Some sources say 'Not Delivered')
12 Aug 44	NS533	653rd BS	1/Lt Ronald Nichols (P) – KIA 2/Lt Elbert Harris (N) – Evaded	Shot down by P-51 over Toulouse
13 Aug 44	MM370	654th BS	1/Lt Dean Sanner (P) – PoWS/Sgt Augustus Kurjack (8th CCU) – KIA	Mosquito hit by 'friendly' bomb over target
19 Aug 44	NS625	654th BS	1/Lt Raymond Musgrove (P) – KIA 1/Lt Harold Fordham – (N) – PoW	Lost on ops over Germany
8 Sep 44	NS538	654th BS	F/O Russell Whitmer (P) – KIFA M/Sgt Raymond Armstrong (Radar Tech) – KIFA	Exploded mid-air over Kennet, UK

Date	Ser No	Unit	Crew	Circumstances
8 Sep 44	NS593	654th BS	1/Lt Robert Tunnell (P) – KIA S/Sgt John Cunney (8th CCU) – KIA	Shot down by ground fire, Crashed near Plantlunne, Germany
24 Sep 44	NS570	653rd BS	1/Lt Clayborne Vinyard (P) – PoW1/Lt John O'Mara (N) – PoW	Shot down by night fighter over Germany
22 Oct 44	NS514	653rd BS	Lt Malcolm MacLeod (P) – OK 2/Lt Milford Hopkins (N) – OK	Written off in take-off accdt RAF Tangmere
25 Oct 44	NS582	654th BS	1/Lt George Brooks (P) – KIA 2/Lt Richard Taylor (N) – RTU	Crashed in Belgium
1 Nov 44	NS677	654th BS	2/Lt Vance Chipman (P) – PoW1/Lt William Cannon (N) – PoW	Shot down by flak over Germany
5 Nov 44	MM386	653rd BS	1/Lt Robert Grimes (P) – KIA 1/Lt Clarence Jodar (N) – KIA	Crashed at Wendling, Suffolk after weather recon
5 Nov 44	NS568	654th BS	1/Lt Otto Kaellner (P) – KIA 1/Lt Edwin Cerrutti (N) – Inj	Crashed on landing after *Joker* mission
22 Nov 44	NS630	653rd BS	1/Lt Malcolm MacLeod (P) – KIA 1/Lt Edward Fitzgerald (N) – KIA	Hit trees at Thompson village, 3 miles S of Watton, while trying to land in exceptionally bad weather
22 Nov 44	NS515	653rd BS	1/Lt Russell Harry (P) – KIA 2/Lt Milford Hopkins (N) – KIA	Crashed Gt Cressingham near Watton just after take-off for weather recon mission
27 Nov 44	NS596	654th BS	1/Lt Wallace Rouse (P) – OK 1/Lt Allen Morrow (N) – OK	Crash-landed in France, short of fuel
23 Dec 44	NS638	654th BS	F/O James Spear (P) – KIFA 1/Lt Carroll Bryan (N) – KIFA	Crashed in UK on training flight
2 Jan 45	MT462	416th NFS	Lt Harley Goetz (P) – KIA No details of nav	Crashed after t/o from Pisa, Italy
21 Jan 45	NS509	653rd BS	2/Lt Jerry Roberts (P) – PoW1/Lt Ralph Fisher (N) – KIA	Shot down over Germany

Date	Ser No	Unit	Crew	Circumstances
27 Jan 45	MT475	416th NFS	Capt. John Davis (P) – KIA 2/Lt Hubbard Larsen (N) – KIA	Came down at Lonate-Pozzolo, Italy
29 Jan 45	MM761	416th NFS	1/Lt Frank Janisch (P) – KIA 2/Lt Eugene Franklin (N) – KIA	Crashed after t/o from Pisa, Italy
16 Feb 45	MM765	416th NFS	Lt Donald Johnson (P) – KIA ? (N) – KIA	Crashed after t/o from ALG A.82, Etain, France
8 Feb 45	NS583	654th BS	Capt. Victor Doroski (P) – KIA Capt. Jacob Hochman (N) – KIA	Crashed in Germany during *Joker* mission
28 Feb 45	MM746	416th NFS	Capt. Lawrence Englert (P) – OK 2/Lt Earl Dickey (RO) – OK	Crew bailed out over Italy after combat damage
4 Mar 45	NT247	416th NFS	F/O Quenton Bruton (P) – OK F/O Boone (RO) – OK	Ground looped on take-off from Pisa
5 Mar 45	NT244	416th NFS	Lt Herbert King (P) – OK F/O Prince (RO) – OK	Crashed on t/o Pisa, Italy
16 Mar 45	MM821	416th NFS	Lt Richard Hoover (P) – OK	Written off after landing accident at Pisa, Italy
20 Mar 45	RF996	654th BS	2/Lt Joseph Polovick (P) – PoW 1/Lt Bernard Blaum (N) – PoW	Abandoned over Germany after engine failure
24 Mar 45	NS711	653rd BS	1/Lt Carrol Stubblefield (P) – KIA 1/Lt James Richmond (N) – PoW	Shot down over Germany by USAAF P-47
25 Mar 45	NS752	653rd BS	1/Lt Bernard Boucher (P) – PoW 1/Lt Louis Pessirilo (N) – KIA	Group report says MIA from weather mission
29 Mar 45	NT249	416th NFS	Lt Eldon Bake (P) – KIA 2/Lt Max Galowich (N) – KIA	Crashed after t/o from Pontedera, Italy
31 Mar 45 (Also recorded as 31 May 45)	MT478	416th NFS	1/Lt Joseph Skrinar (P) – KIA No details of nav	Crashed Fano, Italy after t/o from Pontedera

OPERATIONAL LOSSES OF USAAF MOSQUITOES

Date	Ser No	Unit	Crew	Circumstances
3 Apr 45	NS650	654th BS	Lt Col Alvin Podwojski (P) – Interned Capt. Lionel Proulx (N) – Interned	Landed in Sweden after flak damage
3 Apr 45	NS584	856th BS	Lt Col Robert L Boone (CO 858th BS, 492nd BG)	DBR in take-off accident at Harrington
4 Apr 45	NS635	653rd BS	1/Lt Theodore Smith (P) – PoW Col Troy Crawford (Command Observer) – PoW	Shot down by B-24 gunners
9 Apr 45	NS757	653rd BS	1/Lt Robert James (P) – KIFA 1/Lt Terence Hall (N) – KIFA	Crashed at RAF Shepherd's Grove, UK
9 Apr 45	NS792	654th BS	1/Lt John Pruis (P) – KIA 1/Lt Claude Moore (N) – Inj	Shot down by P-51s
9 Apr 45	MM752 (NF Mk 30)	416th NFS	Lt Jesse Bonneau (P) – OK	Crash landing after engine failure at Pontedera, Italy
13 Apr 45	MM387	653rd BS	Lt Robert Gordon (P) – OK Lt J Handren (N) – OK	Landing accdt at Watton. Ac written off.
22 Apr 45	MT482	416th NFS	2/Lt Wesley Kangas (P) – KIA 2/Lt Jack Herron (N) – KIA	Crashed near San Benedetto, Italy
22 Apr 45	NT248	416th NFS	Maj. James Urso (P) – OK 1/Lt Talmidge Simpson (RO) – OK	Damaged by AA fire & crash-landed San Benedetto, Italy
25 Apr 45	NS707	492nd BG	1/Lt James Kuntz (P) – OK 1/Lt Richard Green (N) – KIFA Lt Jean Nater (JE Op) – OK	Crashed Winchfield, Hants, UK
7 Jun 45	MT479	416th NFS	While being ferried back to RAF after service with 416th. Fg Off Brian Armitage (P) – KIA Sgt Sidney Baker (N) – Inj	Crashed 60 miles NW of Lyons, France

Notes
653rd and 654 BS aircraft are PR.XVIs; 416th NFS aircraft are NF.XXXs.
'JE Op' = Joan Eleanor Operator

273

Appendix D

Chronology of USAAF Mosquitoes

Initial Provisioning Correspondence Between US Army and UK Air Ministry
(Source: UK National Archives file entitled *Mosquitoes for the USAAF*)

11 Apr 43

Air Ministry signal to Gen. Arnold regretting that it is impossible to supply the requested twenty-four Mosquitoes to US Forces in North Africa or the UK. It is airframes rather than Merlin 61 engines that are short. Tasks requiring deeper penetration than possible by F-5 must be carried out by RAF Mosquitoes, which are available to meet US needs. Special circumstances in North Africa not forgotten … not possible to allot four Mosquitoes, but every effort will be made to send out two for the PR Wing and maintain them in theatre.

? Sep 43

Under the Arnold/Courtney Agreement,* UK due to provide 120 Mosquitoes to USAAF in 1943, comprising: forty Mk XX from Canada; sixty Mk VI from UK; twenty Mk XIII from UK.
(*Gen. Henry Arnold, Commanding General of the US Army, and Air Chief Marshal Sir Christopher Courtney, UK Air Member for Supply and Organisation).

20 Sep 43

Air Ministry signal RAF Delegation Washington stating fifty Canadian Mk XXs plus thirty UK Mk VIs to be allocated to USAAF.

22 Sep 43

Air Ministry letter to Maj. Gen. Eaker stating allocation to USAAF to be: forty Canadian B.XXs plus twenty UK NF.XIIIs. Possibility revisited of using USAAF Mosquitoes to form an American Met Flt alongside the RAF's 1409 Met Flt 'to be manned by American crews and under the Control of the 8th Bomber Command.' (The problem of obtaining last-minute weather information in target areas had recently been discussed with representatives of the USAAF and the Director of the (UK) Met Office).

1 Oct 43
Dep Chief of Air Staff's conference records Gen. Eaker's acceptance of thirty FB.VIs to form a target weather recon unit. At same time, RAF Del signal that the US would prefer PR.IXs.

2 Oct 43
Air Ministry signal RAF Del, Washington, saying up to Americans to choose between FB.VIs or delayed delivery of PR.IXs.

26 Oct 43
Letter from RAF Del to Air Ministry stating US have requested following allocation: forty Canadian B.XXs, 125 PR Mosquitoes plus forty-three FB.VIs.

1 Dec 43
RAF Del signal Air Ministry saying (1) US have decided the FB.VI not suitable for weather recon unit and (2) they would like quantity of PR.XVIs.

2 Dec 43
Air Ministry signal to RAF Del saying delivery of FB.VIs to be held in abeyance.

2 Dec 43
Air Ministry signals HQ 8th AF and 8th AF Service Command with programme for allocation of PR.XVIs from Feb 1944 onwards.

10 Dec 43
Americans confirm cancellation of FB.VIs.

14 Dec 43
Air Ministry signal to RAF Del saying US have requested NF Mosquitoes including three squadrons in the UK 'to make good the slippage in US P-61 production'.

3 Feb 44

Air Ministry signal RAF 41 Gp and HQ 8th AF that nine [PR.XVI] aircraft from February allocation to be delivered direct from Hatfield to Sta 590 [Burtonwood], of which MM308 and MM311 were being specially modified at Hatfield.

8 Mar 44

RAF Del signal Air Ministry outlining Gen. Arnold's request for additional Mosquitoes for weather recon flights from China in China Sea and North Pacific towards Japan.

19 Mar 44

Air Ministry reply to RAF Del that this not possible as it would be at expense of operational squadrons.

26 Jun 44

Air Ministry Policy Staff advise Vice-Chief of the Air Staff of difficulty of forecasting delivery of Mosquito NF.XXXs. Many are failing their flight test. Americans have failed to produce an efficient night fighter of their own and … 'we are already in difficulties by being forced to maintain the four US NF squadrons in the MAAF with British NF aircraft [ie Beaufighters]'.

Late Jun 44

VCAS writes to Gen. Carl Spaatz (commander of US Strategic Air Forces in Europe) explaining difficulties of providing Mosquito NF.XXXs at present due to: (1) production problems and (2) burden of ops against V-1 flying bombs.

10 Jul 44

Spaatz replies to CAS appreciating these problems but floating possibility of re-equipping two US NF squadrons in *the UK* with Mosquitoes if production rates improve. This could even be done by diverting (US) Mosquitoes from MAAF to UK?

Mid-Jul 44

UK Air Ministry discuss Spaatz proposal 'in-house'. 'Distinct snag in this. The four US NF squadrons in MAAF are currently equipped with Beaufighters. These are being maintained only with difficulty. To divert their replacement Mosquitoes to the UK would mean that the Beaus would have to slog on even longer …'

19 Jul 44

CAS writes to Spaatz saying there is no immediate prospect of this 'horse trading'.

Nov (?) 44

Signal from HQ MAAF to Air Ministry saying 416th NFS has practically re-equipped [with Mosquitoes]. Gen. Eaker (C-in-C MAAF) would review whether the 416th would continue with Mosquitoes after 1 July 1945 or be re-equipped with P-61s after that date. This would depend on course of the war.

12 Dec 44

Signal from HQ MAAF to Air Ministry quoting an extract from a signal from Gen. George Marshall (Gen. of the US Army) to Gen. Eisenhower (Commander Allied Forces): 'Also hereby confirm authorization of procurement action for 40 Mosquito night fighters, consisting of a Unit Establishment (UE) of 12 plus a delivery rate of 4 per month during Dec 44 to Jun 45 for units in Mediterranean Theatre as requested by Eaker.'

16 Dec 44

Signal from Air Ministry to HQ MAAF saying quota of four per month could not possibly be met. Priority requirement for night fighters is for bomber support squadrons in the UK.

Milestones of Operational Events

11 Jul 42	Maj. Elliott Roosevelt takes command of 3rd Recon Gp
10 Dec 42	Col Elliott Roosevelt takes 3rd Photo Gp to North Africa
17 Feb 43	North West African Reconnaissance Wing formed at Algiers; comprised: 682 Sqn + 3rd Photo Gp. CO is Elliott Roosevelt
20 Feb 43	416th NFS activated at Orlando
? Jun 43	USAAF begins taking delivery in US of Canadian-built Mosquitoes (F-8s)
11 Jun 43	416th NFS to RAF Acklington, UK
c.8 Aug 43	416th NFS to N Africa
21 Apr 41	American Ambassador John Winant and chiefs US Service chiefs watch demonstration of Mosquito and other aircraft at Hatfield
2 Feb 44	Mosquito PR.XVI MM310 delivered to Langford Lodge
8 Feb 44	First 416th NFS victory – in a Beaufighter
11 Feb 44	MM337 and '338 delivered to Burtonwood
22 Mar 44	8th Recon Gp (Sp)(Prov) activated at Cheddington
28 Mar 44	801st Bomb Gp (P) established in 8th AF
30 Mar 44	8th Recon Gp becomes 802nd Recon Gp (Sp)(Prov)
12 Apr 44	802nd Recon Gp moves to Watton
17 Jul 44	325th Reconnaissance Wing formed at High Wycombe, UK. (7th Recon Gp, 25th Bomb Gp); CO Elliott Roosevelt
9 Aug 44	653rd Bomb Sqn (Light, Weather Reconnaissance) activated; 654th Bomb Sqn (Heavy, Reconnaissance, Special) activated
4 Aug 44	First *Aphrodite* mission filmed by 802nd
8 Aug 44	802nd Gp becomes 25th Bomb Gp
12 Aug 44	Loss of Kennedy's *Aphrodite* mission filmed by 25th BG
13 Aug 44	801st Bomb Gp redesignated as 492nd Bomb Gp
c.22 Oct 44	654th BS pilots begin testing Joan Eleanor equipment in Mosquito NS676 at Watton
15 Nov 44	First 'live' Joan Eleanor Mosquito mission, in NS676

29 Nov 44	416th NFS collects its first Mosquito NF.XXX11 Dec 44: 416th pilots collect six Mosquitoes from Maison Blanche
17/18 Dec 44	First operational Mosquito mission by 416th NFS
28 Feb 45	First 416th NFS Mosquito victory
15 Mar 45	Joan Eleanor team move from Watton to Harrington
1 Apr 45	Mosquito PR.XVI RG157 arrives at Harrington for the 492nd BG
4 Apr 45	Mosquito TA614 arrives at Harrington for 492nd BG
1/2 May 45	Final Joan Eleanor Mosquito missions, in RG157 and NS740
6 May 45	Last operational USAAF Mosquito mission – a *Bluestocking* – by 25th BG
16 May 45	416th NFS has four P-61s
7 Jun 45	416th's Mosquitoes ferried back to the RAF
9 Nov 46	416th NFS inactivated

Index

Note
N/K = Not Known